The Qualifications Gap

What does it take for women to win political office? This book uncovers a gendered qualifications gap, showing that women need to be significantly more qualified than men to win elections. Applying insights from psychology and political science and drawing on experiments, public opinion data, and content analyses, Nichole M. Bauer presents new evidence of how voter biases and informational asymmetries combine to disadvantage female candidates. The book shows that voters conflate masculinity and political leadership, receive less information about the political experiences of female candidates, and hold female candidates to a higher qualification standard. This higher standard is especially problematic for Republican female candidates. The demand for masculinity in political leaders means these women must "look like men" but also be better than men to win elections.

NICHOLE M. BAUER is Assistant Professor of Political Communication in the Department of Political Science and the Manship School of Mass Communication at Louisiana State University.

T0372710

The Qualifications Gap

*Why Women Must Be Better than Men
to Win Political Office*

NICHOLE M. BAUER
Louisiana State University

CAMBRIDGE
UNIVERSITY PRESS

CAMBRIDGE
UNIVERSITY PRESS

University Printing House, Cambridge CB2 8BS, United Kingdom

One Liberty Plaza, 20th Floor, New York, NY 10006, USA

477 Williamstown Road, Port Melbourne, VIC 3207, Australia

314–321, 3rd Floor, Plot 3, Splendor Forum, Jasola District Centre,
New Delhi – 110025, India

79 Anson Road, #06–04/06, Singapore 079906

Cambridge University Press is part of the University of Cambridge.

It furthers the University's mission by disseminating knowledge in the pursuit of
education, learning, and research at the highest international levels of excellence.

www.cambridge.org
Information on this title: www.cambridge.org/9781108836326
DOI: 10.1017/9781108864503

First published 2020

Printed in the United Kingdom by TJ International Ltd. Padstow Cornwall

A catalogue record for this publication is available from the British Library.

Library of Congress Cataloging-in-Publication Data
NAMES: Bauer, Nichole M., author.
TITLE: The qualifications gap : why women must be better than men to win
political office / Nichole M. Bauer.
DESCRIPTION: New York : Cambridge University Press, 2020. | Includes
bibliographical references and index.
IDENTIFIERS: LCCN 2020006661 (print) | LCCN 2020006662 (ebook) |
ISBN 9781108836326 (hardcover) | ISBN 9781108818896 (paperback) |
ISBN 9781108864503 (epub)
SUBJECTS: LCSH: Women political candidates–United States. | Women in public
life–United States. | Sex role–Political aspects–United States. | Women–Political
activity–United States. | Political participation–Sex differences–United States. |
Elections–United States.
CLASSIFICATION: LCC HQ1236.5.U6 B38 2020 (print) | LCC HQ1236.5.U6 (ebook) |
DDC 320.082/0973–dc23
LC record available at https://lccn.loc.gov/2020006661
LC ebook record available at https://lccn.loc.gov/2020006662

ISBN 978-1-108-83632-6 Hardback
ISBN 978-1-108-81889-6 Paperback

To Daniel
who loved reading and learning
and who always had a good book to recommend.

Contents

Figures

Tables

Acknowledgments

The original idea for this book came from my childhood experiences growing up in a very, very masculine environment. I was raised in a household with three brothers and we lived on a smattering of military bases throughout the country. Needless to say, military bases were, and probably still are, spaces where ideas about masculinity and sex-segregated social roles dominate how people think. I did not readily accept these ideas. The notion that women were inherently unsuited to fly jets in combat and that men were just naturally going to be better at this task was just silly and unfair. I've spent most of my intellectual career trying to figure out why these gendered concepts exist. Writing this book is just one step in a process of trying to understand how gender stereotypes affect the opportunities for women to be successful.

Many colleagues and friends provided support in putting this book together. I had been quietly working on a series of papers intended for journal articles aimed at answering the broad question, What explains the gendered qualification gap that occurs in those elected to political office? My original plan was to simply publish many, many journal articles. I presented one of the papers out of this series, which would later become Chapters 5 and 6, at the Gender and Political Psychology Research Workshop at Tulane University in October 2017. Those in my research group suggested that I put these papers together into a book project. I took their suggestion. I am grateful to the members of that excellent research group, which included Katie Searles, Kris Kanthak, Erin Cassese, Jenn Merolla, Angie Bos, Tessa Ditonto, Becky Bigler, and others at the conference who offered thoughtful insights about this project.

Others who read portions of this book and provided moral support include Carrie Skulley, Sarah Fulton, Monica Schneider, Sarah Oliver, Kathleen Donovan, Allison Archer, Johanna Dunaway, Mary-Kate Lizotte, Samara Klar, Diana O'Brien, Kira Sanbonmatsu, Emily Beaulieu, Christina Wolbrecht, and Mirya Holman. Yanna Krupnikov patiently answered many, many questions about the book writing and publishing process and constantly reassured me that this book was not going to be terrible (if it is terrible, it is not Yanna's fault). Erin Cassese suffered through multiple drafts of this book manuscript and provided instrumental support throughout multiple stages of this book development process, and her advice helped to crystallize and sharpen many of the ideas presented in the following chapters.

I am especially grateful to Tiffany Barnes, who hosted me for a research talk at the University of Kentucky. The political science department at the University of Kentucky provided excellent feedback and suggestions that I used to develop all of Chapter 7. Had that visit not occurred, there would be no Chapter 7 at all.

My colleagues at the political science department and the Manship School of Mass Communication at Louisiana State University provided exceptional feedback on the theoretical concepts and empirical tests I developed throughout the book. I received generous support for this project from the Remal Das and Lachmi Devi Bhatia Memorial Professorship and an Emerging Research Faculty Grant, both received through Louisiana State University. Without this critical financial support, this would be a much, much shorter book.

The data collections for this book, especially the onerous content analyses for Chapter 4, required an army of undergraduate and graduate research assistants, many of whom did this work voluntarily simply because they were interested in the research, including Megan Craig, Rachael Firestone, Caroline Austin, Tatum Taylor, Charlotte Bellotte, Angela McCarthy, and Martina Santia.

Sara Doskow at Cambridge University Press is an excellent editor about whom I cannot say enough positive things. She made this process very, very efficient, almost delightful even, providing transparency, thoughtful advice, and encouragement along the way. She was a pleasure to work with through every stage of this process.

When my younger brother Daniel was in fifth grade, or around then, he had to write a paper on women he admired. I don't remember the details of the assignment. I found it odd and intimidating that he wrote about me. I don't know why he chose me as an admirable woman.

I hadn't done much exceptional at the time. I was simply in the middle of college trying to figure out what I planned to do with the rest of my life. I had definitely done nothing admirable or remarkable. I always meant to ask Daniel about that assignment once he was grown up. Unfortunately, when I was in the very final stages of finishing this book, Daniel passed away unexpectedly. While I will never know why he wrote about me for that assignment, I am quite certain that Daniel did not buy into the idea that women needed to be held to any sort of a higher standard. I do know that I'm grateful to have had three supportive siblings and parents who always showed an interest in my work.

I

The Gendered Qualification Gap

No country can ever truly flourish if it stifles the potential of its women and
deprives itself of the contributions of half of its citizens.
—Michelle Obama

The United States stands out as one of the only democratic nations yet to
elect a woman as the head of state. Over the last fifty-six presidential
elections, just a handful of women even dared to run for the presidency.
Arguably, the most serious female presidential contender is Hillary
Clinton, who ran in both 2008 and 2016. A constant critique Hillary
Clinton faced during both her presidential races is that she lacked the
qualifications necessary to serve as president. Clinton's resume in 2016
included serving as Secretary of State under the Obama administration,
twice winning election to the Senate, having an active role developing
policy as First Lady, and being a lawyer at a top Arkansas law firm.
Clinton faced qualification criticisms from her primary election challenger
and her general election opponent. Trump notably contended that Clinton lacked that "presidential look." The most common "look" sported by
the forty-four presidents who served in office prior to 2016 is that they are
all men. Trump further called Clinton too weak, too frail, and lacking the
stamina necessary for the challenges of the presidency.

The news media contributed, in part, to the narrative of Clinton as
"questionably qualified" for the presidency, discussing Clinton's qualifications frequently with abundant coverage about her role as Secretary of
State in the Benghazi terrorist attacks and her use of a private email
server. For example, a quick news search in the final eight weeks of the

2016 campaign uncovers nearly 200 news stories in the *Washington Post* and the *New York Times* alone about Clinton's use of a private email server during her time as Secretary of State. A news search in the *Washington Post* and the *New York Times* for stories about Trump's tax returns, a major point of contention about Trump's qualifications, uncovered a mere eighty articles discussing his refusal to release these documents. Donald Trump ran for the presidency without ever having served in political office, either appointed or elected, and Trump lacked experience formulating and implementing public policy.

The Shorenstein Center at Harvard University tracked the news coverage received by the primary and the general election candidates throughout the 2016 campaign. In the final two months of the election, 3 percent of Clinton's coverage reported on her leadership or experience, while 3 percent of Trump's coverage also reported on these same qualities, and both candidates received mostly negative coverage. These patterns suggest some parity in qualification news coverage and that the media devoted little space – indicative of a qualification information gap for both female and male candidates. I argue that the news media do not provide enough information about the qualifications of political candidates. The lack of qualification coverage is much more detrimental to female candidates because it leads voters to assume that female candidates lack the qualifications needed for political office. Voters do not form these same disqualifying assumptions about male candidates.

Political qualifications appeared to matter far more for Clinton compared with Trump – at least based on anecdotal evidence. One voter quipped when asked on NPR's Morning Edition Program about his support for Donald Trump during the 2016 election: "How big could he screw up? I mean, what could he do that would be any worse than what's happened with other presidents that weren't effective?" A *Washington Post* contributor to the political blog *The Fix* succinctly summed up why the lack of qualifications was not a problem for Trump: "For millions of Americans in this unusual election year, Trump's lack of government experience is precisely the sort of qualification they're looking for." Trump's sex, and associated masculine stereotypes, made his populist appeal viable among some voters even though he lacked political experience. Had a woman received a major party's nomination to run for the presidency without any political experience, it is hard to believe that voters would see her lack of political experience as precisely the "sort of qualification" they desired.

Qualification criticisms of female candidates did not cease with Clinton's 2016 presidential defeat. Newly minted member of Congress Alexandria Ocasio-Cortez frequently faces gendered qualification criticisms. A Texas city-council member referred to Ocasio-Cortez as a "bimbo" – a frequently gendered insult used to demean women's intelligence.[1] Senior White House Counselor Kellyanne Conway drew attention to Ocasio-Cortez's sex and her age, characterizing her as a "29-year-old congresswoman who doesn't seem to know much about anything."[2] Other commentators piled onto the gendered insults that also highlighted her age, stating that she's "just 'young and naive.' She's stupid. We're talking full-blown dumb-dumb."[3] The qualification critiques lobbed at Ocasio-Cortez attack her based on her gender and sex as well as her age and, implicitly, her ethnicity. Notable about many of these criticisms is that they came after Ocasio-Cortez defeated a longtime Democratic incumbent man in the primary election and then won the general election, thereby proving that she is, at least from the vantage point of her constituents, qualified to represent them in political office.

Scanning the historical record reveals that other women in politics frequently received criticism for lacking the "right" qualifications for serving in political office. Geraldine Ferraro made history in 1984 as the first woman to appear on a major party's presidential ticket, albeit in the much less high-profile vice-presidential slot. Ferraro was not a political novice when Walter Mondale selected her as his running mate. She spent nearly a decade in the House of Representatives and had an extensive background as a prosecutor. Journalists, political pundits, and some voters questioned whether Ferraro had the "fortitude," "experience," and "competency" necessary to take on the Soviet Union and navigate defense and foreign policy issues. A 1984 *Washington Post* article from the presidential race included a quotation from one female voter who summarized her gendered sentiments about Ferraro: "I don't trust the

[1] Scott McDonald, "Texas Councilman Calls Alexandria Ocasio-Cortez 'Bimbo,' Then Apologizes," *Newsweek.com*, February 9, 2019, www.newsweek.com/texas-city-council man-calls-alexandria-ocasio-cortez-bimbo-then-apologizes-1325135.
[2] Joe Concha, "Conway Says Ocasio-Cortez Is '29-Year-Old Who Doesn't Seem to Know Much about Anything," *The Hill.com*, December 11, 2018, https://thehill.com/homenews/media/420751-conway-says-ocasio-cortez-is-29-year-old-who-dont-seem-to-know-much-about.
[3] Chantal Da Silva, "AOC vs. GOP: The Long List of Smears and Insults Hurled at Alexandria Ocasio-Cortez," *Newsweek.com*, February 21, 2019, www.newsweek.com/alexandria-ocasio-cortez-republicans-gop-insults-1335151.

woman. She's gotten very emotional about a lot of things already, and there's going to be lots worse to come." For Ferraro, having political experience was not enough; she did not have the "right" political experience. It's almost as if Ferraro's qualification, and the qualifications of women more generally, just did not count in the same way they would if they were men's.

These qualification attacks occur not just in presidential races but also when women run for lower levels of political office. Pundits and political opponents dismissed Patty Murray as just a "mom in tennis shoes" with little political agency to make a difference when she first became politically active. Murray turned the dismissive insult into a rallying cry during her campaigns for the school board, state legislature, and then the US Senate. Patty Murray won election to the Senate in the critical first "Year of the Woman." Qualification criticisms do not reflect the reality of women's political backgrounds. On average, the women who run for and win political office have *stronger* qualifications compared with the men who run for and win political office (Anzia and Berry 2011; Ekstrand and Eckert 1981; Fulton 2012, 2014). Despite impressive resumes, female candidates frequently counter criticism that they lack the requisite qualifications for political office.

This book examines what I term the "gendered qualification gap." The gendered qualification gap refers to the differences in the quality of female and male political candidates and elected officeholders. Women, in the aggregate, far outpace men in qualifications. Little is known about the causes of the gendered qualification gap at the voter level. I address four critical questions about the gendered qualification gap. First, How do ideas about gender affect what it means to be qualified for political office? Second, What information do voters have about candidate qualifications? Third, Do voters think differently about the qualifications of female candidates and male candidates? Finally, How can female candidates overcome the gendered qualification gap? I argue that voters hold female candidates to higher qualification standards relative to male candidates based on the way underlying ideas about gender shape how voters think about who should and can hold political office.

Holding female candidates to high qualification standards is a subtle but pernicious source of bias that limits the success of women in politics by creating a high entry barrier for women seeking access to the ballot. These steep barriers can limit women's access to the political pipeline, delay women's political careers, and, in the long term, perpetuate women's political underrepresentation. Gendered qualifications point to a serious tension in democratic decision-making. Campaigns condition many voters to seek out and reward candidates who display masculine qualities, such as being competitive, aggressive, and assertive (Conroy 2015; Dittmar 2015). These qualities do not necessarily make for good political leadership once a candidate wins the election (Guttmann and Thompson 2012). Indeed, legislating and leading require qualities that fit into the perceived stereotypic strengths of women, such as being willing to compromise, build consensus, and reconcile competing perspectives (Eagly and Carli 2003; Hibbing and Theiss-Morse 2002).

This chapter lays the groundwork for developing my theory of the gendered qualification gap and the empirical tests I conduct in later chapters. I start by defining the gendered qualification gap, and then discuss current explanations in the literature explaining why this gap occurs. Past research examines how institutional barriers and socialization patterns contribute to the gendered qualification gap, but missing from the extant body of scholarship is how voters contribute to the qualification gap. This is the gap my book fills. Following the discussion of past scholarship, I then outline the plan for the rest of the chapters in this book.

WHAT IS THE GENDERED QUALIFICATION GAP?

The gendered[4] qualification gap persists no matter how you measure political qualifications. Female candidates, compared with male candidates, have more political experience when they run for political office (Fulton et al. 2006) and more impressive professional backgrounds (Carroll and Sanbonmatsu 2013). As incumbents, the gendered qualification

---

[4] Sex and gender are separate but related concepts (Bittner and Goodyear-Grant 2017). The term "sex" refers to a whether a person is biologically male or female. The term "gender" refers to the performance and perception of femininity or masculinity. In this book, I use sex and gender in distinct ways to describe how biological sex differences between women and men gave rise to the separate social roles occupied by women and men, and how those social roles led to the development of gender stereotypes about the qualities attributed to women and attributed to men (Eagly 1987; Eagly and Karau 2002; Prentice and Carranza 2002). These biological origins of qualities associated with femininity and masculinity are essential to explaining women's exclusion from leadership roles. Throughout this book, I use "sex" to refer to the biological assignment of women as women and men as men. When referring to people as female or male, regardless of their biological assignment, I will default to "gender." But, note that gender is most often used to refer to feminine and masculine stereotypes that, in the minds of many voters, make up what it means to be male and to be female. Because "gender" refers to the qualities that make something or someone feminine or masculine, people have genders, but so do objects, ideas, and institutions.

gap widens. Female lawmakers, relative to their male counterparts, pass more legislation and bring home more federal dollars to their districts (Anzia and Berry 2011) – and female incumbents are especially product-ive even when they are in the minority party (Volden, Wiseman, and Wittmer 2013). Current scholarship assumes that female candidates, as incumbents and challengers, develop these impressive qualifications to stave off voter bias (Anzia and Berry 2011). The logic is that female candidates anticipate bias from voters, and, as challengers, they run for political office only when they have the best record and the highest probability of winning (Lawless 2012). As incumbents, women work hard to prevent reelection challengers and to mitigate bias from voters (Branton et al. 2018; Milyo and Schlosberg 2000). This research does not explain the exact role voters play in perpetuating this qualification gap. For example, it is not clear whether voters reward productive female incumbents for their high levels of legislative productivity. This book directly addresses how concepts related to gender affect whom voters see as qualified for political office, and how these perceptions lead voters to hold female candidates to higher qualification standards.

Female candidates win elections at equal rates as male candidates (Seltzer, Newman, and Leighton 1997). It is easy to conclude from this point of parity that gender bias does not contribute to the underrepresen-tation of women in elected office. This conclusion is not quite accurate. Highly qualified female candidates actually win a smaller share of the vote than similarly or less qualified male candidates (Pearson and McGhee 2013). These findings create the impression that female candidates are more likely to win elections by having better qualifications relative to their male opponents. If gender does not affect electoral outcomes, then female candidates would win elections at higher rates than less qualified male candidates – an outcome that, based on empirical research, does not occur. This leads to an intriguing empirical puzzle: *Women win elections at equal rates as male candidates but women win these elections by a narrower vote margin, and these women, on average, have stronger qualifications relative to the victorious male candidates. Do female candi-dates have to be better than male candidates to win elections?*

I argue that outcomes that appear neutral across candidate gender, such as the probability of winning an election, are not necessarily absent of gender biases. Gender-neutral outcomes are often the result of highly gendered processes. Evaluating political candidates is a gendered process for many voters. Political institutions operate under strict norms of mascu-linity (Barnes 2016; Hawkesworth 2003; Homola 2019; Mahoney 2018);

voters hold strongly masculine expectations for political candidates (Holman, Merolla, and Zechmeister 2011, 2016; Huddy and Terkildsen 1993); and the media further reinforce masculine norms through what they choose to cover about political candidates (Conroy 2015; Hayes and Lawless 2016). These masculine norms and expectations affect how voters evaluate the qualifications of political candidates.

CURRENT EXPLANATIONS FOR THE GENDERED QUALIFICATION GAP

I start by outlining how previous research approaches the question of why the women who run for and win political office tend to have more impressive qualifications relative to the men who run for and win political office. I draw on political science research and also scholarship from sociology and social psychology. Extant scholarship identifies three central sources that contribute to the gendered qualification gap: (1) socialization patterns, (2) structural dynamics, and (3) stereotypic biases among voters.

Gendered Socialization Patterns

Gendered socialization patterns affect how people think about their capacity to serve as leaders. Gendered socialization is the process whereby children learn the appropriate roles, norms, and behaviors for each gender throughout childhood. Children can identify the behaviors and activities considered appropriate for boys and for girls in preschool and early elementary school (Bigler and Lieben 2006). For example, young children know that playing with dolls is an activity for girls and that playing with trucks is an activity for boys. Parents, teachers, the mass media, and other important sources of authority discourage young girls and women from displaying leadership qualities and pursuing leadership opportunities.

The socialization of children into separate social roles affects how they think about who can serve in political leadership. Through this socialization process, young girls face social sanctions for displaying power and agency, while young boys receive rewards for the same behaviors (Sadker and Sadker 1986; Sadker and Zittleman 2009). Take, for example, the case of two kindergarten students, one boy and one girl, who both in a rush of excitement to answer their teacher's question forget to raise their hand and just shout out the answer. The teacher is likely to sanction the young girl for failing to follow the appropriate norm of raising one's hand and waiting one's turn to speak. The same teacher, however, is likely to reward the young boy for showing initiative even though he also violated the appropriate norms of class participation. These differential responses signal to girls that agency and initiative is bad while submissiveness is good; and, for boys, agency and initiative is desirable. Based on these gendered socialization patterns, girls grow up learning how to display submissiveness and boys grow up learning how to display leadership.

Young adults operate in environments where they receive positive reinforcement for conforming to gender-based expectations and punishments for violating such expectations. These patterns of socialization affect how people view their role in political life, especially their interest in pursuing political careers. During high school, students engage in activities that build civic skills, such as participating on student councils, playing sports, and pursuing a variety of extra-curricular activities (Burns, Schlozman, and Verba 2004). When these students enter college, the patterns of participation in public life begin to shift. College-aged women lose interest in pursuing political careers, while college-aged men increase their interest in pursuing political careers (Fox and Lawless 2014b; Schneider et al. 2016). The collegiate experience is one that sends implicit and explicit signals to women that public spaces are masculine spaces. Collegiate women interested in pursuing majors and career paths traditionally dominated by men, such as political science, engineering, or computer science, receive less mentoring, encouragement, and support than male students (Baird 2008). The result is a sorting of people into sex-segregated professions such that women end up pushed out of pipeline political careers and men end up pushed into these careers. The women who persist in pursuing careers in male-dominated fields end up with stronger qualifications than the men who choose those same career paths. Surviving in a profession where women receive consistent messages that they simply do not belong means that these women feel pressured to be better than everyone else to prove that they do, in fact, belong.

Gendered socialization leads young people to seek out very different experiences in adulthood. Women's socialization leads them to pursue careers that fulfill communal goals, such as serving disadvantaged populations, rather than pursuing power-seeking goals, such as political leadership (Holman and Schneider 2018; Schneider et al. 2016; Silva and Skulley 2019). These socialization patterns affect, at a basic level, the way people process political cues in discussion networks (Krupnikov et al. 2019). And this socialization process leads women to express less interest in running for political office compared with men. Consequently, women often see themselves as *lacking* the qualifications needed to serve in political office, and this perception persists even if a woman has comparable qualities to a potential male candidate (Lawless 2012). Research finds these gender gaps exist throughout the candidate emergence process, from when individuals initially make the decision to run for political office (Fulton et al. 2006; Ondercin 2016) to when they make decisions about moving up the political ladder (Maestas et al. 2006). A consequence of gendered socialization is that women, in general, run for political office much later in life than male candidates – once the work–life balance is not as much of a burden (Fox and Lawless 2014a). Women also are more likely to consider a run for political office when they have a high probability of winning the election (Maestas et al. 2006; Ondercin 2016). This risk-aversive decision-making process mitigates the trepidation women feel about electoral competition and conflict (Kanthak and Woon 2015; Stoddard and Preece 2015; Sweet-Cushman 2016).

Institutional Barriers

The way party institutions recruit and support candidates affects the gendered qualification gap. Local party networks are more likely to support men's candidacies, and some local party leaders do not believe that women are electorally viable (Sanbonmatsu 2006). Overcoming these perceptual biases means that female candidates need to have exceptional qualifications just to get on the radar of local party leaders. States without strong party organizations have less motivation to recruit female candidates simply because such recruitment requires an investment of time and resources that these party networks lack (Sanbonmatsu 2006). Local party leaders do not need to ask men to run for political office because men self-select into the candidate pool, and this makes it easy for party networks to, often unintentionally, overlook potential female candidates (Carroll and Sanbonmatsu 2013; Crowder-Meyer 2013).

It is important to note that there is considerable variation in recruitment patterns across state and local party networks. Some state party organization consciously recruit women for political office and try to create a culture that promotes equal access to the ballot for women (Bos 2011). Despite the best of intentions, institutional interventions can backfire. Bos (2015) examined whether affirmative action statements read by party leaders at Democratic state nominating conventions encouraged party elites to nominate more women, and the efforts produced the opposite effect. Karpowitz, Monson, and Preece (2017) found, more positively, that directly encouraging women to put themselves forth as candidates at Republican Party nominating conventions increased the number of female candidates running for political office.

Candidate recruitment patterns create barriers to the ballot for female candidates, and there are disparities in how Democrats and Republicans recruit women. I talk more about these differences in Chapter 6, which takes a deep dive into the partisan gender gap. Recruiting female candidates can be especially difficult because socialization patterns lead women to underrate their own political qualifications, and state and local party networks do not always have the resources needed to recruit viable women. While these factors certainly contribute to the gendered qualification gap, these explanations do not offer direct insight into how voters view candidate qualifications across sex.

The Role of Voter Bias

Current scholarship is relatively silent on how voters evaluate the qualifications of political candidates, with a few exceptions. Fulton (2012) asked political elites, including political activists and candidates, to evaluate candidate quality on the actual skills and tasks that legislators perform in public office, including the ability to speak well in public and secure federal dollars for their district. Fulton's research found that receiving a high qualification rating mattered much more for the electoral victories of female relative to male candidates. This research suggests that, among political elites, female candidates have a higher probability of winning elections by being better than the male candidates running against other male candidates. Pearson and McGhee (2013), using objective observational measures of candidate quality rather than subjective perceptions of candidate quality, reinforce the premise that electoral parity comes when female candidates outperform male candidates. It is not clear whether the candidate socialization and selection process causes this qualification gap or if voter bias contributes to the qualification gap. Current approaches to detecting gender bias focus on how sexism, candidate trait attributions, and issue competencies contribute to the electoral success, or demise, of female candidates.

Sexist attitudes reflect the belief that women are simply not suited for filling leadership roles and that men are best fit for political leadership. Mo (2015) found that sexist attitudes can take an implicit or explicit form, with explicit attitudes reflecting an outright preference for male leadership and implicit attitudes reflecting the unconscious beliefs voters have about gender and political leadership. Both implicit and explicit attitudes affect people's willingness to support female candidates (Sanbonmatsu 2002a). The aftermath of Hillary Clinton's 2016 defeat spurred several studies reaching the empirical conclusion that bias contributed to this presidential loss. Holding the belief that men are more emotionally suited for politics (Bracic, Israel-Trummel, and Shortle 2019), having high levels of hostile sexism (Cassese and Holman 2019) and expressing negative attitudes toward women and feminists (Valentino, Wayne, and Oceno 2018) predicted support for Trump over Clinton especially among white Republican women (Cassese and Barnes 2019). Collectively, this research provides evidence that explicitly sexist attitudes can motivate voters to support an arguably less-qualified man over a more-qualified woman.

Feminine stereotypes characterize women as caring and empathetic (Prentice and Carranza 2002), and, in politics, voters stereotype female candidates as having a high level of expertise on issues that reinforce these traits, such as education or health care policy (Huddy and Terkildsen 1993; Schneider 2014a). Masculine stereotypes characterize men as assertive and dominant (Vinkenburg et al. 2011), and, as such, voters associate male candidates with masculine issues such as defense and the military (Holman, Merolla, and Zechmeister 2016). The political relevance of these stereotypes is that feminine traits lead voters to see female candidates as better fit for communal, or supportive, social roles and not masculine, or leadership, social roles. Voters associate masculine traits with political leaders and see feminine traits as less important (Conroy 2015; Holman, Merolla, and Zechmeister 2016; Huddy and Terkildsen 1993).

Voters do not automatically associate female candidates with stereotypically feminine traits, such as emotionality, compassion, or warmth (Bauer 2015b; Brooks 2013), but voters rate female candidates more poorly than male candidates on the stereotypic masculine traits that voters value in political leaders, including experience, knowledge, and political competency (Schneider and Bos 2014). Voters actively seek out information to confirm that female candidates are competent and knowledgeable (Andersen and Ditonto 2018; Ditonto, Hamilton, and Redlawsk 2014). Emphasizing feminine traits in campaign messages, such as a female candidate describing herself as caring, decreases electoral support for female candidates but not male candidates (Bauer 2015a). Gendered traits serve as a source of bias because voters see female candidates as fundamentally deficient in the traits most strongly associated with political leadership.

Another approach to assessing voter bias is through perceptions of issue competencies. Voters see female candidates and lawmakers as having a high level of expertise on issues such as education, health care, the environment, pay equity, and anti-sexual harassment and discrimination policies (Alexander and Anderson 1993). These issues reflect feminine traits, such as compassion (Huddy and Terkildsen 1993). This association between stereotypically feminine issues and female candidates is not, in and of itself, evidence of bias or a qualification gap. Bias emerges when voters associate female candidates with stereotypically feminine issues and form the impression that female candidates lack competency on stereotypically masculine issues including defense, the military, and national security (Holman, Merolla, and Zechmeister 2016) – issues that reflect traits such as strength and authority (Huddy and Terkildsen 1993). Holman, Merolla, and Zechmeister (2016) found that when national security is a dominant national issue, support for female candidates markedly decreases because voters do not think women can handle these issues.

Voter bias can also occur within the political parties based on the intersection between partisan stereotypes and gender stereotypes. Stereotypes about the Democratic Party mirror feminine stereotypes, while stereotypes about the Republican Party mirror masculine stereotypes (Hayes 2005; Winter 2010). Some evidence suggests that partisanship is a primary driver of the way candidates use feminine and masculine stereotypes in campaign messages and in voter decision-making (Dolan 2014). Other research points to a more complicated relationship between gender stereotypes, partisan stereotypes, and female candidates. The feminine nature of Democratic stereotypes leads voters to more strongly associate Democratic women with feminine traits and feminine issues relative to Democratic men and Republican women (Sanbonmatsu and Dolan 2009; Schneider and Bos 2016). Republican women, however, are not strongly associated with the masculine qualities that define Republican partisan stereotypes (Bauer 2018; Hayes 2011). Democratic women, based on the gender–partisan stereotype overlap, more strongly fit into stereotypes of their political party. Feminine stereotypes may not hinder voter decision-making about Democratic female candidates. Republican women, however, face a "lack of fit" problem with their political party (Thomsen 2015).

Limitations of Current Research

Sexism, traits, and issues can affect how voters perceive a female candidate's qualifications and whether voters support female candidates at the polls. These factors, I argue, do not speak as to whether voters hold female candidates to a higher qualification standard relative to male candidates and what these higher standards entail. This book addresses several limitations of current scholarship, including the limitations of observational comparisons, the assumption that gender-neutral outcomes indicate gender-neutral processes, the lack of a distinction between candidate traits and other dimensions of a candidate's political resume, and whether voters have information about candidate qualifications during a campaign.

First, observational data cannot offer insight about how voters evaluate female candidates who have the same qualifications as male candidates because, in practice, actual female candidates often have better qualifications compared with male candidates. Observational research illustrates that lesser qualified male candidates do just as well as compared with better qualified female candidates. The best way to detect bias is to compare the evaluations of female and male candidates with the same set of qualifications. The experimental approach I employ controls candidate qualifications, and I can give female and male candidates the same set of qualifications. There is virtually no "real-world" scenario that pits a female candidate against a male candidate with the exact same qualifications. Controlling for candidate qualifications is necessary because it is this high level of control that allows me to be sure that any negative ratings a female candidate receives are due to her gender and not an actual difference in her qualifications.

Second, extant scholarship does not always examine what information about candidate qualifications voters have during a campaign. Studies that examine the campaign messages of female and male candidates often focus on the gender stereotypic traits and issues candidates emphasize (Dolan 2014), but few studies examine how female candidates talk about their qualifications (for exceptions, see Fridkin and Kenney 2015; Lazarus and Steigerwalt 2018). If voters do not know about the qualifications of female candidates, then it is likely voters will fall back on stereotypes to assume that female candidates lack the qualifications needed for political office. Female candidates, for fear of a backlash for breaking with feminine norms, may not be as likely as male candidates to tout their accomplishments. If female candidates do not talk about their qualifications, the news media are unlikely to discuss a female candidate's qualifications.

Third, previous scholarship finds that directly associating a female candidate with feminine traits reduces the extent to which voters see that particular female candidate as qualified for political office (Bauer 2015a), while associating a female candidate with masculine traits enhances the extent to which voters see that particular female candidate as qualified for political office (Bauer 2017; Schneider 2014a). The gender trait literature suggests that female candidates lack the basic personality characteristics associated with leadership, such as experience, but this literature does not tell us how voters evaluate evidence of a female candidate's actual experience, and how these evaluations might differ across candidate sex. For example, it is not clear how information about a female candidate's political experience and political accomplishments shifts perceptions of gendered traits.

I conceptualize and empirically test qualifications as characteristics distinct from traits. I focus on qualifications as the resumes, backgrounds, or set of experiences candidates bring with them to political office. These experiences, when taken at face value, do not directly have the same gendered attachments as traits. Most individuals classify a trait such as aggressiveness as a masculine trait, but most individuals do not necessarily classify serving in a state legislature as a masculine experience. The political resumes of candidates are often seen as more objective indicators of candidate quality. Political experience is a common marker used to assess the level of a candidate's quality (Maestas and Rugeley 2008). If a candidate won election and served in political office previously, then it is reasonable to infer the candidate has the skills needed to serve in political office again. But holding political office is also a masculine experience. The inherent masculinity of the experiences, backgrounds, and skill sets needed to hold political office are not always recognized or discussed in research on candidate quality. For example, it is thought that being able to argue for one's position is a valuable political skill. But being able to argue a position and advocate for oneself or for others is a skill associated with power and agency, and this is a stereotypically masculine characteristic. It is not clear, however, that there is a gendered link between the resumes of political candidates and perceptions of candidate qualifications.

To summarize, this book fills three critical gaps in the literature on candidate quality, the underrepresentation of women in politics, and the role voter bias plays in evaluations of female candidates. First, I argue that gender-neutral outcomes are not always indicative of gender-neutral processes. Observational comparisons of female candidates with male candidates find lots of parity, but the campaign process is rife with inequities that create greater obstacles for female candidates. Determining the role of bias in evaluations of candidate qualifications without experiments is incredibly difficult because the female candidates who make it to the ballot are, in practice, better than the male candidates. It is not always possible to know if these women win elections because they are better than their male opponents or if another process contributes to these outcomes. The ability to create conditions where two candidates are of the same quality allows me determine the role bias plays in these outcomes. Second, I look at the information environment in which voters encounter female and male candidates to see how the campaign context, including the news media, may contribute to the gendered qualification gap. Third, I use perceptions of qualifications to capture voter bias toward female candidates as an alternative to the more conventional trait and issue competency measures scholars have used in previous research. I examine qualifications as the set of resume factors that candidates bring with them to the ballot. This approach lets me see how seemingly objective factors of candidate quality can be evaluated differently for female candidates and for male candidates, and create steep barriers for women.

CHAPTER OVERVIEW

I start in Chapter 2 with a brief history of women in political leadership. Arguments used to deny women suffrage and the full political rights of citizenship were deeply rooted in stereotypes that women lacked the stamina to excel in public life and that women's proper roles were as mothers and caregivers. These beliefs that women lacked the qualifications needed to operate in political spheres still affect how voters view the political acumen of women running for political office today. I not only discuss the historic exclusion of women from positions of political leadership through the lens of gender stereotypes but also analyze over time public opinion data about the role of women in politics. Polling data offer an optimistic picture about the prospects of electing a qualified woman to the presidency. These data, however, do not provide insight into who constitutes a qualified female political candidate, and how the public might assess those qualifications. I answer these questions in subsequent chapters.

Chapter 3 addresses the question: How do ideas about gender, namely, femininity and masculinity, affect what it means, from the voter's perspective, to be qualified for political office? I apply social role theory to the development of political leadership in the United States to show how masculinity determines the expectations voters have for what a qualified political candidate looks like. Ideas about femininity and masculinity shape the expectations of individuals for the different types of roles and occupations women and men hold. Caregiving roles are bound up in norms of femininity, and there is a link between masculinity and leadership roles: the expectation that leaders have masculine qualities extends back to America's founding, and indeed, well before the United States came into existence. I use two empirical tests of how masculinity influences thinking about political leadership and qualifications.

Chapter 4 asks: What information do voters have about candidate qualifications? More specifically, this chapter hones in on whether there is a gendered information gap. A gendered information gap has the potential to widen the qualification gap because if voters lack information about a female candidate's qualifications, most voters will assume, I argue, that she lacks the qualifications needed for political office. I investigate the qualification information environment through content analyses of campaign websites as well as analyses of news coverage from the 2016 Senate elections. These data allow me to test for imbalances in how candidates present their qualifications to voters. The website analyses show that while there are some similarities in how female and male candidates sell their qualifications to voters – for example, everyone talks about their political experience – important differences also emerge. Female candidates, the results show, talk about their professional experiences much more than do male candidates.

In Chapter 4, I pair the campaign website analysis with an exhaustive content analysis of campaign news coverage of the 2016 Senate candidates. The website analyses offer insights into whether female candidates might undersell their qualifications. The news analyses tell me two pieces of information. First, I can determine whether the news coverage matches the information candidates present on their websites. Second, I can assess, through both the website and the news analyses, whether voters have enough qualification information about female candidates. These results show a disjuncture in the information female candidates provide about themselves and the information presented in news coverage. Most female candidates talk about their political experience, but female candidates receive less political experience coverage relative to male candidates. The benefit of conducting content analyses in this chapter is that the method has a high level of external validity as I can draw conclusions about the actual amount of qualification information voters have about high-profile female candidates running in actual elections.

In Chapter 5, I draw on shifting standards theory, derived from social psychology research, to determine how and when voters hold candidates to gendered typicality standards. These standards provide voters with a comparative metric to assess whether a candidate has the qualifications needed for political office. These standards also clarify the subtle and pernicious role gender stereotypes play in how voters rate the qualifications of political candidates. The experiments I use in this chapter allow me to control the qualification information about candidates to trace how being female affects the way voters use this information in decision-making. I am also able to measure voters' qualification expectations more directly to assess just how high the gendered qualification bar is for female candidates. This chapter shows that less qualified male candidates generally have a baseline electoral advantage over more qualified female candidates.

Stereotypes about women and men influence how voters evaluate the qualifications of political candidates, but stereotypes about gender sharply intersect with stereotypes about political parties. Chapter 6 builds on Chapter 5 and investigates how stereotypes about Democrats and Republicans affect evaluations of Democratic and Republican female candidates. Voters stereotype Democrats as feminine and Republicans as masculine (Winter 2010). These stereotypes, I contend, create a set of gendered partisan-typicality standards that affect how voters select candidates in primary elections. Republican female candidates face obstacles in primary elections where Republican voters are more likely to support a Republican male than a Republican female candidate. Partisan-typicality standards shaped by gender stereotypes contribute to the partisan gender gap in political representation.

Chapter 7 turns to closing the gendered qualification gap. I develop and experimentally test three strategies to close the gendered qualification gap. I show that simply providing voters with more information about female candidate qualifications is not enough to close the gendered information gap, and thereby the gendered qualification gap. Putting qualification information in a context that tells voters that female candidates have more or better qualifications than male candidates effectively closes the gendered qualification gap. Self-promotion does not close the gendered qualification gap. This chapter points to the need for more research on how to disrupt the implicit biases voters bring with them to the ballot.

Chapter 8 highlights the broader implications of this research for women seeking to enter positions characterized by masculine expectations and traditionally dominated by men. The gendered qualification gap applies not only to political leadership but to the many public institutions that underrepresent women. Women, in general, need better qualifications than men to succeed in business leadership, the legal field, STEM industries, higher education, and other institutions traditionally dominated by men. The gendered qualification gap creates steep entry barriers for women pursuing professions that typically underrepresent women. The result is that women are noticeably absent from public life.

2

Fomenting a Gender Rebellion

I long to hear that you have declared an independency. And, by the way, in the new code of laws which I suppose it will be necessary for you to make, I desire you would remember the ladies and be more generous and favorable to them than your ancestors. Do not put such unlimited power into the hands of the husbands. Remember, all men would be tyrants if they could. If particular care and attention is not paid to the ladies, we are determined to foment a rebellion, and will not hold ourselves bound by any laws in which we have no voice or representation.

—Abigail Adams, letter to John Adams, March 31, 1776

Women's exclusion from positions of political power and influence is a constant throughout much of American history. Abigail Adams, wife of future president John Adams, pleaded with him to "remember the ladies" and warned Adams that "if particular care and attention is not paid the ladies, we are bound to foment a rebellion." John Adams responded to his wife that "we know better than to repeal our Masculine systems" and feared being subject "to the despotism of the petticoat." John Adams failed to heed the warning of his wife. Women received virtually no legal or political rights in the early American republic. In the exchange between the Adamses is the concept of politics and government described as distinctly "Masculine systems." Adams made clear that forming governments was the task of men and that including women was a silly if not outright dangerous idea. Politics was a masculine social role and an appropriate domain for men; the political sphere was not an appropriate place for women.

This chapter starts to unpack the question: How do ideas about gender affect what it means to be qualified for political office? The central argument I advance is that feminine stereotypes characterizing women as weak, passive, and best suited for tasks in the home rather than public life long justified women's exclusion from full political life. This exclusion began at the country's founding. I illustrate the influence of these gendered perceptions with a brief overview of women's status in American politics from the time of the nation's founding to the present. I discuss how women, and men, slowly formed a political movement designed to give women more political and legal rights, including the right to vote. Even when advocating for more political rights, women often used arguments steeped in conventional feminine stereotypes as a reason for women's political inclusion rather than exclusion.

Following this historical overview of women's roles in politics, I turn to tracking the presence of women in positions of elected political office in the post-suffrage era, starting with Jeannette Rankin's election to the US House up to the "pink wave" of the 2018 midterm elections. Women's presence in elected political office at the congressional level shows a picture of women's perpetual marginalization in the national legislature. I argue that women's underrepresentation is due, in part, to the incongruence between feminine stereotypes and the masculine ideals voters hold for political leaders. I add in public opinion data tracking public sentiment about support for a "qualified" female presidential contender as early as the 1930s to the present. Conventional public opinion questions about a "qualified" presidential candidate do not clarify what it means to be a qualified female presidential candidate. I close this chapter with an analysis of data from the 2016 American National Election Study to show that perceptions of candidate qualifications affected electoral support for Hillary Clinton in different ways than it did Donald Trump. This chapter illustrates how feminine stereotypes shape the debates Americans have about the appropriate role of women in political life. Perceptions of femininity and women's appropriate roles always contrasted the more masculine ideas about political leadership. The historical overview and data analyses provided in this chapter set up a central theoretical and empirical question addressed in this book: What does it mean for a woman to be qualified? and Do qualifications matter differently for female candidates relative to male candidates?

REMEMBER THE LADIES?

The new American democracy never quite seriously considered providing women with the basic rights of citizenship. Women did not need the full rights of democratic citizenship because their husbands would vote in the interests of the entire household (McConnaughy 2013). A system known as coverture defined women's legal status. William Blackstone, the English jurist, described coverture in the following way: "By marriage, the husband and wife are one person in law: that is, the very legal being or existence of the woman is suspended during the marriage . . . under whose protection, and cover, she performs everything" (Blackstone 1765). The husband's legal status quite literally "covered" his wife. The purpose of coverture was to "protect" women, thereby forcing women into a dependent legal and political status. The implication is that women did not exist as independent persons separate from their husbands and that women had very few political or legal rights. Husbands and fathers subsumed the legal status of women under this system. There were some exceptions, such as in the case of widows, who had some limited voting and property rights (Kerber 1980). For the most part, the legal and political status of a woman depended on her legal relationship to a man. Seeing women as persons in need of protection illustrates how stereotypes of women as meek and passive undergirded the American political system from the start.

Women were not exactly quick to "foment a rebellion" against the patriarchal power system. Many women accepted their subordinate social status and subscribed to the idea of separate social roles for women and men. The idea of separate social roles for women and men operates from the premise that women's biological abilities, namely, that women can have children, relegated them to serving in roles as homemakers, caregivers, and nurturers – essentially having children destined women to childcare duties. Men, unconstrained by childbearing, were the better sex for participating in public life and taking on key leadership roles. Women's participation in public life, when it did occur, was often through stereotypically feminine roles such as performing charity and social welfare service (Skocpol 1992).

Some women expanded their caregiving roles to include more overt forms of social activism through participation in the abolition movement. The female leaders involved in abolition, including Sojourner Truth, Lucy Stone, and Elizabeth Cady Stanton, lectured, wrote, and fund-raised alongside men. Through participation in the abolition movement, women upheld many of the ideas associated with feminine social roles, such as promoting a more morally virtuous community, but they also received opportunities to exercise leadership. In 1840, 200 female abolitionists organized and attended the World Anti-Slavery Convention held in London. The convention, however, did not permit women's attendance. The convention even barred Lucretia Mott and Elizabeth Cady Stanton, both of whom organized the gathering, from appearing on the convention floor. Women's exclusion from the event, which would not have been possible without women organizing and planning it, prompted Mott and Stanton to organize a meeting to discuss the status of women in public life.

Women gathered for the first time to seriously discuss securing the rights of citizenship at the 1848 Seneca Falls Convention, held in Seneca Falls, New York. Attended by luminaries in both the abolition and suffrage movement such as Lucretia Mott, William Lloyd Garrison, Elizabeth Cady Stanton, Susan B. Anthony, and Frederick Douglass, the convention produced a Declaration of Sentiments modeled on the Declaration of Independence. The Declaration made a cautious case for providing women with the full rights of citizenship. The resolutions in the Declaration made what were at the time extreme statements that "woman is man's equal," that women ought to have access to education, and that laws excluding women from public institutions have no "force or authority" because women did not participate in the creation of such laws. Some members of the convention considered the idea of women's suffrage quite radical, and adding this goal to the agenda sparked controversy. Many of the women and men in attendance, including Lucretia Mott, thought that women's suffrage went too far, while others, such as Frederick Douglass, argued that securing the vote was fundamental to securing women's citizenship. Ultimately, the Declaration set forth suffrage as a clear goal to work toward. The women who gathered at Seneca Falls did not appear to seriously discuss the prospect of women running for and holding political office.

Radical in many of its objectives, the Declaration of Sentiments also preserved stereotypic distinctions about the appropriate roles of women and men. One resolution stated that "inasmuch as man, while claiming for himself intellectual superiority, does accord to woman moral superiority, it is pre-eminently his duty to encourage her to speak, and teach, as she has an opportunity, in all religious assemblies." The notion of women as morally superior to men reflects a separate-spheres ideology. Women should not cross over into men's social roles, and men should not cross over into women's social roles. Were women to, for example, take part in politics, the inherently corrupt and dirty nature of politics would hinder the ability of women to perform their natural roles as mothers.[1] Women's

---

[1] The stereotype of women as less corrupt in politics continues today, and women can gain an advantage after a political corruption scandal (Barnes and Beaulieu 2014; Barnes, Beaulieu, and Saxton 2017; Brown, Diekman, and Schneider 2011), but women can also

responsibility of raising children and preparing them for citizenship required protecting them from the negative influences of politics and power (Banaszak 1996). The early suffragists turned this argument around and argued that women's moral superiority makes them better equipped to select the more virtuous leaders at the ballot (Skocpol 1992). The moral superiority argument did not exactly shift political sentiment in favor of expanding suffrage, but the suffragists were certainly onto an important idea. Women had qualities, based on stereotypic notions, that would make them *better* at the task of democratic participation because participating in democracy requires that citizens not always act in their own self-interest but in the community's good. Working to support others through selflessness, care, and compassion fits into the stereotypic social roles of women.

The half-century after the Declaration of Sentiments saw the push for women's enfranchisement move incrementally. A key moment in the fight for suffrage occurred on Election Day 1872 when Susan B. Anthony and a small group of women marched to the polls and voted. Almost two weeks after the election, the police arrested Anthony and several other women for voting illegally. A judge found Anthony guilty and fined her $100, nearly $2,000 in today's currency. Anthony used her sentencing to make a fundamental point about the status of women in a democracy that denied them the most basic rights: "Robbed of the fundamental privilege of citizenship, I am degraded from the status of a citizen to that of a subject; and not only myself individually, but all of my sex, are, by your honor's verdict, doomed to political subjection under this, so-called, form of government."[2] A government that intentionally excluded the participation of half its citizens based on sex was not, in the eyes of Anthony, a government with the legitimacy needed to punish her for violating the law. Anthony never paid a penny of the fine.

For much of the latter half of the nineteenth century, the suffrage movement trudged along. Women continued to use the tenets of separate-spheres ideology as a reason to support women's suffrage (Banaszak 1996). Women argued that if they were to prepare children, especially young boys, for the responsibilities of citizenship, they needed a voice in shaping government policies through the right to vote. Women's

face disproportionately large punishments if caught in a scandal (Barnes, Beaulieu, and Saxton 2018).

[2] "Sentencing in the Case of United States vs Susan B. Anthony," http://law2.umkc.edu/faculty/projects/ftrials/anthony/sentencing.html.

heightened morality, virtue, and purity, according to the suffragettes, made them the better sex for creating government systems that served the people rather than government systems that served the power-seeking goals of individual men (McCammon and Campbell 2001). Few women argued that they, in fact, had the masculine traits and abilities needed to hold political office.

The suffrage movement picked up momentum in the early twentieth century. At the end of the nineteenth century, several newly admitted states granted women the right to vote, with Wyoming[3] being the first to grant women's suffrage in 1869, followed by Utah, Colorado, and Idaho (McConnaughy 2013; Teele 2018). Many factors contributed to this newfound momentum including some suffragists who shifted away from a strategy of peacefully petitioning male government leaders and instead adopted a more militant approach. Following the example set by the militant strategies of the British suffrage movement, American women marched, protested, and even chained themselves to the gates of the White House. The police tossed many of these militant protestors into jail where women began hunger strikes that led police officials to force-feed these women. Accounts of women tied down and force-fed through a tube garnered the public's attention through often sensationalized news coverage of the atrocities.

The militant tactics of the suffrage movement in the early twentieth century grabbed the nation's attention in a way that the suffrage movement of the past had not. These strategies were also noteworthy because they demonstrated a shift away from the concept of separate spheres for women and men. Militant suffragists, led by Alice Paul, explicitly repudiated feminine stereotypes about women's purity and morality. The militant suffragists displayed qualities that reflected the masculine stereotypes that aligned more closely with stereotypes about politics. A militant suffrage strategy was not without its critics, especially among fellow suffragists, and there is debate about how much this strategy contributed to the passage and ratification of the Nineteenth Amendment (McConnaughy 2013). Opponents to militancy within the suffrage movement stuck with the strategy of using feminine stereotypes to make a strong case in favor of women's suffrage. The debates within the suffrage movement illustrate

---

[3] Even though Wyoming was the first state to grant women the right to vote nearly 150 years ago, Wyoming, in the present, lags far behind other states in women's political representation as women hold only 15.6 percent of seats as of 2019.

how gender stereotypes influenced the way Americans thought about the appropriate social roles women could adopt.

WOMEN IN POLITICAL OFFICE

While suffrage leaders chained themselves to the White House and petitioned state governments, a woman won election to the US Congress just before passage of the Nineteenth Amendment. Voters in Montana elected Jeannette Rankin as their member of Congress in 1916.[4] Rankin served just one term, from 1917 to 1919. Rankin left the US House after that term to run for the Republican Party's nomination to the US Senate. Rankin lost the primary but she ran again for the House some two decades later and represented Montana from 1941 to 1943. One hundred years after Jeannette Rankin's congressional victory, Montana has yet to elect another woman to either the House or the Senate.

The Nineteenth Amendment went into effect in 1920. Women did not quite rush to the ballot or run for political office (Corder and Wolbrecht 2016),[5] but women incrementally increased their presence in elected office during the decades post-suffrage. Figure 2.1 traces the history of women serving in the US Congress. In the three-decade period immediately following suffrage, women held a handful of seats in the US House ranging from just one woman to a high of nine women. A number of these female House members served as widows temporarily appointed, or who ran in a special election, to fill the seat of their spouse after an untimely death. The widow's succession to political office was not necessarily the most common way for women to get to political office, but it offered women a viable entrance point into the political system (Gehlen 1977a). Selecting widows to fill the remainder of a spouse's term did not necessarily reflect any belief that the wife was the husband's equal or that she could "fill in" as a substitute for her husband. Political expediency and partisan motivations often led to the appointment of widows (Solowiej and Brunell 2003). Political parties wanting to hold onto a seat could appoint a widow as a placeholder until they could find a "suitable" male candidate to run for the seat (Gertzog 1984). There was an understanding that the widow would follow the party line if she needed to cast any critical votes in the legislature and that she was not there to cause a ruckus.

[4] Montana voted to give women suffrage in 1914.
[5] The gender gap in political participation, including in voting, existed not only in the United States but in other countries as they expanded the right to vote (Kim 2019; Teele 2019).

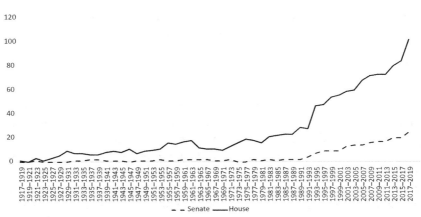

FIGURE 2.1 History of women in Congress

Some twenty or so women filled vacancies in the US House following the death of their husbands, or in one case their father, who died while in the office during this period. Edna Mae Nolan was the first widow House member who ran in a special election in 1922 to fill the seat held by her husband, a member of Congress from California, after his sudden death. Nolan declined to run once she served the rest of her spouse's term, declaring, "Politics is entirely too masculine to have any attraction for feminine responsibilities" (quoted in Chamberlain 1973, p. 50). These widowed members of Congress usually retired after a special election to fill the congressional vacancy. Some of the widowed House women ran to officially fill the seat they held as an appointee, though many of these House widows lost. Margaret Chase Smith filled the House seat held by her husband after he passed away while in office. Smith went onto win election to that same House seat, and later served nearly a quarter-century as a senator from Maine. Lindy Boggs, a member of the House from Louisiana, first ran for the House after her husband, House Majority leader Hale Boggs, died in a plane crash in Alaska. Lindy Boggs decided to run for the seat, won, and held onto the seat for eighteen years. Neither Smith nor Boggs was a political neophyte when they ran for office after the deaths of their spouses. Both played active roles in local politics and in their husband's political campaigns – factors that certainly helped them forge independent political careers.

In the early eras of women's congressional representation, it is not entirely clear that having women in Congress made a substantive difference. Jeannette Rankin's two terns in Congress happened to include America's entrance into both World War I and World War II, and Rankin, as a pacifist, voted against America's entry into both those wars. These behaviors could, arguably, reflect a more feminine way of thinking. Other systematic research suggests that female members of Congress tended to vote on legislation in ways similar to their male counterparts, and conformed to the expectations of the political institution. Frieda Gehlen's (1977b) research on women in Congress in the early 1960s concluded about the similarities between women and men's behavior that "those women who have attained high political office seem to have adapted to the role and its expectations as they exist rather than modifying the role greatly to fit more traditional feminist values and habits" (p. 318). The masculine expectations of political institutions meant that, to be successful in those institutions, individuals often had to conform to masculine norms.

Until 1992 women were still quite rare in Congress as no more than thirty women ever served in the House at the same time; and, just sixteen women ever served in the US Senate before 1992, and of these sixteen women, ten filled vacancies through an appointment upon a sitting senator's death. From 1917 to 1931, with the exception of one woman on one day in 1922, not a single woman held a seat in the US Senate. The lone exception was Rebecca Latimer Felton, the first woman to serve in the US Senate. The governor of Georgia appointed her after a sitting senator died while in office. Nearly 100 years after Felton's appointment, Georgia has yet, as of the completion of this manuscript, to elect a woman to the US Senate.[6] In fact, between 1789 and 2018, a mere fifty-two women served in the Senate, and eighteen states have yet to send a woman, via appointment or election, to the US Senate.

The proverbial "Year of the Woman" in 1992 appeared to mark a turning point in women's political representation. Record-setting numbers of women ran for the US Congress, spurred, in part, by the way the US Senate handled, or failed to handle, the accusations of sexual harassment levied against then Supreme Court nominee Clarence Thomas by law professor Anita Hill. A telling incident occurred when a group of female House members marched to the Senate office buildings to attend the judiciary committee's hearings. The female House members could not gain access to the hearings, as they were told there were "no strangers" allowed in the Senate. Multiple candidates, including Carol Mosley Braun, Lynn Yeakel, and Barbara Boxer,[7] credited the Thomas hearings

---

[6] Georgia Governor Brian Kemp, in 2020, appointed Kelly Loeffler to the Senate. This means Georgia has had two women appointed to the Senate but yet to elect a woman to the Senate.

[7] Barbara Boxer moved up from the House to the Senate at the time, and she was part of the group of female House members who attempted to attend the Thomas hearing who were turned away for being "strangers" to the Senate.

and Hill's treatment by the Senate judiciary committee as a major factor motivating their campaigns for political office (Witt, Paget, and Matthews 1994; Wolbrecht 2000). Other factors such as a high number of open-seat races also propelled women to success during this election cycle (Cook and Wilcox 1994). Some of the 1992 female contenders advanced an argument that their gender gave them a unique and much needed perspective to politics and that the outsider status of women could change the way the mostly masculine Congress operated. After the 1992 election, the number of women in the US Senate increased from one, Barbara Mikulski, to five. The number of women in the US House also increased substantially from twenty-eight women to forty-seven.

The 1992 election cycle was a watershed moment for women in politics, but the momentum of that year did not quite carry over to future elections. While the numbers of women running for office slowly increased, the numbers of women winning and holding a seat in the House or the Senate inched up slowly. After the "Year of the Woman," women held 9.5 percent of seats in the House and the Senate combined. In the aftermath of the 2016 election, the year a woman first ran for the presidency as a major political party's nominee, women's representation stood at just under 20 percent of both congressional chambers. In fact, women failed to gain any new seats in Congress after 2016. Another way to think about the pace of women's representation is that across thirteen elections between 1992 and 2016, women's numbers in Congress increased by less than 1 percent, or about four members, each election cycle. If women's representation continues at this pace, women will achieve parity with men in the legislature in the next fifty election cycles, or in the next 100 years – assuming there is no decline in women's representation.

Many of the previous barriers that prevented women from pursuing political office no longer exist. Women have the legal authority to manage their finances, buy and sell property, and vote. Women's entrance into high-profile positions of political leadership is slow. As of 2019, just around 373 women ever served in the House or the Senate, going back to Rankin's election in 1916. This means that the total number of women to ever serve in Congress from 1789 through 2019 is still *less* than the total number of men, about 408, currently serving in the US Congress. Vermont, along with Idaho, at no point in its history elected a woman in its congressional delegation. This is striking considering that Vermont became a state in 1791. A century after the passage of the Nineteenth Amendment, women are still minority political actors.

The 2018 midterm elections may signal the start of the rebellion portended by Abigail Adams some 240 years ago. Record numbers of women ran for seats to Congress, state legislatures, and gubernatorial offices across the country. The start of the 2019 congressional term saw women's representation catapult from 19 percent to just over 23 percent of the House and Senate combined. If women's representation continues to keep the 4 percent pace set in 2018, as opposed to the 1 percent pace of the past two decades, women will achieve parity with men in Congress sometime between 2040 and 2050. Post-2018, women also increased their presence in state legislatures from an average of 25 percent to an average of 29 percent. But the rates of women's representation vary considerably across the states. Women hold just over 50 percent of congressional seats in Nevada and 47 percent in Colorado. In West Virginia and Mississippi women hold just under 15 percent of seats in the state legislature. Women's representation in state-level executive offices is even more bleak. Prior to 2018, women held six out of fifty gubernatorial offices. At the start of 2019, women will hold nine gubernatorial offices – an all-time high. Despite these recent gains, nearly twenty states have yet to elect a woman to the state's top executive position. Lower levels of office serve as a key pipeline to higher levels of office, and small numbers of women at the local and state level means that there will be smaller numbers of women running for Congress or the presidency.

THE HIGHEST AND HARDEST GLASS CEILING – STILL INTACT

Hillary Clinton's failed 2008 and 2016 presidential runs marked critical opportunities to elect a woman to the highest and, arguably, most masculine political office. Clinton was not the first woman to run for the presidency. Victoria Woodhull was the first woman to run for the presidency in 1872[8] and 1876, followed by Belva Lockwood in 1884 and 1888. These women certainly garnered press attention, often less than favorable, for their presidential runs, but few took them seriously as presidential contenders and neither won any electoral votes. The news media and the public treated these two women as humorous oddities rather than as political activists making a point about the marginalized role of women in public life. *Harper's Weekly* in 1872 depicted Woodhull as the devil in a cartoon about her candidacy, and one article in

---

[8] The age requirement for the president set forth in the constitution rendered Woodhull unqualified in 1872 as she was just shy of thirty-five.

1884 mocked Belva Lockwood's failed candidacy by declaring that she "left a pattern for her ballots. They will be cut bias, the scalloped edges trimmed with jet lace and knotted fringe gracefully looped at the corners and fastened with a bow of pink ribbons." Nevertheless, Woodhull and Lockwood made arguments about the inability of women to access education, gain economic independence, and control their bodies. At the time, many of the ideas put forth by these women were extreme.

After Belva Lockwood's presidential run in 1888, virtually no serious female contenders made a presidential run. In 1964, Margaret Chase Smith, the Republican senator from Maine who first entered Congress as a widow, ran for the Republican Party's nomination. In 1972, two women of color, Shirley Chisholm and Patsy Mink, ran for the Democratic Party's nomination. The candidacies of Chisholm and Mink stand out because both ran for office in the middle of upheaval regarding women's roles and fierce public debate about the role of women in the United States. The country was on the cusp of rapid changes in the public status of women as access to birth control became available to women; Congress passed its first pay equity law in the previous decade; and the Equal Rights Amendment was about to go to the states for ratification.

Women's paths to power, right up to the 2016 presidential election, remained blocked. Many factors deter women from pursuing the presidency. Serious presidential contenders need political experience in elected office of some kind such as the Senate or a gubernatorial seat. The low number of women in presidential pipeline offices means that the pool of viable female presidential contenders is smaller relative to men in those pipeline offices. Even when women have political experience, as did Smith, Chisholm, and Mink, the public, political elites, and the mass media never took these women seriously as presidential contenders. Their political experience was not the "right" type of political experience needed to serve in the country's highest, most powerful, and, arguably, most masculine political office.

Some eighty years ago, Gallup started periodically asking Americans about their willingness to vote for a woman for the presidency. The fact that Gallup included this question eighty years ago is somewhat striking given that virtually nobody thought seriously about the potential of a female president. Gallup did not ask this question every year, nor even every presidential election cycle; as such, the responses offer momentary snapshots about Americans' willingness to vote for a female presidential contender. The question always included a caveat: "if she were qualified in every other respect." The fact that Gallup included the qualification

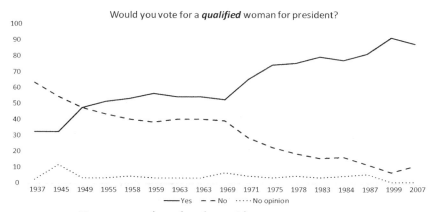

FIGURE 2.2 Vote support for a female president

caveat is important because this suggests that respondents might evaluate a female nominee's qualifications differently from those of a male nominee. Moreover, it is not entirely clear what a qualified female presidential candidate looks like. The question shows interesting shifts over time in how Americans feel about the prospect of voting for a "qualified" woman for the presidency. Figure 2.2 graphs the results of this question from 1937 to 2007. Americans started out skeptical about putting a woman into a position of political power.

In 1937, an overwhelming 64 percent of Americans declared they would not vote for a woman for the presidency even if "she were qualified in every other respect." Opposition to supporting a qualified woman for the presidency slowly diminished throughout the next decade. In 1949, public sentiment shifted when 48 percent of Americans said they would vote for a woman and 48 percent of Americans said they would not vote for a female president. It was just before this upward trend began that Gallup introduced another change in how the question was asked. Starting in 1945, Gallup added a little more information to the question, including, "If the party whose candidate you most often support nominated a woman for the presidency."

Since 1950, the percentage of the American public stating their willingness to support a female candidate for the presidency shifted upward. The high point of American support for a female president came in 1999, with 92 percent of Americans indicating they would vote for a qualified woman. But this upward positive shift reflects that most respondents will support a qualified woman, whatever that substantively means, if the respondent's political party nominated her.

Asking about support for a female presidential candidate is tricky. Such a question asks about a hypothetical candidate rather than an actual person. Questions about women can trigger social desirability bias that leaves respondents feeling pressured to produce a favorable response. Respondents who say they would not vote for a woman for the presidency risk being labeled as sexist. Streb et al. (2008) conducted a list experiment to detect social desirability in the "support for a female president" polling question. The list-experiment method limits the potential for social desirability bias to lead to an overreport in support for a female candidate. The method presented half the experimental sample with a list of four phrases about policies or politics, such as "the way gasoline prices keep going up," and asked the participants to indicate how many of the items made them upset or angry, but not which items made them upset or angry. The other half of participants received the exact same list of items presented in the baseline group but added "a woman serving as president" as the fifth item. Again, participants in the "woman serving as president" treatment group indicated how many but not which items made them angry or upset. The authors then compared the number of items that made participants upset in the baseline group with the treatment group. The logic is that if a woman serving as president *does not* trigger social desirability bias, then the same number of items should make people upset in both conditions. If a woman serving as president triggers social desirability bias, then participants should indicate that *more* items make them upset in the treatment compared with the control group. The authors found that participants indicated that more items made them upset in the woman as president treatment group. In fact, about 26 percent of participants indicated that a woman serving as president made them angry. Burden, Ono, and Yamada (2017) followed up on this research ten years later to see whether public sentiment about a woman serving as president shifted in the wake of Clinton's 2008 and 2016 presidential runs. Just half as many people, 13 percent, expressed anger over the prospect of a female president. This means that a somewhat substantial number of respondents who say they will vote for a qualified woman may not have any intention or desire to support a female presidential candidate.

A good number of Americans who indicate positive support for a female president in polls may not actually support a woman for the presidency. Another way to gauge public support for a female president is with Gallup's question that asks, "Do you think voters are ready for a woman president, or don't you think so?" Figure 2.3 tracks America's readiness from 1996 through 2016. Most poll respondents feel that America is ready

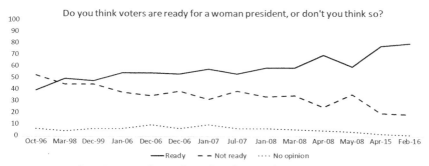

FIGURE 2.3 American readiness for a female president

for a woman to sit in the Oval Office, but this level of positive support is somewhat lower compared with the level of positive support in the qualified presidential candidate question. Looking at how respondents felt about America's readiness for a woman in the White House in 1999, the year that vote support on the qualified woman question reached its zenith at 92 percent, shows that significantly fewer – 48 percent – thought Americans were ready for a female president. In February 2016, just eight months before Americans got the chance to vote for a female president, 80 percent of participants thought America was ready for a female chief executive, while 19 percent thought Americans were just not ready.

Polling data alone suggest that Americans might be willing and ready to support a qualified female candidate's presidential bid. Some of these positive responses may be a product of social desirability where poll respondents offer socially acceptable responses that do not reflect their true intentions or attitudes. The positive responses indicated in the polling data may also be due to partisan affinity effects where respondents will support a female nominee as long as she belongs to their political party. Another limitation of poll questions about America's willingness to vote for a "qualified" woman for the presidency is that it is entirely unclear what it means to be "qualified" for the presidency and what a "qualified" woman looks like. Pundits, journalists, and voters wrote off many of the previous women who ran for the presidency as lacking the necessary presidential qualifications, even though many had good qualifications.

QUALIFICATIONS AND THE CASE OF HILLARY CLINTON

Pollsters throughout the 2016 campaign regularly asked the American public about the qualifications of Clinton and Trump for the presidency. The "qualified for the presidency" question is a staple of election season

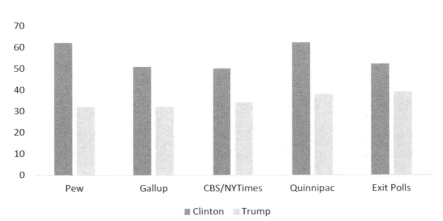

FIGURE 2.4 Qualifications and 2016 presidential candidates

polls. I compiled the percentage of participants who rated Clinton as qualified for the presidency and Trump as qualified across five major polls throughout the 2016 election. Figure 2.4 presents these data. Across the polls, a majority of respondents consistently rated Clinton as highly qualified for the presidency. At no point during 2016 did a majority rate Trump as qualified for the presidency. A high qualification rating did not translate into enough electoral support for Clinton, and a low qualification rating did not hurt Trump at the polls.[9] These patterns, while descriptive, suggest that qualifications mattered in different ways for Clinton and Trump.

The American National Election Study (ANES) does not directly ask respondents to indicate whether a candidate is very or not very qualified but asks participants to rate levels of candidate knowledge. Knowledge is not the same as candidate qualifications, but certainly knowledge is a characteristic that relates to candidate qualifications. It is reasonable to expect that participants will rate an unqualified candidate as not very knowledgeable. Did perceived levels of knowledge factor into voter decision-making in 2016?

Based on nearly eighty years of polling data and the polling data from the 2016 presidential campaign, it is reasonable to expect that respondents will rate Clinton more positively on knowledge relative to Trump,

---

[9] Clinton won approximately 3 million more votes than Trump in the popular vote but lost in the electoral college. The important takeaway is that Trump's lack of qualifications did not hurt him, especially among more conservative voters in rural districts where Trump secured enough votes to win in the electoral college.

and her positive ratings on knowledge should boost her level of vote support. My expectation is that Clinton will, in fact, receive higher knowledge ratings compared with Trump, but these knowledge ratings will not necessarily lead to more vote support. The logic of the gendered qualifications gap means that voters will expect a female presidential contender to be more knowledgeable than her male opponent, but this will not necessarily afford her any electoral advantages. A male candidate, in this case Trump, will receive an automatic advantage because his sex fits with the masculine perceptions of who looks like a leader. As such, if there is a gendered dimension to qualifications, this analysis should show two effects. *First, Clinton should receive a more positive rating on knowledge relative to Trump.* Just to make it onto the ballot, Clinton has to have more impressive qualifications compared with a male candidate. Feminine stereotypes of women lacking the qualities needed for masculine social roles create a high qualification bar for women (Ditonto 2017). *Second, Trump, even though he will not receive positive ratings on knowledge, will receive more support electoral support relative to Clinton.* A low knowledge rating for Trump will simply not matter for voters because Trump still fits the masculine image of the presidency.

I used logistic regression models that predict the effect of perceived candidate knowledge levels on vote choice. A logistic regression model allows me to estimate the effect of candidate knowledge ratings on vote choice for Clinton and for Trump. Logistic regression is the most appropriate modeling choice here because the outcome variables are dichotomous, taking on the value of 1 if the respondent reported supporting the candidate and 0 otherwise. This type of regression model calculates the logarithm of the odds, or the "log-odds," for the value of 1 in the outcome variable, support for Clinton or Trump, given the candidate knowledge ratings, the key predictor, and a set of other relevant control variables. Using the log-odds values, which are difficult to directly interpret into substantive outcomes, I then calculated the predicted probability of expressing vote support for the candidate based on whether the respondent rated the candidate negatively or positively on the knowledge rating while accounting for the "usual suspects" that predict vote choice. The models each included controls to account for those other factors that typically condition affect for presidential candidates, such as party, ideology, income, region, gender, race, and education levels.[10]

---

[10] See the Appendix to Chapter 2 for the full set of regression models.

Just looking at the distribution of responses rating Trump and Clinton's levels of knowledge shows that Clinton outperformed Trump, as expected. Clinton received a high or moderately high knowledge rating among 54 percent of respondents, while Trump received a high or moderately high knowledge rating among 21 percent of respondents. This pattern, so far, offers support for a gendered qualification gap. The second component of the gendered qualification gap argues that these positive ratings on candidate knowledge will not carry over into electoral support. In other words, just because a voter thinks a female candidate is knowledgeable, or otherwise highly qualified, does not necessarily mean the voter will support the female candidate at the polls.

Figure 2.5 displays the level of vote support among respondents who rated the candidate as having little knowledge, a moderate amount of knowledge, and a high level of knowledge based on the logistic regression models. Being knowledgeable does not provide a boost for Clinton. At every level of perceived knowledge, respondents had a higher predicted probability of supporting Trump relative to Clinton. Participants who rated Trump as having a low level of knowledge had a 0.13 (13 percent) probability of voting for him, while participants who rated Clinton as having a low level of knowledge had just a 0.05 (5 percent) probability of voting for her, $p < 0.01$. Participants were more willing to support the male presidential candidate whom they saw as lacking knowledge rather than support an unknowledgeable female presidential candidate.

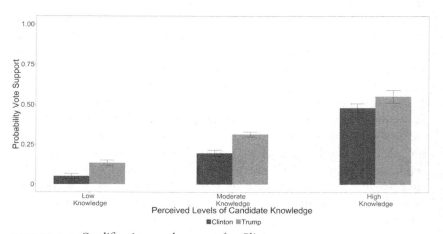

FIGURE 2.5 Qualifications and support for Clinton.
Note: 95 percent confidence intervals included. See Appendix to Chapter 2 for full regression model results.

These patterns fit with the expectations of a gendered qualification gap and reflect the gendered perceptions Americans hold about whether men or women have the qualification needs for leadership.

Perceived levels of candidate knowledge are not the only factors that influence voter decision-making. It is possible that knowledge mattered little in Trump's evaluations because forces such as partisanship weighed more heavily in the minds of voters. The regression models I estimated controlled for respondent party, but I also estimated models that controlled for whether a respondent belonged to the same party or a different political party than the candidate. If co-partisans are less likely to support Clinton relative to Trump when both types of respondents rate them as having low levels of knowledge, this suggests that Clinton's sex might factor into how participants use perceptions of knowledge in decision-making. To test this relationship, I estimated logistic regression models with an interaction between co-partisanship and knowledge ratings. The interaction term between co-partisan status and knowledge ratings lets me test whether the effect of perceived candidate knowledge is conditional on the partisan relationship between the respondent and the candidate. I include the full results from these models in the Appendix to Chapter 2, and I summarize the key findings.

At high levels of knowledge, co-partisans are just slightly more supportive of Clinton, a 0.64 predicted probability, relative to co-partisans who rate Trump high on knowledge, a 0.59 predicted probability, but these rates of support do not significantly differ. At low levels of knowledge, co-partisans are not quite as likely to support Clinton, a 0.12 predicted probability, relative to Trump's support among co-partisans, a 0.28 predicted probability – and these differences are statistically significant, p < 0.01. Co-partisan voters who view Clinton as lacking knowledge are not as strongly motivated by partisan concerns to vote for her compared with Trump's co-partisan supporters, who seem more willing to overlook his low knowledge ratings.

It is possible that the knowledge patterns I uncovered in the preceding analyses occurred in electoral years where there were no female candidates on the ballot and that these patterns are not emblematic of any gendered qualification gap. Using the over-time ANES data, I replicated my analyses using the Democratic and Republican presidential candidate ratings for 1980, the year the knowledge question first appeared on the survey, through 2012. In the Republican presidential candidate vote support models, knowledge ratings consistently have a positive and significant effect on electoral support. In the Democratic vote support models, knowledge ratings have no statistically significant effect on whether a respondent reported voting for the Democratic candidate. Estimating the results year-by-year shows a similar null effect. Prior to 2016, the presidential candidates in both political parties were all men. Ratings on perceived knowledge, a dimension of qualifications, either helped the candidate's electoral prospects among voters or had no significant effect.

Having knowledge is not the same thing as being qualified, but it is reasonable to assume a high correlation between the two concepts. When voters think about what makes a candidate qualified for the presidency, it is likely they will think about whether a candidate has the intellect needed for tackling the tough policy problems facing the nation. A low knowledge rating did not matter for many of Trump's supporters. I argue that this is due, in part, to the inherent link between being male, masculinity, and political leadership. Trump, by virtue of his sex and the gendered assumptions about masculinity this leads to, does not need to have knowledge. A high knowledge rating is not quite enough for Clinton to close the qualification gap. I argue throughout the next several chapters that when voters make assessments about who is qualified and what it means to have solid qualifications, voters are really looking for a male or a masculine candidate.

WHAT HAPPENED TO THAT REBELLION?

John Adams and the other founders certainly forgot to "remember the ladies." It took 142 years for the country to grant women the full rights of citizenship in the US Constitution with the ratification of the Nineteenth Amendment. One hundred years after the passage of that amendment, women still face marginalization at the highest levels of political leadership. Many women and girls felt the sharp sting of defeat after Clinton's unexpected loss, and women received a clear message that they did not belong in public life. Rather than sitting back and taking the defeat quietly, many women and male allies rose up in protest (Campbell and Wolbrecht 2019). Women gathered in Washington, DC, and in cities across the country, and across the globe, in a Women's March to protest the marginalization of women's voices and experiences in public life. The protests that occurred were not necessarily a spontaneous rebellion; they were the result of the coordinated efforts of groups long dedicated to lifting up the voices of marginalized communities (Berry and Chenoweth 2018). The goal was not just to protest Clinton's loss and Trump's victory but to stand against the marginalization of women, and for communities of color, those who identify as LGBTQ+, and other underrepresented groups. Millions of women and allies marched in January 2017. One year later, women gathered again, albeit in smaller though still impressively large numbers, to hold a second Women's March. The Women's March encompassed people from diverse backgrounds and political ideologies unified under the common goal of increasing the voices and presence of women in public life.

The Women's March and the record number of women who ran for office in 2018 may be part of the rebellion promised by Abigail Adams. This rebellion, in the modern era, consists of women protesting their marginalization in public spaces. The "pink wave" occurred at the congressional level and at the state and local level where more women put their name on the ballot, and more women won elections. The anger, angst, and anxiety felt among many at the outcome of the 2016 presidential election may, in fact, be laying the groundwork needed to make significant future gains in women's representation. Campbell and Wolbrecht (2019) found that young girls, especially Democratic girls, expressed more interest in political participation, especially protesting, after the 2016 election. Even though Clinton lost, many women identified her as a role model who inspires them to run for political office in the future (Bonneau and Kanthak 2018). Having more women enter the political pipeline in lower levels of office ensures a steady stream of candidates garnering the experience needed to run for higher levels of political office in future elections.

This chapter began by addressing one of the four central questions guiding this book: How do ideas about gender affect what it means to be qualified for political office? This chapter illustrated how the United States constructed a political system that used feminine stereotypes and sex-segregated social roles to exclude women from political life. Even the suffragists who fought for women's full inclusion in the Constitution often used feminine stereotypes as a reason to grant them voting rights. Indeed, feminine stereotypes have long shaped women's political participation. Feminine stereotypes and beliefs about women's appropriate roles as caregivers and not leaders are still used to exclude women from positions of power and leadership. Women who run for political office face questions about who will care for their children when they serve the

public – questions infrequently asked of male candidates.[11] A consequence of the association between women, feminine stereotypes, and
private roles in the home is that it can make it difficult for the voting
public to see women as viable political leaders.

In the modern era, there is a clear puzzle among the public about
having a woman in the presidency. Polling data show that Americans
will vote for a female presidential candidate of their own political party –
as long as she was qualified in every other way. It is not clear what
constitutes a qualified female presidential candidate, and whether a qualified female presidential candidate looks exactly like a qualified male
presidential candidate. Moreover, the analyses of the relationship
between candidate qualifications and vote choice in 2016 suggest that
qualifications appeared to matter in very different ways for Hillary Clinton, the first woman to run for the presidency as a major political party's
nominee, and Donald Trump, her male opponent. Trump supporters
were more willing to vote for him even though they rated him negatively
on knowledge, a key dimension of candidate qualifications. Even though
Clinton received more positive knowledge ratings than Trump, she did
not receive as much electoral support. I argue that part of how voters
define political qualifications is through the lens of masculinity, and the
association between leadership and masculinity creates an obstacle for
female candidates. In Chapter 3, I turn to how masculinity shapes the way
Americans think about what it means to be qualified for political office.

---

[11] However, some reporters in the 2020 lead-up are trying to level the playing field by
asking male candidates about their children and childcare arrangements. Anna North,
"We Asked the Dads Running for President What They Do for Child Care," *Vox.com*,
May 28, 2019, www.vox.com/policy-and-politics/2019/5/22/18633044/2020-election-
democrats-child-care-kids-men.

3

No Place for Women

The selection of General George Washington, who rose to prominence as a military commander, as the first president in 1789 set the tone that military prowess and physical strength are necessary for good political leadership. Many political leaders in early American history rose to fame through military experience, and many political candidates still tout military experience and all-around toughness as an asset. Andrew Jackson earned a reputation as a ruthless military commander in the War of 1812. William Henry Harrison and his running mate John Tyler won the presidency in 1840 with the slogan "Tippecanoe and Tyler too," a reference to the Battle of Tippecanoe, also in the War of 1812. Americans chose the leader of the Union Army, General Ulysses Grant, to lead in the aftermath of the Civil War. Prior to becoming president Theodore Roosevelt led the Rough Riders in the Spanish-American War – combat experience some would argue Roosevelt sought out specifically to burnish his political credentials for the presidency. This seemingly intrinsic connection between military leadership and political leadership reinforces the notions of politics as a masculine endeavor.

Electing military commanders and generals as political leaders is not unique to the American experience. Indeed, as Chapter 2 discusses, the link between masculinity and political leadership developed over millennia and exists across time and across many communities and cultures. There are ample examples of nondemocratic leaders who displayed masculinity, such as Julius Caesar, King Henry VIII, and even examples of women such as Catherine the Great, but these leaders were not necessarily chosen because they displayed masculinity, and they certainly were not chosen through a democratic process. Rather, nondemocratic leaders, such as kings who ascended to power via the divine right of monarchs, learned to display masculinity as a way to hold onto their power (Bederman 1995; Ducat 2004). The demand that leaders, even nondemocratic ones, display masculinity cements the idea that being a leader requires being masculine. The most foolproof way to be masculine is to be male. Another way for aspiring politicians to show masculinity is to have experience in masculine institutions, with the military being, arguably, one of the most masculine institutions. The election of military leaders in a democracy, especially the choice of a military general as the first president, matters in the American democratic framework because masculine credentials became a criterion by which voters chose political leaders.

Dwight Eisenhower is the last military commander elected to the presidency,[1] but a seemingly unbreakable link between the masculinity of the military and the American image of a quintessential political leader persists today. Political candidates regularly engage in masculine behaviors on the campaign trail. Indeed, presidential campaigns often consist of "manly men doing manly things in manly ways" (Duerst-Lahti 2007, p. 87). Ronald Reagan frequently presented himself in the classic image of the rugged American cowboy. In the 2004 presidential election, George W. Bush reminded Americans of his National Guard service, while John Kerry talked about his tours of duty in Vietnam. Sometimes attempts at masculinity backfire. Democratic presidential nominee Michael Dukakis famously appeared outfitted in military combat garb while riding a tank – a ploy that inspired mockery rather than faith in his masculine leadership. Dukakis's instinct that Americans wanted to see a political candidate who could command and lead the country, while poorly executed, was not off the mark. Meredith Conroy (2015) conducted an extensive analysis of the news coverage received by presidential candidates in the modern era and found that, quite overwhelmingly, when it comes to news coverage it is masculinity that dominates the press. The news media pay attention to the masculine behaviors of candidates, highlight masculine traits, and rely on gendered conflict frames to create a competitive narrative between two political contenders. It pays, through earned media coverage, to be masculine.

Candidates highlight masculinity at lower levels of office. Take, for example, the role of guns in campaign ads. It is typical for congressional

---

[1] Eisenhower was certainly not the last military commander to pursue the presidency. As recently as 2004, General Wesley Clark ran for the Democratic Party's presidential nomination.

candidates to talk about, hold, and shoot guns. Joe Manchin, a West Virginia Democrat, aired a campaign ad where he shot the printed text of the Affordable Care Act thrown up into the air. Jason Kander, who ran for the Senate in 2016 to represent Missouri, aired an attention-grabbing thirty-second campaign spot that featured him assembling a gun while blindfolded. Kander lost the election but received praise for his "bold" ad. Georgia gubernatorial candidate Brian Kemp also featured guns in a 2018 Republican primary ad with the candidate talking to a teenage boy about dating Kemp's daughter while deliberately pointing a gun at the boy. Guns represent strength and authority. They are literal tools of power and destruction.

The need for candidates to tell voters that they are tough and aggressive can pose an inherent obstacle for female candidates. The easiest way for political candidates to display masculinity is to talk about their experiences participating in masculine institutions. This task is not quite so easy for female candidates. Masculine institutions, such as the military, business, and the legal field, all historically excluded women. To be sure, women are not entirely absent from the masculine institutions that serve as pipelines into politics, but the roles of women in these institutions often reinforce femininity rather than masculinity. In the business sector, women are not likely to be in top executive-level positions but are more likely to work in the human resources department (AAUW 2016) – a role that reflects feminine rather than masculine qualities. Women's historic exclusion from masculine institutions makes it more difficult for women to talk about masculine experiences they simply do not have.

Being masculine requires some creativity and risk-taking on the part of female candidates. Joni Ernst conquered this challenge in her 2014 Republican Senate primary in Iowa with a campaign ad talking about her experiences growing up on a farm castrating pigs. The image of the "Midwestern farmer" evokes a classic masculine image that harkens back to that classic American cowboy image that resonates with Americans. Farming requires physical strength, grit, and the willingness to take risks – all stereotypically masculine qualities (Koenig et al. 2011). Ernst's message was also credible. Not only did she have her farm experience to fall back on, but she served in Iraq as a member of the National Guard – giving her that coveted military experience. Other female candidates struggle to credibly show masculinity. Alison Lundergran-Grimes did not fare so well with her masculine campaign approach. She received considerable flack for airing a campaign ad that featured her shooting a gun. This image of a woman engaging in a typically "masculine" behavior did not sit well with voters, as many saw the ad as lacking authenticity and credibility. The 2018 midterm elections featured a number of female military veterans and women with experience in the CIA and other intelligence agencies, which are, arguably, masculine institutions. Female candidates such as MJ Hegar, Amy McGrath, Gina Ortiz-Jones, Chrissy Houlahan, Elissa Slotkin, and Mikkie Sherrill, just to name a few, all ran, in part, on their masculine records. Not all of these women won their elections – most of the losses came from partisan dynamics in gerrymandered districts – but direct experience in masculine institutions gave them the credibility needed to campaign on masculinity.

Chapter 2 illustrated how femininity shaped women's marginalized political status from the founding of the United States up to the present. Women's exclusion from political roles is nothing new in US history. Separate-spheres ideology, with women serving roles in the home and men serving roles in public, determined the appropriate role for women for well over a hundred years in the United States. Even suffragists fighting for the right of women to vote did not necessarily challenge the idea that women were the purer, more moral sex, and that women are best suited for roles as mothers and caregivers. These stereotypes, I argue, limited the ability of women to fill leadership roles. Chapter 2 traced the slow progress of women into political leadership roles throughout the twentieth and into the twenty-first century.

Chapter 3 continues to answer the question: How do ideas about gender affect what it means to be qualified for political office? I develop my core theoretical argument that there is an intrinsic link between what it means to be qualified for political office and ideas of masculinity. The concept of gendered qualifications means that voters will hold masculine ideas about who can serve in political leadership roles. To explain this connection, I draw on social role theory. Social role theory argues that the performance of women and men in separate social roles sets the expectations for which sex is best suited for filling specific social roles, especially the role of being a political leader (Eagly and Karau 2002). Social role theory explains the deeply embedded association between men and masculinity as well as how masculinity influences who voters see as qualified political leaders.

I apply social role theory to the study of political qualifications to illustrate how seemingly objective metrics of candidate quality, such as political experience, have an inherently gendered component. The research on candidate qualifications has not connected these concepts to gender stereotypes to better understand how measures of candidate qualifications can pose obstacles for female candidates. This is a critical theoretical contribution. Women's historic exclusion from public life means that many women often have difficulty gaining entrance into the political pipeline institutions necessary to have the qualifications needed for political office. These pipeline institutions include higher education, prestigious law firms, and top business companies – and these are institutions that do, on average, underrepresent women. The women who successfully gain entrance into masculine institutions end up with better qualifications than many of the men who also come through those institutions. The perception that candidates should follow a narrow political path that often involves participation in public institutions dominated by men leads to the expectation that candidates with more feminine careers, such as nursing or teaching, are not qualified.

I use two empirical analyses to highlight how masculinity affects who Americans see as fit for filling political leadership roles. First, I use a simple visualization task to test the premise that when voters think about political leaders they think about men. I adapt the classic "draw a scientist" task from social psychology research, and recruit an online sample of adults to find pictures of leaders using a Google image search. The vast majority of leader images selected by participants, indeed about 90 percent, are images of men. Second, I conduct an experiment that asks participants to evaluate a hypothetical candidate that has a classic masculine background or a candidate that has a more feminine background that reflects the experiences in institutions where women are more likely to participate. This experiment tests the contention that voters prefer candidates who come from masculine backgrounds. I find that voters, in fact, preferred the candidate with the more feminine background. The argument set forth in this chapter shows that masculinity affects how voters think about candidate qualifications in subtle ways.

A SOCIAL ROLE PERSPECTIVE ON POLITICAL LEADERSHIP

Social role theory argues that stereotypes about whether women or men can perform certain roles stems from the observed performance of women and men in separate social roles. The segregated social roles held by women and men evolved from early communities that needed to balance safety and protection needs with their nourishment and procreation needs (Eagly 1987). Early, pre-industrial revolution communities, required protection from leaders, and providing this protection required physical strength. Leadership in early communities needed individuals who could

provide sustenance through hunting; performing this role required individuals capable of leaving the community for long periods of time. Men
were physically more suited to filling these roles (Wood and Eagly 2012).[2]

Women certainly have physical strength, but the biological roles of
women as mothers made it more difficult for women to engage in physically strenuous tasks that also required them to venture away from home
for long periods of time. Women instead performed communal tasks
through caring for small children and engaging in agricultural tasks closer
to home. According to social role theory, the division of women and men
into separate roles emerged, initially, from basic innate differences
between women and men (Eagly 1987; Eagly and Karau 2002; Wood
and Eagly 2012). Protecting and feeding communities required brute
physical strength and the ability to travel away from home for long
stretches of time, making men better suited for filling these roles. Protecting communities no longer requires any physical strength, but the classification of these roles as masculine persists. The continued performance of
women and men in these separate social roles shapes the broader stereotypes about gender that now exist.

Even though there is no need for a political leader to have physical
strength, masculine traits largely define the qualities required to serve in
the masculine social roles originally performed by men. Observing men in
positions of power as well as observing leaders displaying masculinity
reinforces this connection between being male, being masculine, and
being a leader. Female leaders who rise to positions of power frequently
reinforce the perception that politics is a masculine endeavor because
these successful women often "look like men," so to speak. Margaret
Thatcher earned the nickname the "Iron Lady" because she showed
aggressiveness and strength while serving as prime minister. A social role
perspective would argue that Thatcher had to perform masculinity for
acceptance as a legitimate and valid leader.

Giving birth to and caring for children is a social role that does, to
some extent, still require the unique biological capacities of women. Only
women can give birth, and caring for newborns, through behaviors such
as breastfeeding, places explicit physical demands on the bodies of
women. The biological fact that only women get pregnant and give birth
leads to the idea of gender essentialism. Gender essentialism argues that

---

[2] Women still participated in food procurement through farming and gardening closer to
home. The difficulty of traveling away from home for longer periods of time made men
more suited for hunting.

women and men have innate and natural skills that relegate them to separate social roles (Coleman and Hong 2008; Heyman and Giles 2006; Taylor 1992). According to this argument, women, because they are the only sex biologically equipped to give birth, are innately better at caring for children, homemaking, and engaging in other caregiving and communal tasks. Gender essentialism justifies the perpetuation of sex-segregation in social roles, justifies sexist beliefs, and contributes to prejudicial and discriminatory attitudes toward women (Brescoll and LaFrance 2004; Glick et al. 2004; Roberts et al. 2017; Wilton et al. 2018). If women are "naturally" destined to perform caregiving tasks, then, according to gender essentialism, men are destined for leadership.

Women reinforce gender essentialism through occupations that reflect supportive social roles such as working as childcare providers, teachers, nurses, secretaries, or assistants. For example, the occupation of being a schoolteacher involves caring for children and requires that those serving in that role be warm, compassionate, nurturing, and patient – all traits that reinforce the communal roles of women as mothers. Even occupations that, on their face value, do not seem to have much to do with communality still reinforce the supportive roles of women. Being an executive assistant is an occupation frequently, though not exclusively, filled by women. The task of being an executive assistant involves providing support to a more prominent and more powerful individual in a company or an organization. An executive assistant might not be required to be compassionate and nurturing in the same way a teacher or a nurse is, but the job still reinforces the supportive roles women fill. The gender essentialism argument makes it difficult for women to enter into professions traditionally dominated by men.

Women who enter male-dominated professions by becoming lawyers, doctors, or professors are seen as going against the roles they are "naturally" suited to performing. Women who hold high-profile jobs traditionally held by men, such as being the CEO of a major corporation, often find themselves performing many communal tasks such as fetching coffee for people, organizing birthday parties for employees, and taking the minutes at meetings.[3] Women often just "fall into" these roles, even if they are a chief executive at a company, such as Sheryl Sandberg recounting her time as an executive at Google or Facebook refilling coffee mugs

---

[3] Adam Grant and Sheryl Sandberg, "Madame C.E.O., Get Me a Coffee," *New York Times*, February 6, 2015, www.nytimes.com/2015/02/08/opinion/sunday/sheryl-sandberg-and-adam-grant-on-women-doing-office-housework.html.

at meetings. When women are not around to fill these roles, men manage to fetch their own coffee without a problem. The women in traditionally male-dominated professions often face hostility, resistance, and backlash for breaking with feminine norms (Heilman and Okimoto 2007; Heilman, Block, and Martell 1995). A female lawyer who is good at her job may receive a penalty for being bad at feminine tasks or lacking feminine traits. Women face barriers entering stereotypically masculine roles because these are high-status, high-prestige, and frequently high-paying roles, and women doing the work conventionally done by a man are seen as going against the grain of the "natural" skills and abilities of women.

While it is difficult for women to cross over into masculine roles, it is not quite as difficult for men to cross into feminine roles – though it is not often that men choose to step into these roles.[4] There are few biological barriers preventing men from caring for children, performing supportive tasks, or working in communal occupations. The low status and low prestige of "women's work" means, however, that some men will resist performing these roles. The roles, occupations, and tasks performed by women are not considered important or essential tasks for survival. Indeed, much of the work that women do – caring for children, providing for the home – is unpaid work. As such, if there is no monetary value placed on the tasks women do, it is thought that anyone can perform "women's work," even though this is important work.

There is a perception that men who perform "women's work" will suffer a loss of status, prestige, and masculinity. For instance, there are a number of jokes that mock men in nursing as well as men who work in other seemingly "feminine" professions. However, research in social psychology shows that this perceived backlash toward men who do not fit into masculine roles does not occur (Moss-Rascusin, Phelan, and Rudman 2010). Research suggests that men who perform feminine tasks often get overrewarded for being caring, kind, warm, or compassionate without losing stereotypically masculine qualities such as being authoritative, tough, assertive, or aggressive (Moss-Rascusin, Phelan, and Rudman 2010). Think about the father who receives lavish praise from strangers

---

[4] Economist Betsey Stevenson argues that it would be better for men to step into more communal roles because it can increase the prestige associated with work perceived to be menial and less important. Stevenson, "Manly Men Need to Take on More Girly Jobs," *Chicago Tribune*, December 7, 2016, www.chicagotribune.com/opinion/commentary/ct-masculine-men-feminine-jobs-20161207-story.html.

for holding his baby while his wife does the grocery shopping. All the father is doing is holding his child without dropping the child, a fairly basic task, but when he performs this stereotypically feminine task he is seen as "such a great father." Few strangers praise women who hold their baby and shop for groceries at the same time. When women perform tasks traditionally done by men, such as being the major breadwinner, they do not always receive the same type of lavish praise for performing a masculine role that men receive for performing a feminine role.

Not only do men receive praise for performing "women's work," but when men move into social roles previously held by women, those roles become more prestigious, more high status, more high paying, and more masculine (Levanon, England, and Allison 2009). Jobs once seen as menial, tedious, and unimportant, such as computer coding and programming, were once roles that women dominated. As the field of computer programming grew in importance and prestige, more men moved into these jobs and effectively transformed the field from "women's work" to one that shuts women out of its ranks. The opposite happens when women start to dominate professions once dominated by men. Take the occupation of schoolteacher. Throughout the 1800s, teaching school was more of a man's job; there were unmarried women who were teachers but they left their jobs once they wed. As women increased their ranks as schoolteachers and men left the profession, the pay, prestige, and status with the job all declined (Levanon, England, and Allison 2009). Men, by virtue of the higher status associated with their social roles, have more flexibility to shift into and out of counter-stereotypic roles. Women do not have this luxury.

Social role theory identifies how individuals develop ideas about *who* can serve in political leadership. Leadership requires masculine qualities readily associated with men. A consequence of this association is that feminine traits are valued far less in political leaders relative to masculine traits. When asked to list the traits desired in political leaders, individuals identify masculine traits as among the most important qualities for leaders, including strength, authority, and aggressiveness (Huddy and Terkildsen 1993). The American National Election Study regularly provides respondents the opportunity to list five items they like (or dislike) about the presidential candidates. The ANES provides a set of master codes that classifies these responses into a variety of traits, issues, and other common qualities provided by respondents. I measured the frequency with which participants listed feminine and masculine qualities as something they liked or disliked about the Democratic and Republican

presidential candidates.[5] Out of the 23,514 items listed as a "like" about
the presidential candidates between 1972 and 2004, 13 percent of the
items listed reflected masculine qualities, while 7 percent reflected feminine qualities, and this is a significant difference, $p < 0.01$. Masculine
traits are "must have" qualifications for political leaders. Feminine traits
are not absent from the list of qualities participants desired in political
leaders, but these are considered as less important characteristics compared with masculine qualities. Among the dislikes, there are far fewer
differences in the extent to which respondents listed masculine and feminine qualities. About 3 percent of respondents listed a masculine quality
as a dislike, while only 1 percent listed a feminine quality as a dislike, and
these values are marginally significant at $p < 0.10$. The substantive difference between listing a negative masculine trait and a negative feminine trait
is not that large qualities for average citizens participating in politics.

The masculinity of politics not only shapes perceptions about *who* can
serve in political leadership but affects how candidates self-select to run
for office, and it affects who participates in politics at the citizen level.
Oliver and Conroy (2017) asked city council members to identify how
strongly they saw themselves as having feminine and masculine traits. The
authors found that those serving in political office, even at the city council
level, overwhelmingly have more masculine qualities relative to feminine
qualities. McDermott (2016) measured how average citizens associated
themselves with femininity and masculinity. She found that among average citizens, those most likely to participate in politics through activities
such as voting, protesting, or talking about politics were individuals who
had masculine dominant sex-types. Not only are masculine traits "must-
have" qualities for potential political leaders, but masculine traits are also
"must-have" qualities for average citizens participating in politics.

The Inherent Masculinity in Measures of Political Qualifications

Most scholars measure candidate qualifications through political experience, professional jobs, and academic credentials (Bond, Fleisher, and
Talbert 1997; Branton et al. 2018; Carnes and Lupu 2015; Carson,
Engstrom, and Roberts 2007; Folke and Rickne 2016; Milyo and Schlosberg 2000; Stone, Maisel, and Maestas 2004), with political experience
considered by many to be the best metric of candidate quality (Maestas

---

[5] I classified the responses based on the classification of the master codes provided by the
ANES into feminine and masculine traits developed by Winter (2010).

and Rugeley 2008; Stone, Maisel, and Maestas 2004). Taken at face value, these metrics appear gender-neutral. It is reasonable to infer that a candidate who previously won election to political office has the requisite qualifications for winning election to political office again. Candidates with political experience will have fundraising networks and established coalitions of supporters. Defining political qualifications through this narrow lens contributes to the perception of qualifications as masculine in three ways: first, women are less likely to have experience in the typical political pipeline institutions; second, this narrow conceptualization of political qualifications excludes alternative ways of gaining skills and resources through participation in more feminine institutions; and third, it is not clear how voters evaluate a candidate's political, professional, and academic credentials.

First, women are less likely to have experience in the typical political pipeline institutions because, historically, women have had difficulty gaining access to these institutions. The pool of potential female contenders with backgrounds in these institutions is likely to be smaller than the pool of potential male contenders with comparable backgrounds (Lawless and Fox 2010). Higher education is a domain that excluded women for much of American history.[6] Certainly, all-female education institutions existed during the colonial era and the early period of American history. Many of these all-female institutions had narrow academic scopes, operating as "finishing colleges" where women learned the social and cultural norms associated with being a good housekeeper; these institutions trained women to serve as teachers or as members of religious organizations. The narrow scope of women's education reinforced the distinction that women belonged in the private sphere, filling feminine social roles, and not in public life, filling masculine roles. It was not until 1920 that Harvard admitted women, and even then, it was just the School of Education that accepted female students. Admitting women to the School of Education locked women into communal social roles. Princeton and Yale did not begin fully admitting women until 1969. It was not until the latter half of the twentieth century that most colleges and universities in the United States admitted female applicants.

Historically, gaining access to a political pipeline institution, such as law school, means that a female applicant generally had to have better undergraduate GPAs, better test scores, and better resumes compared

---

[6] To be sure, for much of American history colleges and universities were inaccessible to women, people of color, and nonelite white men.

with male applicants because law schools were not going to admit female and male applicants in equal numbers. After gaining acceptance to law school, female students then had to survive in an institution where they were often made acutely aware of their minority status. Supreme Court Justice Ruth Bader Ginsburg sometimes recounts a story of her time at Harvard Law when the dean invited the small class of women to a dinner and then admonished them for taking the place of male students.[7] Hillary Clinton spoke of a similar backlash that she experienced when she was the only woman sitting to take the Law School Admissions Test. Fellow test-takers taunted her for taking the seat of a man who would be drafted into Vietnam because of her ambition.[8] Given these barriers, many women feel pressured to be better than their male colleagues in order to gain acceptance in an institution where they are constantly reminded that they do not belong.

Second, most people in political office come from very similar backgrounds, and the relative lack of diversity in political backgrounds can limit how scholars view what makes a candidate qualified. Examining the backgrounds of female and male members of the House from the 114th congressional session shows few differences across candidate sex on some of the basic metrics of qualifications. Most members of the House had some prior political experience. A key difference is that 78 percent of female House members held a prior elected office before serving in the House of Representatives compared with 68 percent of male House members, $p < 0.10$. The fact that female House members in this congressional term were more likely to have prior political experience aligns with the general expectations of the gendered qualification gap. Female House incumbents were just as likely as male House incumbents to have completed an undergraduate or postgraduate degree. Most House members came from one of three professions: the legal field, a business background, or the military. Thirty-two percent of men who served during this term in the House of Representatives came from the legal profession, and 25 percent of women also came from a legal background, and this is not a

---

[7] Philip Galanes, "Ruth Bader Ginsburg and Gloria Steinem on the Unending Fight for Women's Rights," *New York Times*, November 14, 2015, www.nytimes.com/2015/11/15/fashion/ruth-bader-ginsburg-and-gloria-steinem-on-the-unending-fight-for-womens-rights.html.

[8] Glenn Kessler, "Hillary Clinton's Story of a Vietnam Era Confrontation over Law School Admissions," *Washington Post*, September 14, 2016, www.washingtonpost.com/news/fact-checker/wp/2016/09/14/hillary-clintons-story-of-a-vietnam-era-confrontation-over-law-school-admissions/.

statistically significant difference. The business world is a common profession for men in Congress, with 26 percent of men coming from a business background, though 16 percent of women also come from the business sector, $p < 0.10$. The most substantial gender gap in backgrounds is that 18 percent of House members members have military experience of some kind, but only three veterans in the House were female, $p < 0.05$ – but this is narrowing with the increasing numbers of female veterans running for the House.

The resource model of political participation argues that individuals learn the basic skills needed to participate in politics through participation in public institutions (Verba, Schlozman, and Brady 1995). Institutions such as higher education or the legal or business professions provide individuals with the critical reading, writing, speaking, and analytical skills needed to excel in political leadership. Participation in masculine institutions is not the only way to learn these skills. Many of the modes in which women engage in politics go unrecorded in the literature (Baxter and Lansing 1983; Bourque and Grossholtz 1974). For example, success in the legal profession requires power, agency, and a host of other masculine traits, and these are also seen as important qualities in politics. But being successful in politics also requires the ability to find common ground and build consensus across diverse interests. These are skills potential candidates can learn through volunteer organizations such as working in a Parent Teacher Association, the nonprofit sector, or professions such as teaching, nursing, and social work (Schlozman et al. 1995). These alternative paths of developing political qualifications are not always considered to be "good" qualifications of candidates.

The narrow lens of defining political experience and political participation is one that not only affects how scholars examine candidate quality but also affects how scholars measure other aspects of political engagement such as political knowledge. Asking political knowledge questions about the names of Supreme Court justices or party leaders in Congress often shows that women have lower levels of knowledge than men. But asking questions about politics that are more relevant to women or that women may pay more attention to, such as the names of female political leaders, shows an increase in women's political knowledge (Jerit and Barabas 2017; Lizotte and Sideman 2009; Ondercin and Jones-White 2011). A similar gap occurs when asking women and men about political engagement. Women are less likely to participate in politics through behaviors such as fundraising, and women do not talk about politics with their peers as much as men do (Verba, Schlozman, and Brady 1995).

These are masculine ways of expressing political preferences that women do not necessarily do as much as men due to gendered norms of socialization as well as the limitations on financial resources that permit campaign contributions (Schlozman et al. 1995). I argue that the narrow lens through which scholars, pundits, campaign strategists, and the media define qualifications can limit the ability of women and other, nontraditional candidates to work their way through the political pipeline.

Third, it is not clear how voters consider candidate qualifications when deciding which candidates to support. Certainly, incumbency benefits political candidates through support from name recognition, fundraising networks, and having a distinct policy record on which to run (Fenno 1978; Maestas and Rugeley 2008; Mayhew 1974; Sellers 1998). There is evidence that voters sometimes use more "fuzzy" metrics to assess political candidates, such as considering candidate likability, relatability, or whether they want to have a beer with a candidate (Campbell et al. 1960; Miller, Wattenberg, and Malanchuk 1986). It is not entirely clear how voters consider candidate "resumes" when deciding whom to support, and gender stereotypes intersect to shape the way voters evaluate the political, professional, and academic accomplishments of female and male candidates. This is a critical gap in the literature. I conduct two empirical tests to investigate whom and what voters think about when they think about political leaders. In other words, How much do voters think about men and masculinity when they think about political leadership?

THINK LEADER, SEE A MAN?

I start with a simple empirical test of the premise that when voters think about leaders, they think of men. I used a visualization technique developed in social psychology research. Social psychology researchers measure how voters think about the roles women and men fill through a task that asks students, generally school-aged children, to "draw an image" of a scientist. The task allows scholars to see the types of images children associate with the role of a scientist. Children overwhelmingly draw an image of a man rather than a woman when asked to draw a scientist (Chambers 1983). Applying this task to political leadership allows me to see whom and what voters think leaders look like.

For this task, I asked a sample of adults to visualize political leaders. Rather than asking adults to draw images of a political leader, I recruited 195 participants to find an online image that best exemplifies political

leadership through Amazon's Mechanical Turk – a sample of technologic-
ally sophisticated adults (Klar and Krupnikov 2016). The instructions
simply asked participants to find an image of a political leader. Participants provided the link to the image they found. Following the approach
of Klar and Krupnikov (2016), I downloaded all the photos and then
relied on two independent coders to assess the image of each content. *The
general expectation is that most participants will select images of men as a
typical male leader.* This comes not only from the long-standing historic
link between masculinity and leadership but also from the overrepresen-
tation of men in political leadership roles.

The images participants found fit into several overarching categories:
current or former elected officials in the United States or abroad, women,
and cartoon characters. The most common images provided were of men,
as 90 percent provided a link to a male leader. The most frequent
individual featured was Barack Obama (20 percent), followed by Donald
Trump (12 percent). This is not surprising given that Obama and Trump
are the most recent US presidents. A good number of the images were of
contemporary, nonpresidential officeholders, including John McCain,
Paul Ryan, and Bernie Sanders. Nearly all the male leader images are
official photos taken in political office or of the leader engaging in
political activities.[9] For example, several participants provided "action"
shots of members of Congress holding hearings.

The broad expectation for this task was that participants would
provide images of men, but part of the social role theory argument is
that the historic presence of men in leadership roles limits the ability of
voters to think of women as typical leaders. These expectations bear out
in this simple test. Female photos were rare. A mere 9 percent of
participants linked to an image of a woman. Hillary Clinton was the
most common female image provided, followed by Elizabeth Warren.
Linking to images of Clinton and to Warren is not surprising given their

---

[9] It is possible that Google's search algorithms affected the images participants selected
(Emily Cohn, "Google Image Search Has a Gender Bias Problem," *HuffPost.com*, December 6, 2017, www.huffpost.com/entry/google-image-gender-bias_n_7036414). One way
to get at how these algorithms affected the outcome on this task is to look at how much
time participants spent completing the task. Participants spent an average of 6.24 minutes
(SD = 3.48 minutes) searching for photos. The range of time participants spent completing
the search task spans from 1 to 19 minutes. Participants who spent less time, especially
those spending 1–3 minutes completing the search task, are perhaps more likely to have
relied on the top of the list images to complete the task, which are the images likely to come
from search algorithms. Seven participants, out of 195, spent less than 3 minutes completing the task.

prominence in US politics over the last few years. The results suggest that Americans have a very narrow image of political leadership, and this is largely a masculine image. I build on this first empirical test with an experiment to investigate how gender shapes the way voters evaluate the qualifications of political candidates. When people think about leaders, they think about men because most leaders have been men. But do voters want candidates with experience in stereotypically masculine political pipeline institutions?

GENDERED QUALIFICATIONS AND VOTER DECISION-MAKING

Social role theory leads to the prediction that voters value masculine experiences in political candidates, such as serving in the military or even just being a lawyer. The literature on candidate qualifications compounds this expectation. Candidates with previous political experience, work in political pipeline professions, and college degrees are generally considered high-quality candidates. The implication is that more communal, or feminine, backgrounds, such as community organizing, volunteer work, and the nonprofit sector, hold less esteem from the perspective of voters. I test the assumption that candidates with masculine qualifications will fare better than candidates with more feminine backgrounds. Many of the emerging women motivated to run for political office come from these more feminine backgrounds. New Orleans mayor LaToya Cantrell, the first black woman to lead the city, started her career as a community activist working to put New Orleans back together after Hurricane Katrina. Cantrell's background reinforces the stereotypic roles of women as keepers of the community. Political elites do not always see these highly engaged women as potential contenders, and many of these women do not consider themselves viable candidates because they do not come from the masculine backgrounds more typical of candidates (Lawless and Fox 2010). I conducted an experiment designed to test how voters view feminine and masculine qualifications.

The social role theory argument suggests that voters will place a higher value on masculine over feminine qualifications. Most political candidates come through the same political pipeline: law school, lower level of political office, and then a run for Congress. Photos of women were rare (Maestas and Rugeley 2008; Stone et al. 2006). This leaves little room for female candidates who may come through a different, more feminine, pipeline, such as work through community engagement and service in local office (Sweet-Cushman 2018). Based on the candidate quality literature, voters should prefer the "high-quality" candidates that come from a conventionally masculine background, as outlined in the candidate background prediction.

Candidate Background Prediction: Voters will prefer the masculine candidate background over the feminine candidate background.

The logic of this prediction means that candidates with backgrounds such as that of Mayor Cantrell should not fare as well as candidates with from more stereotypically masculine political pipelines.

The experiment tracks how voters evaluate the qualifications of political candidates absent information about whether the candidate was female or male. I intentionally excluded information about whether the candidate was female or male because the goal of this experiment is to identify how voters evaluate the gendered qualifications of candidates rather than how voters evaluated female candidates with feminine or masculine backgrounds. Excluding information about whether the candidate was a woman or man offers a more conservative test of how voters value feminine and masculine backgrounds. A female candidate paired with a feminine background is likely to receive a negative evaluation relative to a male candidate compared with a masculine background or even compared with a female candidate with a masculine background (Bauer 2015a, 2017). Only manipulating the gendered backgrounds gives me a conservative estimate of any negative effects of feminine and masculine qualification sets.

The two biographies focused on the participation of candidates in masculine and feminine institutions. The masculine resume read:

McCann is running for a seat to Congress. At the law firm, McCann was a partner, worked with major business clients in the state, and developed a reputation for an aggressive approach in the courtroom. Prior to serving in the law firm, McCann worked tirelessly as an advocate for the state's business interests, and worked with military veterans. McCann is a longtime resident of the state. McCann graduated from a top law school at the top of the class. McCann, throughout the campaign, has pledged to bring a tough approach to politics.

This biography emphasized the candidate's participation in stereotypically masculine institutions, including experience in business, legal, and military institutions. This set of experiences encompasses the typical backgrounds of lawmakers in political office and the qualities partisan gatekeepers use to delineate high-quality from low-quality political candidates. The feminine resume provided the following information:

McCann is running for a seat to Congress. As a state legislator, McCann served as the party leader, chaired the education committee, and developed a reputation for bringing compromise to the legislature. Prior to serving in the legislature, McCann worked tirelessly as an advocate for women and children, and volunteered for many community organizations including the Parent Teacher Organization. McCann's family are longtime residents of the state. McCann graduated from a small liberal arts college. McCann, throughout the campaign, has pledged to bring a caring approach to politics.

This set of qualifications highlights the candidate's participation in more feminine institutions, including work with community organizations, local schools, and children – all of which reinforce the supportive, or more communal, roles traditionally performed by women.

Participants rated the candidate's qualifications for Congress, favorability, and vote support. These three outcomes offer insight into whether there are differences, based on gendered backgrounds, in how voters develop impressions of candidate qualifications and how these impressions can affect whom voters select at the ballot.[10] If results follow expectations, then voters should prefer the masculine over the feminine biography. The civic skills literature argues that participation in stereotypically masculine institutions provides potential candidates with the skills needed to excel in campaigns and political office (Verba, Schlozman, and Brady 1995). Moreover, research on the stereotypes voters associate with leadership suggests that voters prefer masculinity over femininity in political candidates (Conroy 2015; Miller, Wattenberg, and Malanchuk 1986), even in female candidates (Holman, Merolla, and Zechmeister 2016; Huddy and Terkildsen 1993).

Using a series of two-tailed t-tests, I compared the feminine and masculine backgrounds. Figure 3.1 graphs the average candidate evaluations on the three major outcomes across the feminine and masculine background conditions. To compare the three outcomes, I rescaled each variable to range from 0 to 1. Higher values indicate that a higher proportion of participants rated the candidate positively on each variable. The results offer somewhat mixed support as to whether voters prefer feminine or masculine backgrounds. The female candidate's rating on the qualification outcome was 0.07 points (7 percent), higher than the rating of the male candidate, $p < 0.01$. On favorability, the results flip. The masculine background receives 0.16 point (16 percent), a more positive favorability rating relative to the feminine background, $p < 0.01$. When it

---

[10] The Appendix to Chapter 3 includes more details about the precise questions.

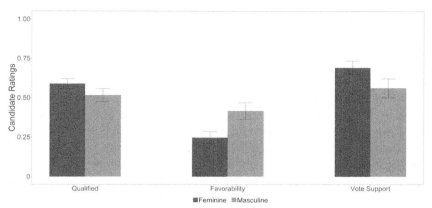

FIGURE 3.1 Voter responses to candidates from feminine and masculine backgrounds.
Note: 95 percent confidence intervals included. Variables range from 0 to 1 with higher values indicating that a higher proportion of participants rated the candidate positively.

comes to vote support, 70 percent of participants indicated they would vote for the candidate with the feminine background, while 56 percent of participants expressed electoral support for the candidate with the masculine background, $p < 0.01$. On two of the three outcomes, the feminine background performs better than the masculine background.

These results suggest that participants might not always prefer a candidate that comes from the conventionally masculine political pipeline paths, but that candidates with divergent backgrounds can succeed as well. Participants rated the feminine background more positively when asked to rate candidate qualifications for Congress and when asked their level of vote support. The feminine background described the candidate's experience with compromise in the legislature and the candidate's work advocating for marginalized groups. These are experiences that speak more to the communal skills that lawmakers need in order to get things done in legislative institutions (Guttmann and Thompson 2012). When given the option of supporting a candidate with the skills needed to possibly break through legislative grandstanding and gridlock in Congress, voters prefer that candidate. An important caveat about these results is that the end of the study asked participants to indicate whether the candidate they read about was a woman or a man. Neither treatment included any information about whether the candidate was female or male. Seventy percent of participants thought the feminine background belonged to a male candidate, and 80 percent of participants thought the

masculine background also belonged to a male candidate. While participants favorably rated the feminine background, they still thought that
candidate was a man.

The results of this experiment suggest that voters favor candidates with
feminine backgrounds, but these results do not exactly overturn the
conventional wisdom that candidates need experience in masculine institutions. A path forward for female candidates may be to balance feminine
and masculine qualifications in campaign messages. Many of the female
candidates who ran in 2018 offer some insights into what these strategies
might look like. Two of the most attention-grabbing campaign messages
in 2018 came from military veterans Amy McGrath, a Kentucky House
candidate, and MJ Hegar, a Texas House candidate. Both candidates
aired ads that highlighted their masculine military credentials and also
highlighted their outsider status as women in an institution that created
rules and barriers designed to exclude their participation. Highlighting
their status as trailblazing women in masculine institutions suggests that
these women can also be trailblazers in Congress – another masculine
institution. Moreover, both women showed images of their more "feminine" qualifications. MJ Hegar's announcement video featured her bal-
ancing a small child on her hip while talking about taking on the
Pentagon's ban on women in combat roles, an image that reminds voters
that she is not only a veteran but a mother as well. While neither
candidate won their election, largely due to partisan dynamics in their
districts, the strategies of both candidates suggest that female candidates
can leverage their status as women in masculine institutions.[11]

OVERCOMING ENTRENCHED MASCULINITY

This chapter builds on Chapter 2 and continued to address the question:
How do ideas about gender affect what it means to be qualified for
political office? I argue that there is an intrinsic link between being male,
masculinity, and political qualifications. Indeed, political campaigns are
rife with examples of candidates seeking to outdo their opponent on just
how masculine they are, whether it is shooting a gun at random objects
thrown into the air or talking about castrating hogs. Social role theory
argues that these masculine displays, as ridiculous as some of them seem,
make sense because leadership is intrinsically linked to masculinity.

---

[11] The defeats of McGrath and Hegar have not deterred them from politics as both are now
running for the Senate in 2020 in their respective states.

The historic exclusion of women from masculine institutions makes it difficult for women to obtain the "masculine" qualifications valued in political leaders. It is only in the last half-century that women can formally enter higher education and pursue legal and business degrees that help them pursue careers in the legal industry or in major corporations and industries. The women who gain access into traditionally masculine institutions, such as the legal field, must overcome stereotypic biases that they do not belong in such professions. The result is that the women who survive in these institutions end up being better than their male counterparts. In short, these women must be better to prove that they belong. This gendered pressure for women to outperform men contributes to the gendered qualification gap in politics.

I argue that the masculine perceptions of political leadership create a high qualification bar for female candidates. A typical masculine qualification set for a candidate might include a degree from an Ivy League institution, a stint in the military, a graduate degree either through law school or business school followed by work in the legal or the business profession, and then a run for political office. These institutions teach individuals many of the skills conventionally associated with leadership and allow individuals to build the networks needed to be political leaders. Women face barriers entering each of these institutions. Women's participation in these institutions has increased over time, but women still face obstacles in pursuing careers in stereotypically masculine institutions. Women make up over 50 percent of students in law schools but make up a minority of partners in top law firms across the country.[12]

This chapter used a simple empirical test to show that when voters think about political leadership, most think about men. The adapted "draw a leader" task found that only 9 percent of participants found an image of a female leader when asked to find an image of a "typical leader." This is not surprising. Over 75 percent of members of Congress are men and every one of the forty-five presidents in the United States have been men. Even in the 2018 "pink wave" midterm elections, nearly 78 percent of the congressional candidates who ran were still men. The image of a man as a typical leader is one deeply ingrained into the way many people, not just Americans think, about leadership. I also used an experiment to test the assumption that voters will prefer candidates with the masculine background that most candidates and officeholders, female

---

[12] "Women in Law: Quick Take," *Catalyst*, October 2, 2018, www.catalyst.org/research/women-in-law/.

and male, tend to have. The experiment found that voters did not necessarily prefer a masculine profile. A more feminine profile that reflects participation in more feminine institutions, such as experience in local community organizations, outperformed the more typical masculine profile. This experiment shows that voters do not necessarily prefer candidates with the more masculine profiles. The implication is that there may be more opportunities for candidates, including but not limited to female candidates, with diverse qualification backgrounds to succeed at the polls.

In the next four chapters, I present rigorous empirical tests probing how the gendered qualification gap operates in American politics. These chapters examine how candidates, the news media, and voters contribute to the gendered qualification gap. I start Chapter 4 with an examination of a gendered information gap. Detecting the presence of a gendered information gap is important because if voters do not have adequate information about a female candidate's qualifications, they will be more likely to fall back on feminine stereotypes that can harm a female candidate's electoral chances. Voters are less likely to assume that a male candidate lacks the appropriate political qualifications based on his sex because being male and being a leader go hand in hand. A gendered information gap can also create a high bar because this means female candidates may have to work harder to let voters know they have the qualifications needed to excel in political office.

4

A Gendered Information Gap

On December 31, 2018, Senator Elizabeth Warren posted an online video announcing her candidacy for the 2020 Democratic presidential nomination. The video traced Warren's personal story from growing up in Oklahoma to when she delayed her academic career for the sake of her marriage to her successful career as a law professor at Harvard. Warren sat in a kitchen and talked about herself to voters. The day after Warren announced her candidacy for the presidency in 2020, *Politico* published an article declaring that Warren will probably struggle with likability among voters. Polling data about Warren's likability and favorability gave no indication that the Massachusetts senator was anything but likable. Indeed, Warren consistently maintained high approval ratings in her state, and she had just won reelection that November with 60 percent of the vote. The only thing that appeared to make Warren unlikable is the fact that she declared her candidacy for the presidency. *Politico*'s article questioning Warren's likability plays into a long-standing trope that ambitious women are not likable women.[1]

Warren is not the only woman to face scorn for her ambition. Take, for instance, the case of Kirsten Gillibrand, who led the call for Senator Al Franken's resignation when it came to light that he engaged in behaviors that violated the personal space and boundaries of women in ways that women found uncomfortable and demeaning. One op-ed criticized Gillibrand for taking advantage of Franken to position herself for a 2020 presidential run, declaring: "For Gillibrand, nearly every move seems to be a

[1] Natasha Korecki, "Warren Battles the Ghosts of Hillary," *Politico.com*, December 31, 2018, www.politico.com/story/2018/12/31/elizabeth-warren-hillary-clinton-1077008.

self-serving playing of the angles. While it's not surprising to see a
politician behave this way, Gillibrand seems to be an especially egregious
practitioner of the finger-in-the-wind politics that so many voters can no
longer abide."[2] Regardless of the motivations behind Gillibrand's advo-
cacy on the issue, the message is clear: a woman in politics should not
show ambition. Few media outlets question the motives of male politicians who may also take "self-serving" positions designed to advance
their own careers.

The ambition-shaming, of course, does not stop with Gillibrand.
Shortly after Amy Klobuchar announced her 2020 candidacy, the *New
York Times* published the now-infamous "comb-salad" article that framed
Klobuchar as a "bad boss."[3] Certainly, some of the behaviors reported by
Klobuchar raise alarm, but those same behaviors from a male boss are
often seen as signs of a strong leader rather than a tyrant. Not to be left
out, *USA Today* reported on a brief romantic relationship between
Kamala Harris and former San Francisco Mayor Willie Brown, who took
credit for launching her career.[4] This narrative sets Harris up as a woman
who uses sexuality for career advancement rather than using her intellect
and work ethic. Threading these examples together is the criticism that
women should not violate the prescribed social roles for women and that
women who violate the expectations set by feminine stereotypes can suffer
a gendered penalty their male colleagues do not necessarily have to worry
about. The roots of the gendered penalties that women face for straying
from feminine norms go back to the tenets of social role theory laid out in
Chapter 3 – women are innately suited for some tasks, such as homemaking, and are not innately suited for leadership.[5] The news media's

[2] Ciro Scotti, "The Trouble with Kirsten Gillibrand," *The Daily Beast*, January 5, 2018, www.thedailybeast.com/the-trouble-with-kirsten-gillibrand?via=twitter_page.

[3] Matt Flegenheimer and Sydney Ember, "How Amy Klobuchar Treats Her Staff," *New York Times*, February 22, 2019 www.nytimes.com/2019/02/22/us/politics/amy-klobuchar-staff.html.

[4] William Cummings, "Former S.F. Mayor Willie Brown Writes about Dating Kamala Harris, Appointing Her to Posts,"*USAToday.com*, January 27, 2019, www.usatoday.com/story/news/politics/onpolitics/2019/01/27/willie-brown-kamala-harris-san-francisco-chronicle-letter/2695143002/.

[5] There is a long history of shaming women who stray from their child-rearing roles. Political scientist Robert Lane wrote during the second wave of the women's movement that "working girls and career women who insistently serve the community in volunteer capacities, and women with extracurricular interests of an absorbing kind are often borrowing their time and attention and capacity for relaxed play and love from their children to whom it rightfully belongs" (Lane 1965, pp. 354–355, quoted in Bourque and Grossholtz 1974).

focus on whether women should even be running for political office draws attention away from the qualifications of these women. Moreover, these patterns in news coverage also illustrate a gendered information gap where the news media are less likely to highlight the qualifications of female political candidates relative to male political candidates.

This chapter answers the question: What qualification information do voters have about the qualifications of female candidates? I test for a gendered information gap in two ways. First, female candidates may not market their qualifications as aggressively as male candidates for fear of being shamed for their political ambition and facing a backlash for violating social norms that women should be modest. Second, a gendered information gap can also emerge in the way the news media cover the qualifications of female candidates. These two sources of an information gap, I argue, are linked. The news media frequently rely on campaign communication directly from political candidates when developing stories (Darr 2016; Gershon 2012a); as such, if female candidates are not talking about their qualifications, then it is unlikely the news media will talk about qualifications. I argue that a gendered information gap can contribute to the broader gendered qualification gap because without qualification information about female candidates, voters may be more likely to assume that female candidates *lack* the qualifications needed for political office, but voters may not make this same assumption about male candidates.

This chapter builds on the social role argument of political qualifications developed in Chapters 2 and 3 to investigate how feminine norms of female modesty shape the self-promotion behaviors of female candidates and how masculine definitions of political leadership affect how the news media talk about political qualifications. Few studies measure whether there are differences in the self-promotion behaviors of female and male candidates, and this is an important gap in the literature that I fill. I start by developing a set of theoretical expectations about the self-promotion strategies of female candidates. I then describe the data collection I undertook using the campaign websites of the 2016 female Senate candidates and their male opponents to test how women self-promote on the campaign trail.

Following these data analyses, I turn to my second empirical test of the gendered information gap using news coverage. I review previous research on how the news media discuss the qualifications of female candidates differently from those of male candidates. Much of the existing work on news coverage of female candidates has yet to examine the extent to which the campaign strategies of female candidates drive the coverage female candidates receive. If news coverage that appears biased when comparing coverage for female candidates to coverage for male candidates is, in fact, driven by the communication strategies of female candidates, then the coverage disparities may not be come from bias on the part of reporters. Using previous research as a guide as well as the results of the website analyses, I derive expectations about how the news media will promote the qualifications of female candidates. The goal with these two empirical data collections is to connect research measuring how female candidates talk about qualifications on campaign websites with how the news media, in turn, talk about those very qualifications in news coverage. If female candidates do not discuss their qualifications, it is unlikely that the news media will discuss their qualifications. Without news coverage, it is unlikely that voters will have qualification information about female candidates.

HOW DO FEMALE CANDIDATES MARKET THEIR QUALIFICATIONS?

Much of the current scholarship focuses on how candidates deploy gender-stereotypic traits and issues in campaign communication. Dolan (2014) finds that female candidates emphasize the same types of issue and trait priorities as co-partisan male candidates. Other scholars find that female candidates draw on issues and traits that reflect feminine stereotypes more frequently compared with male candidates (Gershon 2008; Herrick 2016; Schneider 2014b). Investigating the role of stereotypic traits and issues certainly lends insight into how female candidates think about overcoming biases among voters rooted in feminine stereotypes. Using masculine traits and issues suggests that female candidates consciously try to fit into the masculine image of political leadership. Drawing on feminine traits and issues suggests that female candidates might want to gain a unique advantage over their male opponents. Trait and issue competencies can affect broader perceptions of candidate qualifications, but these studies do not speak to how voters evaluate the political experiences or backgrounds of candidates.

Fridkin and Kenney (2015) measured how female and male Senate incumbents talked about legislative successes, a key component of candidate qualifications, through official Senate websites and press releases. The authors found that female incumbents were just as likely to showcase policy accomplishments compared with male incumbents on their campaign websites and in press releases. Promoting policy achievements is an important component of how voters assess candidate qualifications, and it appears that female candidates give voters this type of critical information. Lazarus and Steigerwalt (2018) also analyzed how members of Congress share information about legislative accomplishments with constituents by examining the frequency of trips back home and how lawmakers use the franking privilege. The franking privilege allows members of Congress to use the postal service without cost to send official communication to constituents. The authors found that female lawmakers frequently use both tools, sometimes more than their male colleagues, to keep in touch with their constituents.

Together, these two studies suggest that female incumbents provide constituents with information about their legislative productivity – a key part of candidate qualifications. Female incumbents do not undersell themselves on legislative productivity; but it is not clear how female challengers tell voters about their qualifications. Most female candidates who run for political office do so as relatively unknown challengers (Ditonto and Andersen 2018; Palmer and Simon 2001). Challenger candidates have an even greater need than incumbents to tell voters about their qualifications. My approach builds on the work of Fridkin and Kenny (2015) and Lazarus and Steigerwalt (2018) to examine how both female incumbents and challengers market their qualifications to voters. I expand on this scholarship to include more than just legislative productivity as a metric of qualifications. I also include any mention of experience at other levels of elected political office, along with professional backgrounds and academic credentials. My approach offers a comprehensive overview of how candidates incorporate, or fail to incorporate, qualifications into campaign messages.

Why Might Female Candidates Undersell Their Qualifications?

It seems counterintuitive that a candidate running for political office would avoid talking about the qualifications they bring with them to the ballot. Running for political office is a major life decision, and female candidates, perhaps more so than male candidates, are "in it to win it." It seems reasonable to expect female candidates to do everything possible to maximize their odds of an electoral victory. The motivation to win leads to the expectation that female candidates will not undersell themselves. A competing perspective argues that women worry about facing a gender-motivated backlash for breaking with gendered norms. Bragging about oneself violates the feminine norm of modesty – and from this perspective, female candidates might hesitate before talking about their accomplishments. I outline these two competing perspectives.

First, the strategic emergence literature starts with the observation that female candidates believe that voters will assume they lack the qualifications needed for political office. Female candidates see the campaign landscape as fraught with gendered expectations and believe voters will see them as lacking the masculine qualities needed to serve in political office (Dittmar 2015). Research shows these perceptions are frequently accurate (Schneider and Bos 2014). Moreover, voters actively seek out information about the competencies of female but not about male candidates (Ditonto, Hamilton, and Redlawsk 2014), again reinforcing the premise that female candidates must prove they have the "masculine" qualifications needed for political office. The perception of a gendered campaign environment can pressure female candidates to show voters that they "look like men." This gendered pressure should motivate female candidates to aggressively market their qualifications to voters. If this gendered pressure bears out, then female candidates will not be less likely to emphasize their qualifications relative to male candidates.

Another reason why female candidates may tout their qualifications is that when women run for office, they aim to maximize their odds of victory (Lawless and Fox 2010). Carroll and Sanbonmatsu (2013) describe the decision to run for political office as a "relationally embedded process." Women do not simply wake up one day and decide to run for city council, Congress, or the presidency. Rather, women seek feedback and input from multiple outlets, including family members, friends, community leaders, and political gatekeepers. Women consider how running for political office will upset their professional and family balance, including the impact such a decision will have on their spouses and children. In short, women take longer to decide to run for political office. Women also are more likely to run for office when the odds of winning an election are very high (Fulton et al. 2006). Men, on the other hand, are more willing to run for office even if their victory is a long shot, and men are willing to run for office multiple times if they do not win on their first attempt. Talking about how qualified you are for political office is a strategy that can maximize the odds of an electoral victory for a female candidate. The strategic candidate emergence literature leads to the following prediction about the self-promotion behaviors of female candidates:

Strategic Emergence Prediction: Female candidates will not promote their qualifications less than male candidates.

This prediction does not necessarily mean that a female candidate will self-promote more than a male candidate, though a female candidate might, but that female candidates will not underpromote their qualifications relative to their male counterparts.

The second perspective, the gendered backlash theory, draws on social psychology research showing that women who "self-promote" can face a gender-based backlash (Rudman 1998). Prescriptive feminine stereotypes set the expectation that women should be warm, kind, and deferential – these are traits others expect women to display. Proscriptive feminine stereotypes set the expectation what women should not be boastful, brash, or assertive. The prescriptive and proscriptive stereotypes designating what women should and should not do link back to the social roles of women. The traits that women should embody are traits associated with communal roles, and the traits that women should avoid are associated with power-seeking roles considered more appropriate to, or "natural," for men. The potential of facing a social norm violation may limit the extent to which women engage in self-promotion. Anecdotally, the examples of "ambition-shaming" at the beginning of the chapter suggest that women who engage in behaviors that violate feminine norms face pushback for doing so, and these criticisms can limit other female candidates in down-ballot races from engaging in self-promotion.

Psychology research affirms that women can, in fact, face sanctions for violating stereotypic proscriptions (Moss-Rascusin, Phelan, and Rudman 2010). For example, "bossy" is a negative adjective used to admonish young girls who show initiative, while young boys who show leadership skills receive praise for being bold. Political science research also confirms that female candidates can, in fact, face a gendered backlash for violating feminine norms such as failing to compromise in Congress or engaging in campaign negativity (Bauer, Yong Harbridge, and Krupnikov 2017; Krupnikov and Bauer 2014; Vraga 2017). The socialization processes discussed in Chapter 1 condition women to avoid behaviors that violate feminine norms, and this means less self-promotion for female candidates. The stereotype backlash prediction delineates the effects of gendered socialization on female candidate's self-promotion behaviors:

Stereotype Backlash Prediction: Female candidates will promote their qualifications less than male candidates.

The stereotype backlash perspective argues that female candidates might undersell themselves to voters. Pressure to conform to stereotypic feminine norms can create an information gap because female candidates will avoid talking about their qualifications or downplay them. Evidence of this effect will occur if female candidates talk about their political, professional, and academic qualifications less than male candidates. The stereotype backlash model creates a tension for female candidates. Female candidates who talk too much about themselves can face a backlash for being too brash, too selfish, and too outspoken. Consequently, it is likely voters will see female candidates who do not talk about themselves as lacking the experience and competency needed for holding political office.

These two theoretical perspectives lead to divergent expectations about whether female candidates will promote or downplay their qualifications. The strategic candidate emergence literature suggests that female candidates anticipate bias from voters, and telling voters about qualifications is a strategy that can mitigate such bias. Stereotype violation theory suggests that female candidates will avoid breaking with feminine norms, and self-promotion is a break with expectations that women be modest, meek, and humble. A finding that female candidates talk about their qualifications at the same rate or more frequently as male candidates aligns with the expectation set forth in the strategic emergence literature. Moreover, this result also suggests that there may not be a gap in the information voters have about candidate qualifications. A finding that female candidates incorporate qualifications in messages less frequently than male candidates offers evidence of the stereotype backlash expectation. Support for the stereotype backlash theory means that female candidates may albeit inadvertently, contribute to a gendered information gap. Such an information gap contributes to the qualification gap because without information, voters may assume that female candidates lack the qualities needed for political leadership.

I investigate the presence of a gendered information gap using the campaign websites of Senate candidates in 2016. Campaign websites are valuable tools for assessing the marketing strategies of candidates, for several reasons. First, campaign websites are accessible messaging tools widely used by nearly all candidates (Druckman, Kifer, and Parkin 2009; Fridkin and Kenney 2015; Herrick 2016). Developing a campaign website requires modest financial resources and little technical skill, making this communication platform relatively accessible to candidates in high- and low-profile elections. Second, campaign websites are important platforms candidates use specifically to talk about themselves (Druckman,

Kifer, and Parkin 2009). Nearly every campaign website has an "about me" section completely dedicated to the personal narrative of the candidate. If there is any communication platform where candidates are most likely to include their qualifications, it is on a campaign website. Druckman, Kifer, and Parkin (2009), for example, found that websites dedicate most of their content to establishing the qualifications of political candidates. Third, campaign websites "offer an unmediated, holistic, and representative portrait of campaigns" (Druckman, Kifer, and Parkin 2009, p. 343). Information on campaign websites is not filtered through the news media but goes straight from a candidate to a voter. Campaign website developers see voters, especially undecided voters, as their primary target audience (Stromer-Galley, Howard, and Schneider 2003). Candidates tailor the information on campaign websites specifically to reach voters. Fourth, the formulaic nature of campaign websites increases the likelihood that candidates will talk about similar types of qualifications. This platform offers a conservative estimate of any differences between female and male candidates in self-promotion.

The data include all the female Senate candidates running in 2016 and their male opponents.[6] I use Senate races rather than House races because these races are more visible, and Senate seats are, in general, more competitive than House seats. Sixteen women ran for the US Senate in 2016. There are twelve elections that featured a female candidate running against a male candidate, and two elections that included a female candidate running against another female candidate. Including female candidates and male opponents allows me to test differences in self-promotion within the context of a single electoral race. Of the sixteen women in the election, three ran as Senate incumbents, and three women ran as Republicans. This partisan skew reflects the wide partisan gap in women's representation, as most of the women who run for political office do so as Democrats. Despite the limited number of Republican women running in 2016, there is more diversity in the women running for the Senate compared with past election cycles. The campaign featured two all-female elections – an infrequent occurrence. Four women of color pursued Senate seats in 2016 with multiple states electing a woman of color to the Senate for the first time, and the first transgender candidate ran for the Senate as well.

---

[6] The Appendix to Chapter 4 includes more information about the female and male candidates included in the data analyses.

Two research assistants coded the landing page and the "about me" page of each Senate campaign website.[7] Table 4.1 summarizes the website coding scheme, and the observational differences that should emerge in the qualification messages of female and male candidates. There are several ways that candidates can include qualification information on campaign websites, such as through legislative accomplishments, experience in lower levels of elected office, professional achievements, and academic accomplishments. Legislative accomplishments include a candidate describing sponsored bills or more aggressive behaviors, such as taking credit for a major legislative accomplishment. For example, several Senate incumbent candidates listed bills sponsored about gun safety – a major issue leading up to the 2016 elections. If female Senate incumbents spend less time talking about legislative accomplishments compared with male Senate incumbents, this offers evidence of an underselling effect. Challenger candidates can talk about their legislative accomplishments in other levels of elected office. Most lawmakers who pursue a Senate seat are not political neophytes but have experience in the US House or serving in state legislative chambers (Maestas and Rugeley 2008). If female candidates do not self-promote, then they should be *less* likely to talk about political experience. The professional background category includes any type of professional experience that did not require winning election to public office. Candidates had a range of professional experiences, whether it was working as a grocery store clerk (as was the case for Misty Snow, the Democratic nominee running for the Senate in Utah) or working in the business sector (such as Loretta Sanchez's experience working as a financial analyst for Boeing).

The research assistants coded each site for any discussion of the candidate's academic credentials. Most candidates for political office hold graduate degrees, whether it is a JD, MBA, or medical degree. Candidates also might write about where they went to high school and where they pursued an undergraduate degree, in an attempt to make them seem more relatable to the average voter (Carnes and Sadin 2014). Over the last two

---

[7] Two coders read each news article to ensure a high level of accuracy and intercoder reliability of at least $\alpha = 0.80$. Some of the discussion of political, professional, and feminine qualifications involve making subjective judgments about the content of news coverage.

TABLE 4.1 *Qualifications in candidate communication*

Qualification metric	Coding method	Observable expectations
Political qualifications	Time in the Senate as incumbent Previous experience in lower levels of elected office Legislative productivity, such as bills sponsored, co-sponsored, or passed or hearings held	Strategic Emergence: Female candidates will discuss political qualifications *comparably to or more* than male candidates. Stereotype Backlash: Female candidates will discuss political qualifications *less* than male candidates.
Professional qualifications	Any discussion of the jobs/careers of candidates not including elected political experience	Strategic Emergence: Female candidates will discuss professional qualifications *comparably to or more* than male candidates. Stereotype Backlash: Female candidates will discuss professional qualifications *less* than male candidates.
Academic qualifications	Any mention of where the candidate attended primary or secondary school, universities, or college for undergraduate or graduate degrees Any mention of the degrees earned by candidates, including a BA, BS, MA, MPA, MBA, PhD, JD, or MD	Strategic Emergence: Female candidates will discuss academic qualifications *comparably to or more* than male candidates. Stereotype Backlash: Female candidates will discuss academic qualifications *less* than male candidates.
Feminine qualifications	Discussion of family members, relationship to family members such as being a wife/husband, mother/father Any "first female" experiences of the candidate, such as being the first female partner at a law firm or the first woman to serve in a combat role	Strategic Emergence: Female candidates will discuss feminine qualifications *less* than male candidates. Stereotype Backlash: Female candidates will discuss feminine qualifications *more* than male candidates.

decades, women increased their ranks in higher education and in graduate programs. Women receive more than half of the undergraduate degrees and about half of the law degrees awarded each year. If women do not self-promote, then they should be less likely to draw attention to their academic credentials compared with men.

Political, professional, and academic accomplishments are the most common objective variables that scholars use to measure political qualifications. These qualification metrics reflect the masculine paths that most political candidates follow to political office. Women may choose to market their qualifications by drawing attention to their different paths to political office, such as their roles as mothers and caregivers (Carroll and Sanbonmatsu 2013). The research assistants recorded any mention of the candidate's family, the candidate's status as a mother or father, or any mention of the candidate being the "first woman" to accomplish something. There are several possibilities for how feminine qualifications might emerge in campaign messages of female candidates. First, female candidates run for office to pursue communal goals (Schneider et al. 2016), and it is reasonable to expect that female candidates discuss communal experiences that reflect their motivation for pursuing political office. Second, female candidates may feel pressured to "look like men" and be *less* likely to talk about their families or their status as a woman on campaign websites. If this effect occurs, then female candidates should be *less* likely to mention families and communality relative to male candidates. Third, it is also possible female candidates will discuss their families to "soften" their image and prevent a gendered backlash for breaking with feminine norms if they do choose to promote their qualifications. Discussion of family allows female candidates to have it both ways, so they can talk about their qualifications without worry about a backlash for breaking with feminine norms.

To analyze the data, I created a dichotomous variable for each of the qualification metrics: political, professional, academic, and feminine experiences. A value of 1 indicates that a candidate mentioned one of these qualification metrics on the landing page or the "about me" page of the campaign website, and a value of 0 indicates that a candidate did not mention this qualification metric. I undertook a systematic investigation of the differences between female and male candidates but also other factors, such as incumbency status, partisanship, and the competitiveness of an election, to develop regression models predicting the likelihood a candidate emphasized their political qualifications. I estimated a series of logistic regression models that predicted whether a website included information about a specific qualification metric.[8]

There are two competing expectations for how female candidates may promote their qualifications based on the strategic emergence literature in political science and the self-promotion literature from the social psychology. Two observable outcomes can offer support for this first perspective. First, female candidates may talk about their qualifications at the same rate as male candidates, and I would expect male candidates to actively talk about all their qualifications on their campaign websites. Second, female candidates may be more likely to self-promote compared with male candidates. Male candidates, especially given the high rate of male incumbents in the data, may not talk about their professional experience often, but this is an aspect that female candidates, given the status of many as challengers, might be more likely to include along with political and academic experience. The strategic emergence approach argues that female candidates are most likely to run for political office when their odds for winning elections are at their highest. As such, female candidates will do everything they can to maximize their chance of victory and will not shy away self-promotion.

Evidence for the self-promotion perspective would emerge if female candidates have a lower predicted probability of talking about their qualifications, especially their political, professional, or academic credentials, relative to their male opponents. The observable implication of this perspective is that female candidates will be less likely to include qualification information on their campaign websites compared with their male opponents. The self-promotion argument suggests that female candidates will worry about a backlash for violating feminine norms of modesty if they "brag" about their accomplishments too much, and this will pressure female candidates to downplay their qualifications.

Figure 4.1 displays the predicted probability that a female candidate talked about a specific aspect of qualification on their campaign website. Overall, there are many similarities in the self-promotion patterns of

---

[8] The Appendix to Chapter 4 includes descriptive data documenting how candidates, based on whether they are female or male, partisanship, and incumbency status, discussed qualifications on their websites. The analyses include control variables for whether the candidate was female, candidate party, whether the opponent was female, incumbency status, the competitiveness of an election, and whether the race was an open seat. I clustered the errors at the state level to account for any unobserved heterogeneity across each election. The Appendix to Chapter 4 includes the full logit model results.

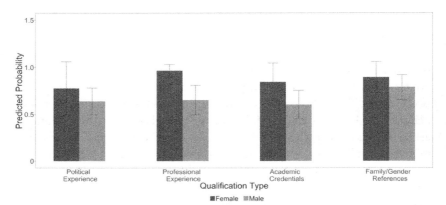

FIGURE 4.1 Candidate qualifications on campaign websites.
Note: 95 percent confidence intervals included. Each bar displays the probability that a candidate mentions a type of qualification on their website based on the results of logit regression models. The Appendix to Chapter 4 displays the full models.

female candidates and their male opponents. The candidates had very high predicted probabilities of talking about their political, professional, academic, or feminine qualifications. The predicted probability that female candidates discussed their political experience in 2016 was 0.77, and the predicted probability for male candidates was 0.63; these differences are not statistically significant. The relatively high probability that a female candidate highlighted her political experience is important because all but three of the female candidates in 2016 ran as challengers, most against long-term incumbents. There is also no statistically significant difference between female and male candidates in the probability that candidates emphasized their academic credentials on their campaign websites. Female candidates, based on these initial analyses, were not afraid of a self-promotion backlash in 2016, but appeared to be maximizing their opportunities for electoral success. The findings fit with the expectations of the strategic emergence expectation.

Being a female candidate had a significant effect only in the professional experience model. The predicted probability that a female candidate talked about professional experience was 0.95, while the predicted probability that a male candidate talked about professional experience was 0.58; this difference is statistically significant, p < 0.05. These results suggest that it is quite probable that nearly all female candidates will talk about their professional experiences on their campaign websites. The findings, again, fit with the expectations of the strategic emergence rather than the self-promotion model. Female candidates used their websites in 2016 to give voters as much qualification information as possible to maximize their odds of success. The findings suggest that there is not a gendered information gap on the campaign websites of female candidates.

A third interesting finding from these models is that female candidates are just as likely to mention their families and to reference themselves through gendered roles (e.g., such as being a mother) relative to male candidates. The predicted probability that female candidates mentioned their families was very high at 0.90, and the predicted probability for male candidates was somewhat lower at 0.78, but these values do not differ significantly from one another. The gender-role incongruity between feminine and masculine social roles suggests that female candidates might downplay femininity, but this does not appear to be the case. Despite these similarities, female candidates may talk about their families for different reasons than male candidates. Talking about their wife or children can soften the image of a male candidate so that voters will see him as both tough and sensitive. Many female candidates without children or spouses can face scrutiny for being unconventional women. For female candidates, mentioning families can mitigate a potential backlash for a social role violation.[9]

To better understand the quantity of information on a candidate website available to voters, I created a qualification score indicating the number of qualification items a candidate included on their campaign website. The qualification outcome variable ranges from 0, indicating that a candidate talked about *no* qualifications on their campaign website, to a value of 4, indicating that a candidate talked about all four types of qualifications on their campaign website. A value of 4 indicates that a candidate provided voters with a high level of information. Of course, this variable accounts for the information available to voters on these websites and not whether voters accessed and read this information.

I estimated ordinary least squares (OLS) regression models, including controls for being a female candidate, partisanship, incumbency status, electoral competitiveness, an open seat, and whether the opponent was

---

[9] Figure 4.1 isolates the self-promotion strategies of male candidates running against female candidates. To see whether male candidates behaved differently when they are running in races against a female opponent, I calculated the predicted probabilities of male candidates in a sample of all-male races employing a self-promotion strategy on a website when the opponent was female compared with when the opponent was male. There are no differences in the self-promotion strategies of male candidates based on whether the opponent was male or female.

TABLE 4.2 *Amount of qualification information on campaign websites*

	Female candidate	Female candidate by party interaction	Female candidate by incumbency
Female candidate	0.721* (0.392)	0.815 (0.490)	0.366 (0.475)
Democratic candidate	−0.461 (0.341)	−0.434 (0.397)	−0.383 (0.342)
Female × Democrat	−	−0.142 (0.620)	
Incumbent candidate	−0.437 (0.351)	−0.455 (0.361)	−0.636 (0.395)
Female × incumbent	−	−	1.100** (0.501)
Competitive race	0.266 (0.236)	0.272 (0.241)	0.286 (0.237)
Open seat	0.004 (0.296)	−0.006 (0.298)	0.045 (0.300)
Female opponent	−0.057 (0.365)	−0.044 (0.370)	0.008 (0.366)
Campaign funds, logged	0.196*** (0.044)	0.196*** (0.045)	0.209*** (0.046)
Front-runner status	0.103 (0.196)	0.100 (0.201)	0.154 (0.215)
Constant	−0.127 (0.825)	−0.132 (0.833)	−0.403 (0.904)
Observations	61	61	61
Pseudo R^2	0.2898	0.2642	0.2898

Note: The outcome variable is the number of qualification items about a candidate present on each website. The variable ranges from 0 to 4, and I estimated the models using OLS models. Standard errors in parentheses. * $p < 0.10$, ** $p < 0.05$, *** $p < 0.01$.

male or female, with the errors clustered at the state level. I used an OLS model because the outcome variable resembles a continuous variable in range. Table 4.2 displays the results. The coefficient for the female candidate variable suggests that female candidates provide voters with 0.72 *more pieces* of individual qualification information compared with male candidates. When it comes to the quantity of qualification information, female candidates outperform male candidates, and this suggests that female candidates are not the source of the gendered qualification gap.

I also estimated models with interactions between female candidates and incumbency as well as between female candidates and partisanship. The partisan interaction model shows no significant differences based on the interaction between being a female candidate and being a Democratic candidate. The incumbency interaction model shows a significant relationship. The key difference is between female and male incumbents. Female incumbents, on average, include 3.81 qualification items on their campaign websites, while male incumbents include 2.35 qualification items, $p < 0.05$. Female incumbents are more likely to face reelection challengers (Branton et al. 2018), and this potential for a competitive reelection bid can certainly motivate female incumbents to proactively market their qualifications to voters. Female incumbents not only are providing more information about their political experience, which as incumbents they have plenty to talk about, but are also emphasizing their professional backgrounds more than male incumbents.

Female incumbents in 2016 presented voters with a diverse range of qualification information. Voters who visited Senate incumbent Lisa Murkowski's website, for example, learned about the federal dollars Murkowski secured for Alaskans but also learned about her work as an attorney in Anchorage before she started her political career. A voter who visited Senate incumbent Richard Burr's campaign website would learn about his time in the US House and his work on the intelligence committee but might not learn about his professional career in the business industry. Female challengers also highlighted their qualifications extensively and provided, on average, 3.35 pieces of information on their websites, and male challengers provided 2.99 pieces of information, but these values do not differ from one another at a statistically significant level. While female challengers provide voters with somewhat less information than female incumbents, the difference in the values is not statistically significant.

Looking more closely at which female challengers are not talking about their qualifications offers some useful insights. All the female incumbents in the sample highlight their political, professional, and academic qualifications, and all the female incumbents make some mention of their families. Most female challengers with political experience and who spent time in political pipeline professions (i.e., the legal field) talked about these qualities on their campaign websites. But not all the female challengers had political experience, such as regular Senate candidate in New York Wendy Long or first-time Senate candidate in Louisiana Caroline Fayard, and this means that these candidates do not have much to talk about in the way of political experience.

The first test of the gendered information gap highlights two key findings. First, female candidates do not undersell their qualifications, and when it comes to professional experience, female candidates present more information on this metric relative to male candidates. Second, female candidates actually present voters with *more* individual pieces of qualification information compared with male incumbents and challengers. These findings fit with the strategic candidate emergence prediction. The second test of the gendered information gap turns to measuring whether the news media echo the qualification messages disseminated by female candidates.

NEWS MEDIA COVERAGE OF CANDIDATE QUALIFICATIONS

Accessing information about candidates through campaign websites requires some motivation on the part of voters. Voters more frequently learn about candidates through news coverage, and candidates are key agenda-setters for the news media (Boydstun and Aelst 2018; Darr 2016; Groeling 2010). In other words, reporters turn to campaign communication, including websites, to determine what to talk about when covering a political candidate. The first set of analyses found that female candidates provide more qualification information relative to male candidates. The second half of this chapter examines whether the news media's coverage of female candidate qualifications mirrors the self-promotion patterns found on candidate websites. If an agenda-setting effect occurs, then the news media should provide more information about the qualifications of female relative to male candidates. If the news media undersell female candidates, then it is likely that voters will not have information about the qualifications of candidates. Without information, voters are likely to assume that female candidates *lack* the qualifications needed for political office, and this can dampen electoral support. Gendered patterns of news coverage can perpetuate a gendered information gap among voters and, ultimately, contribute to the gendered qualification gap.

The scholarship on gender differences in candidate news coverage offers a set of relatively mixed expectations about the potential for gender bias. Early scholarship found that women received *less* news coverage than male candidates (Kahn and Goldenberg 1991). The coverage that female candidates received focused on horse race coverage and the novelty of women as candidates (Kahn 1992), which leads voters to see female candidates as unlikely to win the election (Kahn 1994). Gender differences in news coverage did not always disadvantage female candidates depending on the election cycle. In 1992, emphasizing feminine stereotypes benefited female candidates when women's issues dominated the national electoral agenda (Kahn 1994).

Female candidates receive *more* news coverage about their hair, hemlines, and husbands (Heldman, Carroll, and Olson 2005). For instance, much of the news coverage surrounding Sarah Palin's nomination to the vice-presidential slot in 2008 focused on her wardrobe and her physical appearance (Burns, Eberhardt, and Merolla 2013; Carlin and Winfrey 2009; Miller and Peake 2013). Certainly, there are instances of male candidates receiving appearance-based coverage. John Edwards received critical news coverage in the lead-up to the 2008 Democratic primaries for spending $400 on a single haircut. The difference is that the news media still talk about the substantive policies of male candidates while also talking about their appearance. Female candidates, especially those running against male opponents, receive appearance-based coverage and receive less substantive issue coverage (Dunaway et al. 2013; Turcotte and Paul 2015).

Lawrence and Rose (2010) conducted an extensive analysis of the news coverage received by Hillary Clinton, Barack Obama, and John McCain during the 2008 Democratic and Republican presidential primaries. Masculine news norms formed in largely masculine newsrooms led the news media to cover Clinton very differently from her male counterparts. The focus on the "horse race" framed Clinton's electoral prospects negatively, even when Clinton was a front-runner. Negative horse-race coverage increases the perception that women are unlikely to win the election. The news media also views candidates as "characters" in a broader political story, and the focus on character over policy occurred more frequently for Clinton compared with Obama and McCain. The different type of coverage received by Clinton had the effect, if not the intent, of undermining her candidacy. The focus on polling and horse-race coverage and personality over policy occurs when women run at other levels of office as well (Dunaway et al. 2013; Kahn 1994; Lawrence and Rose 2011; Searles and Banda 2019) and is not unique to the American context (Tolley 2016; Ward 2017).

More recent research finds fewer differences in the content of stories about female and male candidates. The news media ascribe masculine traits to candidates, regardless of gender (Hayes and Lawless 2016), suggesting that the news media exhibit no bias toward female candidates. This conclusion may overstate the lack of bias in news coverage for three reasons. First, it is not clear if the news media use masculine traits to describe female candidates because female candidates use masculine traits to describe themselves. Fridkin and Kenney (2015) find that the news media are less likely to incorporate information in the press releases disseminated by female candidates compared with those of male candidates. Second, other research finds that routine news coverage, coverage that occurs when there is not an active campaign, focuses far more frequently on the feminine traits of female candidates (Aaldering and van der Pas 2017). Third, there are marked differences in the news coverage received by white female candidates compared with minority female candidates. Women of color still receive higher levels of coverage about their race, their novelty, and their viability (Gershon 2012b, 2013; Ward 2016).

Much of the current scholarship on differences in coverage for female and male candidates focuses on coverage of feminine and masculine traits and feminine and masculine issue competencies but has yet to examine how reporters talk about the political, professional, and academic experiences of female and male candidates. Certainly, gendered trait and gendered issue competencies are part of the set of a candidate's qualifications that a voter might consider when forming impressions of candidates and deciding which candidate to support. But, as I wrote in Chapter 1, trait and issue competencies are not quite the same as the qualifications that make up a candidate's political resume based on the candidate's experiences in political pipeline institutions. The ability of a candidate to acquire masculine trait or masculine issue competencies may depend, in part, on the candidate's ability to gain entrance into masculine institutions, such as the legal profession or the military – and these are institutions that, historically, are difficult for women to enter.

There are two expectations for how the news media might cover female candidate qualifications. I base the first expectation on the concept of agenda convergence (Hayes 2010). Agenda convergence occurs when a candidate's message matches the media's message. If agenda convergence occurs, then there should be a gendered information gap that favors female candidates. The first set of results found that female candidates discussed their professional qualifications more than male candidates and had a higher qualification score than male candidates based on the website analyses. If the news media follow the cues of candidates, then qualification news coverage should favor female candidates, and I describe this effect in the agenda convergence prediction:

Agenda Convergence Prediction: The news media should be more likely to cover the qualifications of female candidates relative to male candidates.

This first prediction assumes that a candidate's campaign communication materials, beyond their websites, reiterate the messages on websites and that the news media follow and read the candidate's campaign materials. Research suggests that reporters rely on candidate campaign materials (Gershon 2012a; Stromer-Galley, Howard, and Schneider 2003), but it is not clear how this affects qualification coverage.

The second expectation I develop is based on the evidence illustrating the ways that masculine norms and processes affect how the media report on political campaigns in terms of the quality of coverage and the socialization of reporters. From this perspective, there should be a gendered information gap in news coverage that disadvantages female candidates such that they receive less coverage of their political, professional, and academic qualifications. The gendered influences of the newsroom can lead reporters to rely on gender stereotypes when covering female candidates (Heldman, Carroll, and Olson 2005; Zeldes, Zico, and Diddi 2007). This gendered influence should, if it is present, lead to more coverage of the feminine qualifications of female candidates relative to their male counterparts. The second prediction, the masculine news norms expectation, argues that that female candidates will receive less substantial qualification coverage relative to their male opponents:

Masculine News Norms Expectation: Female candidates will receive less political, professional, and academic qualification coverage relative to their male opponents.

The masculine news norms expectation implies that the news media will not necessarily pay attention to the self-promotion strategies that female candidates deploy but will fall back on gender stereotypes about women as lacking the masculine qualities needed for political office.

I analyzed news coverage of qualifications of Senate candidates in the 2016 election using the same set of candidates from the website analyses. A team of research assistants and I analyzed the news coverage from September 1 through Election Day for the female Senate candidates and their male opponents. I examined coverage in both local and national news outlets. Using the Lexis-Nexis database, I conducted a search for news articles that used the candidate's name. The Lexis-Nexis database is not an entirely comprehensive set of news articles that covered the candidate in some way, as not all news outlets upload their content to this electronic database, but this search still yields a relatively comprehensive overview of the articles written about candidates across the electoral cycle (Ridout, Fowler, and Searles 2012).

As with the web coding, two independent coders read each article and determined whether the article discussed candidate qualifications. The news qualification coding mirrors the web qualification coding. The research team recorded each article that mentioned the political experience, professional background, and academic accomplishments of the candidates (see Table 4.1). The data set simply records whether the article included information about a specific qualification metric with a binary variable. I also recorded whether a female author penned an article. To record whether the author was female, I looked for information about the specific reporter through professional websites or social media accounts. I also classified whether the article appeared in a major national news outlet (e.g., *New York Times* or *Washington Post*), a statewide outlet (e.g., *The Hartford Courant* or the *Charleston Gazette-Mail*), a local outlet (e.g., *Richmond County Daily Herald* in North Carolina or the *Reading Eagle* in Pennsylvania), or an internationally based outlet (e.g., *The Guardian* or *The Jerusalem Post*).[10]

The total set of articles included in the analyses is about 3,500. There is considerable variation in the number of news articles that appeared about each candidate, with the values ranging from just two articles about Joe Miller, who challenged incumbent Lisa Murkowski, to a high of 476 news articles about Pennsylvania Senate incumbent Pat Toomey, challenged by Katie McGinty. The average number of articles written about a candidate was 121 articles. This means that between September 1 and November 8, 2016, a candidate had approximately two articles appear in the news about them every day. Looking at the contests that featured a female candidate running against a male candidate, so excluding the all-female races, shows some interesting patterns. There were 955 news articles written about female candidates in races against male opponents; their male opponents received more coverage, with a total of 2,513 articles. Take, for instance, the high-profile Senate race with Republican incumbent Pat Toomey defending his seat against Katie McGinty, a Democratic first-time female candidate. There were 476 articles written about Pat Toomey, while there were 339 articles written about his female opponent Katie McGinty (a difference of 137 articles).

To detect differences between female and male candidates systematically, I estimated a series of logistic regression models predicting the likelihood that a candidate received news coverage of qualifications.[11] These models predict the likelihood that a candidate receives news coverage about qualifications. Figure 4.2 displays the main results. The findings indicate the presence of gendered information gaps. The probability the news media wrote about the political experience of a female candidate is

---

[10] The Appendix to Chapter 4 includes more information about the full set of controls included in the analyses.

[11] The models include control variables for being a female candidate, party, incumbency, and the presence of a female opponent as well as variables reflecting the type of news outlet that covered a story and whether the author of the article appeared to be female. As with the website analyses, I clustered the errors at the state level to account for unobserved heterogeneity at the state level.

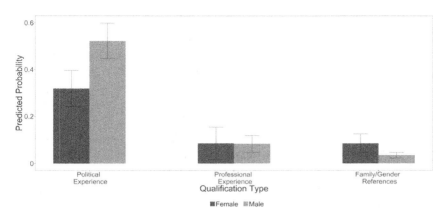

FIGURE 4.2 Predicted probability of receiving qualification news coverage.
Note: 95 percent confidence intervals included. Each bar displays the probability of a
news article reporting on the qualifications of a female and male candidate based on
the results of logit regression models. The Appendix to Chapter 4 includes the full model
results. There were too few cases of academic news coverage, discussion of where the
candidate went to school or the degrees they hold, to include, and I excluded that
category from this analysis.

0.32, while the probability of political experience coverage is 0.52 for a
male candidate, and this 0.20-point difference is statistically significant,
p < 0.01. The website analyses conducted earlier in this chapter found
that female candidates were more likely to report on their professional
qualifications relative to male candidates. If the news media followed the
lead of female candidates in developing their coverage, then there should
be significant differences in professional qualification coverage that favor
female candidates. The findings do not support the agenda convergence
expectations.

The results suggest that the news media follow masculine news norms
that pressure them to favor male candidates who fit into the conventional
image of a political leader. For qualification coverage, relying on masculine stereotypes for male candidates simply means talking about their
political experience, but relying on feminine stereotypes for female candidates means talking about feminine experiences that are incongruent with
political leadership. The results bear out this expectation. Nine percent of
the articles about female candidates reported on their husbands, children,
status as mothers, and other gendered aspects of their qualifications,
while 3 percent of the articles about male candidates reported on comparable qualities, and these patterns are statistically significant, p < 0.05.
While 9 percent does not seem like a substantively large number of

articles, even a small amount of coverage focusing on feminine qualities of female candidates can draw attention to the gender-role incongruity between being a woman and being a leader (Bauer 2015a; Ditonto, Hamilton, and Redlawsk 2014; Lizotte and Meggers-Wright 2019).

What about All-Female Races?

What happens in races with two female candidates running against one another? Do races with two women running against each other receive different types of qualification coverage relative to races with two men running against one another? There were two female-versus-female Senate races in 2016, and they were both high-profile elections. The first all-female Senate race featured Kamala Harris running against Loretta Sanchez in California. This race is atypical because both candidates ran as Democrats in an open-seat race, and both candidates are women of color with a history of holding elected office in the state. The second all-female race was in New Hampshire and featured Republican incumbent Kelly Ayotte running against the Democratic governor Maggie Hassan. This race, much like the one in California, again featured two women with ample political experience. Did the media pay attention to the political experiences of these women?

I compared the news coverage received by these two female candidates with a small matched sample of races featuring all-male candidates with comparable levels of political experience and comparable levels of competitiveness. Comparing the qualification news coverage between all-female and all-male Senate races allows me to see whether there is something about a woman running against a male candidate that alters the way the news media talk about the qualifications of candidates. The competitive context of a woman running against a man could lead journalists to fall back on conventional stereotypes of women as not very qualified for political office when they otherwise might not rely on these concepts. A race with two women running against one another could be treated more similarly to an election with two male candidates.

Figure 4.3 displays the breakdown in the type of news coverage in the all-female Senate races compared with the all-male Senate races. The all-female Senate races received *more* news coverage relative to the all-male Senate races, with nearly 200 more articles, but the content of this coverage still reflects a gendered information gap. The all-female Senate races received nearly 20 percent *less coverage* about political experience compared with the all-male Senate races, and these races also received slightly

FIGURE 4.3 Qualification news coverage in all-female versus all-male races.
Note: Figure displays the percentage of news articles about political, professional, academic, feminine, or some other type of content about the candidates in all-female and all-male races. The female candidates running against one another were Kamala Harris versus Loretta Sanchez in California, and Kelly Ayotte versus Maggie Hassan in New Hampshire. I included two all-male races as comparable as possible to the all-female races for comparison, and these included the Senate race in Wisconsin with Ron Johnson challenged by Russ Feingold and Todd Young running against Evan Bayh.

less professional experience coverage. The all-female Senate races received more coverage about family and children relative to the all-male races.

The feminine qualification coverage is striking in the all-female Senate races because neither Sanchez nor Harris had children, and the two women rarely mentioned their marital status or families. Family made up a considerable bulk of the news media's coverage of Kelly Ayotte. This type of coverage was prominent in the types of coverage female candidates received during October 2016. In early October 2016, the now infamous "Trump tape" became public. The *Access Hollywood* tape featured Trump talking about sexually assaulting women. Ayotte repeatedly had to explain her condemnation of the tape in terms of her status as a mother with small children. Male candidates did not have to explain their support or lack of support for the president in the post-tape stage of the campaign in terms of their status as fathers.

Of course, many male candidates, especially Republican male candidates, did make statements of the "as a father" variety denouncing the Trump tape, but these statements from male candidates did not seem to garner as much media coverage especially when these male candidates waffled around their denunciations.[12] One of the reasons why the news media took Kelly Ayotte to task about her statement against the Trump

---

[12] For more on the influence of fatherhood on male candidates, see Greenlee et al. (2018).

tape is that she was not initially quick to condemn Trump's apparent sexism. Senate candidate Pat Toomey was in a similarly competitive race against Democratic challenger Katie McGinty. Toomey, like Ayotte, initially hesitated in his condemnation of Trump's statements on the *Access Hollywood* tape; Toomey, similar to Ayotte, has young children. Comparing the family coverage received by Ayotte with that received by Toomey illustrates a gendered dynamic, as 12 percent of the articles about Ayotte talked about her family, while less than 1 percent of articles about Toomey referenced his family. The vast majority of Ayotte family coverage is about the Trump tape, and very little of the family coverage of Toomey mentions the tape. Toomey did receive coverage about his ambiguity on the tape, but most of these articles did not reference Toomey's three young children or his status as a father. These patterns, while anecdotal, suggest that the identities of women as mothers are never far from their status as political candidates.

Maybe Female Candidates Were Just Less Qualified in 2016?

Only three of the women running in 2016 ran as incumbents, with the rest of the women running as challengers against more senior incumbent men. Female candidates may have received less qualification news coverage in 2016 because they had fewer qualifications. To test whether the women who ran in 2016 were simply less qualified relative to the more senior men they ran against, I collected biographical data on the political, professional, academic, and feminine experiences of the female candidates and their male opponents who ran in 2016. With this information, I created several types of variables. For political experience, I recorded whether the candidate was an incumbent, whether the candidate had previously held a statewide elected office, had served in Congress but was not a Senate incumbent (i.e., was attempting to move from the House to the Senate), or had served in a state legislature or a local office. For professional experience, I classified the professions and jobs held by candidates based on whether they were traditional political pipeline jobs (i.e., lawyer) or not. I created a series of academic credential variables that recorded whether the candidate had a bachelor's or graduate degree and whether the candidate attended an Ivy League institution.

I compared the levels of political experience across state, local, and national offices, and found that a higher proportion of male candidates, 62 percent, were likely to have served in the US House previously compared with female candidates, 19 percent, and this is a significant difference, p < 0.05.[13] There were no other differences in the proportions of female and male Senate candidates who served in statewide elected offices (e.g., attorney general or governor), state legislatures, or local offices. With the data on the different levels of political experience at which the candidates previously served, I created an overall political experience variable that records the number of offices a candidate previously held before their Senate race. Female candidates, on average, held 1.25 (SD = 0.25) elected positions, and men previously held, on average, 1.77 (SD = 0.28) elected positions, but these differences are not statistically different from one another. Looking at political experience, the single most common metric of candidate quality, there are many points of parity between the female and the male candidates. This means there should be more parity in the news coverage. On the other dimensions included in the analyses, I found no statistically significant differences in the professional experiences of the female and male senate candidates. I also found no differences in the proportions of female and male Senate candidates who held bachelor's or graduate degrees or received degrees from Ivy League institutions. The gendered information gaps in news coverage are not necessarily due to female candidates simply having fewer qualifications relative to their male opponents.

Pairing together the website analysis with the news media analysis highlights the source of the gendered qualification gap. Female and male candidates highlight their political experience at equal rates, but the news media are more likely to highlight the political experience of male candidates rather than female candidates. Female candidates are most likely to use their professional experiences as a selling point on their campaign websites – a pattern that fits with the model of female candidates as strategic campaign actors. The news media report on the professional qualifications of female candidates and male candidates at equal rates. Reporters, however, are more likely to discuss the feminine qualifications of female candidates than male candidates, and this reinforces long-held stereotypes that women do not belong in masculine positions of political leadership.

IS THERE A GENDERED INFORMATION GAP?

The six women running for the presidency in 2020, based on the results from this chapter, may need to work a bit harder to sell their

---

[13] See the Appendix to Chapter 4 for the full comparisons.

qualifications to voters compared with their male candidates. Indeed, the news media have devoted more headlines, column inches, and tweets to the nearly twenty men pursuing the Democratic Party's nomination. FiveThirtyEight measured the amount of media coverage of male contenders for the Democratic Party's nomination just before and just after their presidential campaign announcements. The journalists found that the male candidates tended to receive more coverage after their announcements compared with the female candidates. In fact, the gender-based imbalance in news coverage, in and of itself, became the subject of news reporting. One *Christian Science Monitor* article asked in its headline, "With so many women running for president, why is focus still on the men?" A *New York Times* headline read, "'A woman, just not that woman': How sexism plays out on the trail." Another *Vox* headline queried, "Do male candidates get more coverage than women? It's complicated." This research shows that male candidates do indeed receive more qualification coverage relative to their female opponents.

This chapter centered on the question: What qualification information do voters have about the qualifications of female candidates? Whether voters have qualification information about female candidates and what that information is depends on their information source: a candidate's campaign website or the news media. Female candidates do not undersell themselves. The website analyses found that female candidates are just as likely to emphasize their political, profession, and academic qualifications as their male opponents. This finding supports the strategic candidate emergence literature. Female candidates run for political office when the odds of victory are highest (Fulton et al. 2006), and female candidates maximize their odds of victory by emphasizing their high level of qualifications. Examining the individual pieces of qualification information available to voters on the websites of female candidates reveals that there is slightly more qualification information available on a woman candidate's website compared with the website of her male opponent. Campaign websites are just one communication platform, but it is reasonable to assume that candidates will reiterate the messages on their websites on other communication platforms, such as direct mail, campaign ads, and stump speeches (Fridkin and Kenney 2015). Part of the broader message of a candidate involves sharing their personal narrative, much as Elizabeth Warren did in her announcement video. It does not seem likely that a female candidate would make no mention of relevant political experience on a campaign website but would talk about political experience in a stump speech.

The website analyses found that female candidates included discussion of their families, as did their male opponents. Talking about families is a routine practice on candidate websites and is part of telling the life story of a candidate. But for female candidates the familial discussion could have a different motivation and effect than it does for male candidates. Female candidates may highlight their families, especially their status as mothers, to *prevent* a self-promotion backlash. Dittmar (2015) found in her interviews with campaign consultants who advise female candidates that campaigns regularly make this type of calculated trade-off: if a female candidate is going to engage in a strategy that violates feminine norms, then she also should include something in her message that adheres to feminine norms. References to family are a common way for female candidates to show they are not too masculine. My research does not directly investigate the underlying motivations behind decisions to discuss families on candidates' websites, but this does not mean that the mention of family does not have this softening effect on voters (Deason, Greenlee, and Langer 2015).

Comparing the website with the news media analyses suggests the absence of an agenda-setting effect. The news media are far more likely to cover the political experiences of male candidates and not female candidates, while the news media are more likely to highlight the feminine qualifications of female candidates. The differences in political experience coverage are especially striking given the twenty-point difference in the probability of an article highlighting the political experience of a male candidate relative to a female candidate. This gap cannot be explained by differences in the actual qualifications of female and male candidates. The news analyses found no differences in female and male candidates discussing political and feminine qualifications. The website analyses found that female candidates emphasize their professional experiences more than male candidates, but this slight advantage for female candidates does not carry over into news coverage. The gendered information gap uncovered in the news media analysis on the political experience dimension can have critical implications for the success of female candidates. The comparative context of a female candidate vying against a male candidate can heighten the perceived incongruity between being female and being a leader (Bauer 2020b). Voters may assume, in this comparative context, that male candidates have the qualities needed for political office and female candidates do not (Ditonto 2017).

This analysis relied on only one election year, but this year was noteworthy because of the high visibility of gender throughout the campaign, not only at the presidential level but also among many of the Senate races we analyzed. Several women who ran for the Senate in 2016 did so as female firsts, and the media's reliance on novelty means that these women should have actually received more news coverage than their male counterparts. Kamala Harris and Loretta Sanchez were running to be the first women of color to represent California, and Katie McGinty and Catherine Cortez Masto would have been the first women to represent their states. News norms and values dictate that these women should have received more coverage than they actually did receive. The patterns uncovered in candidate news coverage reflect a broader trend in how masculine news norms and routines determine the way reporters cover political campaigns (Armstrong 2004; Searles and Banda 2019; Zeldes, Zico, and Diddi 2007). Reporters, just like voters, are susceptible to using conventional feminine stereotypes to cover female candidates because these constructs are easy and accessible. The next chapter tests how voters use and evaluate the types of qualification information female and male candidates present on their campaign websites. In other words, How do voters evaluate the qualification information of female and male candidates?

5

Do Voters Expect Women to Be Better than Men?

Project strength, ladies! Set that jaw! If there is a single rule for female politicians – especially those seeking an executive office such as governor or president – it's that they must work harder than male candidates to appear strong and decisive.

—2007 article in the *Washington Post* about the "rules" for
female candidates

In late January of 2016, a record-setting blizzard struck Washington, DC. The blizzard raged for thirty-six hours and covered the nation's capital in nearly three feet of snow. This extreme weather event brought the capital to a near standstill, closing businesses and much of the federal government. The Senate was still in session during the blizzard, but on January 27, the only senators to show up for work were women. Senators Lisa Murkowski and Susan Collins made it to the Senate chamber despite the snowstorm; not one of the eighty male senators made it into work that day. It is not necessarily noteworthy, in and of itself, that only Senators Murkowski and Collins braved the winter weather, as both are from northern states known for cold, icy, and snowy weather. The January 27 Senate session was noteworthy because the only Senate staff members and Senate pages who came to work that day were women. Senator Lisa Murkowski made note of the all-female Senate chamber, stating, "Something is genuinely different – and something is genuinely fabulous."[1]

---

[1] Emily Heil, "Post-Blizzard, Sen. Murkowski Notes That Only Women Turned Up to Run the Senate," *Washington Post*, January 26, 2016, www.washingtonpost.com/news/reli able-source/wp/2016/01/26/post-blizzard-sen-murkowski-notes-that-only-women-turned-up-to-run-the-senate/.

Asked to speculate on why only female senators and only female Senate staffers showed up to the chamber, Murkowski stated, "Perhaps it speaks to the hardiness of women. That put on your boots and put your hat on and get out and slog through the mess that's out there."

This rare all-female Senate session may reflect the "hardiness" of women, but it also reinforces empirical data showing that women, on average, work harder than their male counterparts. Many female politicians face pressure to work harder due to an internalized sense of gendered vulnerability and the anticipation of facing bias among voters (Anzia and Berry 2011; Lawless 2012; Lazarus and Steigerwalt 2018). These fears are not unfounded as male challengers often see female incumbents as weak opponents who will be easy to defeat – a sentiment that reflects conventional feminine stereotypes – and this means that female lawmakers will work harder than male candidates to prevent the primary and general election challenges that female incumbents are more likely to face compared with male incumbents (Barnes, Branton, and Cassese 2017; Lawless and Pearson 2008; Milyo and Schlosberg 2000). I argue that female candidates not only experience gendered vulnerability among party elites and potential reelection challengers but also experience this vulnerability among voters. Voters will, according to my argument, hold female candidates to a higher qualification standard than male candidates. Holding female candidates to a higher standard at the level of voters contributes to the gendered qualification gap because it means that female candidates will be most likely to win elections when they have better qualifications than their male counterparts.

Chapter 4 illustrated how female candidates face a gendered information gap on the campaign trail. Female candidates are not necessarily the cause of this gendered information gap. Indeed, both female and male candidates highlight their political experiences, and female candidates are even more likely to discuss their professional qualifications relative to male candidates. The information gap comes from the news media. The news media are, on average, more likely to talk about the families of female candidates, relative to male candidates, and less likely to talk about the political experience of female candidates. This information gap can create a high qualification bar for female candidates, who may have to work harder than male candidates to get the message out about their exceptional qualifications. Without qualification information, voters may assume that female candidates, based on feminine stereotypes, lack the qualifications needed for political office.

This chapter turns to investigating how voters evaluate female candidate qualifications. The central question guiding this chapter asks: Do voters hold female candidates to a higher qualification standard relative to male candidates? This is a question existing scholarship has yet to answer. Holding female candidates to a higher standard, or even just a different standard, compared with male candidates, can make it harder for women to win elections. I argue that voters do, in fact, expect female candidates to be of a higher quality than male candidates, contributing to the gendered qualification gap. A long-standing empirical finding is that female candidates win elections at rates equal to those of male candidates (Ekstrand and Eckert 1981; Seltzer, Newman, and Leighton 1997). Observational surveys regularly show that voters rate the qualifications of female candidates quite positively – often even more positively than a male candidate's qualifications (see, e.g., Brooks 2013; Dolan 2014; Hayes and Lawless 2016). It is easy to conclude from these findings that female candidates do not face gender bias. This conclusion rests on two implicit and untested assumptions. First, scholars assume that rating a female candidate as "very qualified" or "very experienced" directly translates into electoral support (Brooks 2013; Hayes and Lawless 2016). Second, previous scholarship assumes that a female candidate rated as highly qualified or highly experienced looks just like a male candidate also rated as highly qualified or highly experienced (Dolan 2014). These approaches do not address the role voters play in perpetuating the gendered qualification gap where female candidates are held to higher, or different, qualification standards than male candidates.

Drawing on a theory of shifting standards from social psychology research, I identify three gendered qualification standards voters will use to evaluate female and male political candidates: a gender-typicality standard, a female politician standard, and a role-typicality standard. The argument I develop suggests that voters will use these standards at different stages of the impression-formation process to evaluate the qualifications of female and male candidates. I argue that voters will use gender-typicality standards to evaluate female and male candidates when forming initial impressions about whether candidates have the minimum skills needed for political office. Under gender-typicality standards, voters will evaluate a female candidate according to whether she has more or fewer minimum skills than a "typical woman," and voters will compare a male candidate against a "typical man." Gender-typicality standards will most prominently affect female challengers. I argue that for female incumbents, voters will use a standard that reflects both feminine and masculine stereotypes: the female politician standard. With this standard, voters will compare a specific female incumbent with the prototypic image of a female politician – a stereotype that consists of negative feminine qualities and positive masculine qualities. The use of these standards creates the illusion that voters rate female candidates positively. These positive ratings, I suggest, will not necessarily lead to increased vote support because voters will shift to a masculine role-typicality standard to make inferences about whether a candidate can fill the role of being a political leader. With masculine role-typicality standards, voters will compare a female and a male candidate with the masculine image of a political leader, thereby advantaging male candidates and disadvantaging female candidates.

I use two original survey experiments to test how and when voters shift the standards they use to evaluate candidate qualifications. An experimental approach allows me to control the qualifications of female and male candidates so that the only factor that varies between two candidates is whether they are female or male. Real-world elections cannot guarantee this level of control, which allows me to isolate the role that a candidate's status as female has in perceived qualification ratings because women in actual elections generally outperform men in terms of qualifications. These two experiments also vary the different contexts that affect the use of gender-typicality or role-typicality standards in qualification evaluations. The gender-typicality experiment examines how a female candidate's incumbent status affects how voters evaluate her minimum skills for serving in political office. The gender-typicality experiment also tests if voters shift to a female politician standard for female incumbents. The role-typicality experiment investigates how running against a male opponent affects the broad inferences, or assessments about electability, viability, and ultimate vote choice decisions made about female candidates. Together, these experiments isolate how voters rate female candidate qualifications, and when voters will hold female candidates to a higher standard than male candidates.

The use of stereotypic standards explains a puzzling phenomenon. Female candidates, in polling data and in actual practice, receive high marks for their strong qualifications (Fulton 2012), but female candidates only break even with male candidates in electoral returns (Seltzer, Newman, and Leighton 1997), and female candidates win elections by smaller margins than male candidates (Pearson and McGhee 2013). If there were no bias in voter decision-making, then female candidates would win elections by larger vote margins than male candidates.

I argue that the use of shifting gendered standards explains, in part, these dynamics. In this chapter, I start by defining and describing gender-typicality, female politician, and role-typicality standards, and based on these standards I develop a set of hypotheses about how and when voters will use them to evaluate female and male candidates. I then present the results from two original experiments that illustrate how voters use these gendered standards to evaluate female candidates. I conclude this chapter with a discussion about the implications of these gendered standards.

GENDER-TYPICALITY STANDARDS

As Chapter 3 discussed, the prolonged performance of women and men in separate social roles gave rise to stereotypes about whether women or men are better suited to serve in specific social roles, such as being a caregiver or a leader. These sex-segregated social roles shape the occupations that women and men pursue, the tasks that women and men perform in their occupations, and the broader social expectations about the traits men and women possess. When people hold beliefs that either men or women are better suited to fill a specific role or occupation, then it is likely that corresponding gender stereotypes will be the standard of judgment people use when deciding who has the qualifications necessary to serve in that specific role (Biernat and Manis 1994; Kunda, Sinclair, and Griffin 1997). The role of a "political leader" is a highly masculinized role. Voters prefer political leaders to have masculine traits and have a high level of expertise on masculine issues (Holman, Merolla, and Zechmeister 2016; Huddy and Terkildsen 1993). Given these strongly gendered expectations, voters will use gender stereotypes to evaluate the qualifications of women and men to fill these roles. I argue that voters start to form impressions of candidate qualifications by evaluating female and male candidates according to the gender stereotype that matches their status as female or male, and in this section, I explain how these gender-typicality standards work.

A common "compliment" women receive is that they are good at a task, skill, or activity "for a girl." This phenomenon plagues female athletes, female CEOs, and other exceptionally qualified women. This qualifier suggests that if a woman were a man, her accomplishment would not be quite as exceptional or noteworthy. The "for a girl" language sets a low bar for women operating in typically masculine roles and indicates the use of a gender-typicality standard to evaluate the accomplishments of women. Gender-typicality standards use a "within-group standard of judgment" where a woman or a man is compared with stereotypes of a "typical woman" or a "typical man" (Biernat and Kobrynowicz 1997). The within-group standard of judgment consists of the beliefs voters have about the skills and abilities of women and men, in general. Stereotypes create the set of within-group standards voters can use to assess the qualifications of individual candidates. People will form these within-group evaluations because they need a comparative anchor when forming impressions of other individuals (Campbell, Lewis, and Hunt 1958; Postman and Miller 1945). Essentially, stereotypes are comparative anchors that ease the task of decision-making. Gender stereotypes provide individuals with an easy and accessible comparative metric they can use to evaluate the qualities of an individual woman or man (Biernat and Manis 1994).

Gender-typicality standards will affect how voters form impressions about the minimum skills of political candidates. Biernat and Kobrynowicz (1997) describe minimum skill judgments as "the *minimal level* of an attribute that is expected from a group" (p. 546). Minimum skill assessments do not necessarily include decisions about whether to hire a job candidate for a specific position or whether to vote for a political candidate, but they are still important evaluations. Minimum skills are more like "quick and dirty" assessments about whether a person has the baseline qualifications needed to do the job. For example, a person using a gender-typicality standard to evaluate the qualifications of a female applicant for a job as a trial lawyer, a stereotypically masculine profession, might start by evaluating whether the woman is aggressive enough to handle the back-and-forth argumentation of the courtroom. Stereotypes about a typical woman, in general, characterize her as not very aggressive and as more conflict-avoidant, and this means that the female job applicant needs to meet a relatively low standard to demonstrate that she is aggressive enough to handle a little conflict in the courtroom. A woman, in this case, just has to be more aggressive than a stereotypic woman and does not necessarily need to be more aggressive than a stereotypic man. A woman who argues just a little bit will likely be seen as very aggressive. Gender-typicality standards apply to men as well, and these standards can create a high bar on minimum skill assessments. Others will see the "typical man" as having the qualities needed for filling a masculine role, and this means that a specific man must work a little harder to show that he is more qualified than the typical man. A man applying to be a trial lawyer will have to prove that he is more aggressive than the average man, whom others will see as aggressive given that this is a quality that fits into stereotypes about men.

Voters will use the gender-typicality standard only to assess whether the woman has the *minimum skills* needed to fill a specific role and will not use this standard to decide whether to hire her to fill that role. Hiring decisions, or broad inferences, require using a role-typicality standard, which I outline in the next section. Voters will use gender-typicality standards to evaluate the minimum skills of a candidate because, in short, these are quick and easy heuristics to use when forming initial impressions about a candidate. In a political context, voters will evaluate a female candidate's qualifications, or minimum skills, for political office based on the extent to which a "typical woman" has the qualifications necessary to serve in political office, and voters will evaluate male candidates based on a "typical man" standard (Biernat and Manis 1994). Being female, in general, is incongruent with serving in political leadership roles (Eagly and Karau 2002). This incongruity creates low expectations for whether a female candidate has the minimum skills needed for political office because the typical woman is perceived as lacking the qualifications for political office. For male candidates, voters will compare a specific male candidate to a "typical man." The congruity between being male, masculinity, and leadership means that male candidates will have a somewhat higher bar to meet on minimum skill assessments.

The gender-typicality prediction outlines the observable implications of this standard. The use of a gender-typicality standard sets a low bar for female candidates to receive a positive rating on minimum skills.

Gender-Typicality Prediction: A female candidate will receive more positive minimum skill evaluations relative to a male candidate.

The key with gender-typicality standards is that more positive evaluations do not necessarily mean that voters are comparing a female candidate with a male candidate. The positive ratings mean that voters see the female candidate as having more minimum skills than a typical woman. Past research does not elaborate the standard of comparison voters use to evaluate qualifications, experience, or knowledge of a candidate. The use of gender-typicality standards explicates the role that gender stereotypes play in evaluations of female and male candidates – and this is a unique contribution of my theory.

ROLE-TYPICALITY STANDARDS

Masculine stereotypes influence who voters see as a viable political leader. These assessments about who can serve in a leadership capacity reflect an evaluation where voters will shift, according to my argument, from gender-typicality to role-typicality standards (Biernat and Kobrynowicz 1997; Foschi 1992). Role-typicality standards are based on the stereotypes associated with a "typical" individual in a specific role. I argue that voters will shift to masculine role-typicality standards to evaluate *who* can fill a distinct social role. I call this decision about who can fill a gendered social role a *broad inference assessment*. Voters will shift to a role-typicality standard because they are no longer thinking about whether a person has the basic qualifications, or minimum skills, to fill a role but are thinking about the active performance of a person in that specific role.

Going back to the example of a trial lawyer, stereotypes of men as aggressive and argumentative define the stereotypic qualities associated with a "typical trial lawyer." Role-typicality standards will disadvantage women vying to fill stereotypically masculine roles because others do not typically see women as having masculine qualities. Even though a woman applying to fill a trial lawyer role may receive an initially positive assessment on the minimum skills needed to fill the role, the female applicant will not necessarily be rated positively on her ability to fill the role of a trial lawyer.[2] This negative broad inference rating comes from the incongruity between the woman's sex, the feminine stereotypes typically ascribed to women, and the masculine stereotypes of the specific role. A man applying to be a trial lawyer will have an advantage over a female applicant even if he initially received a low minimum skills rating.

Applied to a political leadership context, masculine role-typicality standards create a high qualification bar for female candidates and a low qualification bar for male candidates. In this masculine context, role-typicality standards will "bias the evaluations so that a man's performance at a masculine task will be assessed as better than the same performance by a woman" (Foschi 1992, p. 185). Voters will prefer male candidates when it comes to forming broad inferences about whether a candidate can serve in a political leadership role because these broad inferences ask voters to think about how well this candidate fits into the role of being a political leader. When voters think about political leaders, they think about men. As Chapter 3 explained, this association is one that developed over millennia of men serving in leadership. Fitting a male candidate into the masculine prototypical image of a political leader is

---

[2] For feminine roles and occupations, women should have an advantage over men on broad inference decisions according to the shifting standards framework.

relatively easy for voters. Fitting a female candidate into the masculine prototypical image of a political leader is cognitively more difficult for voters. Thus, masculine role-typicality standards create a low qualification bar for male candidates and a high qualification bar for female candidates when it comes to broad inferences.

According to my argument, voters will shift from gender-typicality to role-typicality standards when making judgments about whether a candidate can serve in a specific role and not necessarily whether the candidate has the minimum skills needed to fill a specific role. Broad inference assessments include more than just whether a candidate has the minimum qualifications to do the job, and might include whether a person is seen as a viable contender, whether others are likely to support the candidate, and whether a person plans to vote for the candidate themselves. While minimal assessments and broad inferences seem connected, these are two different types of assessments. A voter might see a male candidate as electable even if she lacks the minimum qualifications needed for political office because of the congruence between masculinity and leadership. Likewise, a voter might see a female candidate as not very electable even if she is very experienced and receives a high minimum skill rating due to feminine stereotypes.

The role-typicality standard means that a female candidate will not have an advantage over a male candidate. The role-typicality prediction outlines the observable effect of this standard.

Role-Typicality Prediction: Female candidates will not have any advantages over a male candidate when voters form broad inferences about the ability of a candidate to fill a leadership role.

This disadvantage is present even when the female candidate may have received more positive evaluations on the minimum skill assessments. Masculine role-typicality standards create a high bar for female candidates when deciding whether a woman can actually fill a leadership post because of the incongruence between being female and being a leader (Eagly and Karau 2002). The gender-role congruity between being male and serving in leadership roles creates a baseline advantage for male candidates. Voters will assume that a male candidate has all the qualities needed to succeed in a political leadership role and that female candidates will have more difficulty succeeding in a masculine role. The use of role-typicality standards explains why female candidates *must* outperform male candidates to win elections. Simply being as good as a male candidate is not enough to secure victory for a female candidate.

FEMALE POLITICIAN STANDARD

Gender-typicality and role-typicality standards explain how and when voters will switch between feminine and masculine stereotypes to evaluate female candidates depending on whether voters are forming minimum assessments or making broad ability inferences about these candidates. The gendered standards voters use can, depending on the status of a female candidate, be a mix of both feminine and masculine stereotypes. The third standard I develop integrates research on the distinct stereotypes voters hold of female incumbents with research on how a candidate's status affects the standards used to form evaluations about qualifications. This third standard, the female politician standard, applies to female incumbents, and I argue that voters will hold female incumbents to a gendered standard made up of both feminine and masculine qualities.

The status of an individual, according to the shifting standards framework, can affect the extent to which others will use a gender-typicality comparison as the evaluative standard used to form minimum skill assessments. When roles are shaped by strongly gendered standards, the sex of an individual determines, in part, their status in relation to that role (Biernat and Manis 1994). For masculine roles and occupations, men automatically have a higher status relative to women. Status can also relate to the experience an individual already has in a specific role. An individual with higher status in a specific role may not be compared with a gender-typicality standard when it comes to minimum skills assessments (Foschi 1992). High-status individuals are those with some experience in the agentic roles they aim to fill. For example, a high-status woman in business might be a CEO or a manger who will have to meet a different minimum ability standard relative to a woman applying for an entry-level position in a corporation.

A female incumbent running for reelection is an example of a high-status woman. The incumbent status cues voters that the candidate has already "fit" into the masculine leadership role at some point, and this differentiates her from a female challenger candidate who has yet to prove her masculine leadership credentials. Previous research shows that female incumbents are evaluated in ways that are distinctly different from female challengers (Fulton 2012; Fridkin and Kenney 2009). A female challenger running for election to the Senate or the House either for an open-seat election or in a bid to unseat an incumbent is a comparatively low-status woman in the political system – and voters will evaluate her minimum skill abilities according to a gender-typicality standard. Female challenger candidates, even if they have some political experience, are still likely to be unknown to voters and lack incumbency status. More high-profile and more senior female incumbents, such as long-term incumbent women, may not have to meet a gender-based within-group standard of comparison. I argue that female incumbents will have to meet a gendered standard based on the stereotypes voters hold of female leaders, and these stereotypes include a mix of feminine and masculine qualities.

Female incumbents will not be judged in terms of their minimum qualifications because they have already met these minimum qualifications by virtue of their current office. Instead, they will be judged against a "female politician" standard. This unique stereotype category creates an alternative, but still gendered, standard. Female incumbents will be held to this higher standard, while nonincumbent female challengers will be evaluated based on the weaker gender-typicality standard. Schneider and Bos (2014) describe this standard where participants stereotype female politicians as lacking warmth and compassion, qualities conventionally associated with women, but see female politicians as being educated, competitive, ambitious, and confident, qualities conventionally associated with both masculinity and political leadership – though voters do not associate these masculine qualities with female leaders as strongly as they do with male leaders. Incumbency status creates the expectation that a typical female politician has a high level of skills, and a specific female incumbent may have more trouble meeting this standard relative to a female challenger. Female incumbents will not have the same low bar to meet as female challengers when it comes to minimum skill assessments. Female challengers will be held to the low bar of the gender-typicality standard. The female politician prediction outlines these effects:

Female Politician Prediction: Female incumbents should receive lower minimum skills ratings relative to female challengers.

The observable implication of the female politician standard is the difference in minimum skills evaluations of female incumbents relative to female challengers. There will still be differences in the minimum skill ratings between female incumbents and male incumbents, with female incumbents still receiving more positive evaluations relative to male incumbents. I argue that the female politician standard will come to bear on minimum skill evaluations of female incumbents more so than on broad inference assessments. In broad inference assessments, voters will shift from a female politician standard to a masculine role-typicality standard.

The difference between incumbents and challengers matters most for female candidates rather than male candidates. Incumbency and challenger status will not matter as much for male candidates, and this goes back to gender-role congruity. Men, by virtue of their sex and the corresponding masculine associations, have a higher status within politics, and this higher status occurs when they are challengers and when they are incumbents. Indeed, Schneider and Bos (2014) found few differences in the stereotypes associated with male leaders and men in general. This is not to say that voters will evaluate male incumbents differently from male challengers, but that the gendered standards used to evaluate male incumbents and male challengers will not necessarily differ.

GENDER-TYPICALITY EXPERIMENT

I test the presence of gender-typicality and the female politician standard with an experiment that manipulates candidate sex and the incumbency status of a candidate. I manipulated candidate sex with names, Carol or Chris Hartley, and female and male photos. The candidate was either an incumbent or a challenger running for election to the US House of Representatives. I manipulated the incumbency and challenger status of the candidate because this lets me test how the status of a woman in the political system affects the use of female politician standards as opposed to the gender-typicality standard or the role-typicality standard. I excluded partisan labels in this first study to ensure that partisan affinity does not affect the results (Badas and Stauffer 2019).[3]

I use a newspaper article for the manipulation because this treatment resembles how most voters learn about elections (Darr 2016), and research shows that media coverage of candidate qualifications, such as competency, differs for female candidates compared with male candidates (Bligh et al. 2012). In the challenger condition, the candidate was a state legislator moving up to a seat in the US House. The challenger stimulus provided information about the legislative productivity of the candidate while serving in the state legislature, including committee service and bills sponsored and passed, as well as information about the professional background of the candidate. The challenger text read:

Carol/Chris Hartley is running for a seat to Congress after having served in the state legislature for a single term. As a state legislator, Hartley did not serve in any

---

[3] I include details about the sample's demographics and the experimental design in the Appendix to Chapter 5.

leadership positions, but was a member of several committees though she/he sponsored no bills that became law. Before serving in the state house, Hartley had a small law practice with several clients throughout the state. Carol/Chris Hartley attended the State University where she/he received both her/his bachelor's degree and her/his law degree.

The incumbent condition mentioned that the candidate just finished a first-term in the House, is a member of multiple committees, and sponsored bills but they did not become law. The text read:

Congresswoman/man Carol/Chris Hartley is running for reelection. Hartley just finished her/his first term in the House of Representatives. Hartley serves on several committees. During the last legislative term, Carol/Chris Hartley sponsored bills to bring federal dollars to the district to repair roads and build a new community center – but was ultimately not successful. Hartley sponsored no bills that successfully became law. Carol/Chris Hartley has a reputation of refusing to work across the partisan aisle to get things done.

It is important to note that I did not vary the qualification information between the female and male candidate conditions. I control the information in this way because this allows me to isolate how the candidate's status as a woman, when the qualifications of candidates are exactly the same, affects the way voters evaluate those very qualifications.

The first outcomes I measured asked participants to rate the minimum skills of each candidate.[4] The minimum skills included working hard; being organized, determined, principled, able to stand their ground; being compromising; consensus-building; willingness to engage in bipartisan behavior; sharing credit with others; public speaking; and working well with others. I developed this measure based on existing scholarship on the basic skills legislators need to serve in public office (Bauer 2020b; Fulton 2012). For example, being in public office requires lawmakers who can, at a basic level, engage in public speaking, whether it is speaking in the legislature or speaking at small events with constituents. Participants indicated whether or not the individual possessed each skill. I combined the individual legislative skill ratings into a single scale of *minimum skills*.[5] The minimum skills scale ranges from 0 to 12 where each value indicates the number of skills a candidate possesses. I combined the skills into a single measure because voters generally want candidates who can display excellence on as many skills as possible. Support for the gender-typicality prediction will emerge if the female candidate receives a more

---

[4] See the Appendix to Chapter 5 for information about the skills pretest.
[5] Cronbach's $\alpha = 0.8622$, indicating that this scale has a high level of internal consistency.

positive rating than the male candidate. This more positive evaluation comes from the lower expectations voters hold about the abilities of women to fill masculine leadership roles. Support for the female politician prediction will emerge if the female challenger receives a more positive rating relative to the female incumbent.

I also measured general election viability assessments as a type of broad inference. I predict voters will use role-typicality standards to make these decisions, but I include this measure in this study to illustrate the way that positive minimum skills assessments do not necessarily lead to positive outcomes. I ask about viability as a proxy for vote choice. Asking directly about vote choice in an experiment with a single candidate is difficult because there is no alternative option presented (Brooks 2013). Moreover, asking about vote choice in an experiment about a female candidate can trigger social desirability biases and lead to an overreport of support for the female candidate (Krupnikov, Piston, and Bauer 2016). Viability assessments not only ask about the ability of the candidate to win the election, which requires using a masculine standard to assess the chances of victory, but also require participants to think about whether the candidate will face bias among other voters in the electorate, and asking about the potential for bias among others can lead to more accurate assessments because the question can alleviate social desirability pressures (Claassen and Ryan 2016). Regarding the viability question, it is important to note that because this study presented no opposing candidate in the election, it is likely that participants will assume that the female candidate will face a male opponent. The assumption of a male opponent increases the likelihood of using masculine role-typicality standards. I coded the viability outcome as 1 if participants indicated the female candidate is likely to win the election and 0 otherwise. If my theory is correct, participants will rate the female candidate more positively than the male candidate on the minimum skills measure, but the female candidate will not receive more positive evaluations than the male candidate on viability.

Gender-Typicality Results

The gender-typicality prediction argues that the female candidate should be held to a lower standard of minimum skills relative to a male candidate. If results follow expectations, then the female challenger should receive a higher minimum skill rating relative to the male challenger, and the female incumbent should also receive a higher skills rating than

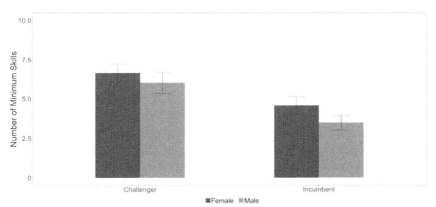

FIGURE 5.1   Gender-typicality and minimum skills.
Note: 95 percent confidence intervals included.

the male incumbent. The left side of Figure 5.1 displays the average number of skills attributed to the female and male challenger candidates. Participants rated the female challenger with 6.65 minimum skills (SD = 2.88) and the male challenger with 6.03 minimum skills (SD = 3.44). The female challenger is attributed with 0.62 more skills than the male challenger. This difference fits the expectations of the gender-typicality prediction, but does not quite reach conventional levels of statistical significance.[6] The female challenger received a slightly more positive skills rating relative to the male challenger because voters compare her with the low bar set by a "typical woman" standard.

The right side of Figure 5.1 shows a wider gendered qualification gap in the incumbent conditions. Participants rated the female incumbent with 4.58 minimum skills (SD = 2.88) and the male incumbent with 3.49 minimum skills (SD = 2.34), $p < 0.01$. Participants rated the female incumbent as having 1.10 more minimum skills than the male incumbent. The difference in the minimum skills ratings of the female and male incumbent suggests that the two candidates, who had the same set of qualifications, are not held to the same standard. According to the logic of the gender-typicality prediction, the female incumbent has more skills than a "typical woman." It is not necessarily the case that the female incumbent has more skills than the male incumbent. The results from this

---

[6] Using a two-tailed t-test, these values do not significantly differ ($p = 0.1730$), but using a one-tailed t-test ($p < 0.10$), there is a marginally significant difference.

first experiment offer partial support for the use of gender-typicality standards. The patterns of higher evaluations for the female candidate relative to the male candidate fit with the expectations, but these qualification gaps are statistically significant only between the incumbent candidates.

Voters do not hold the same stereotypes about female leaders that they do of women in general, and the female politician prediction argues that voters will hold the female incumbent to a different type of gendered standard relative to the female challenger. To test this prediction, I compared how the incumbency versus challenger status of the female candidate affects the skills rating. Evidence of the female politician standard will emerge if there is a difference between the female challenger and the female incumbent. The low status of the female challenger means that voters will not necessarily compare her with a female leader but will compare her with a "typical woman." The female challenger should be held to a significantly lower feminine gender-typicality standard relative to the female incumbent, who should be held to a more stringent, slightly more masculine, typicality standard. This means the female challenger should receive a *higher* minimum skill rating relative to the female incumbent. Participants rated the female challenger as having 2.07 more skills than the female incumbent, $p < 0.01$. This finding fits with the expectations of the female politician prediction. The female challenger has an even lower bar to meet for minimum skill assessments compared with a female incumbent with experience in political office.

Comparing the skill ratings of the male incumbent and the male challenger also shows a significant difference between these two male candidates, $p < 0.01$. But this does not necessarily mean that voters are comparing the two male candidates based on the same type of gender-typicality standards they use to evaluate the female candidates. It is entirely possible, and even reasonable, that participants hold a male incumbent to a higher *masculine* qualification standard due to his status as an experienced leader and that participants are more willing to cut the male challenger some slack, so to speak, due to his status as a political newcomer. The female candidates, both as challengers and as incumbents, receive more positive evaluations relative to the male candidates. The second part of this theory argues that these positive evaluations will not lead to positive broad inference ratings. If the results follow expectations, then the female candidates will *not* receive more positive evaluations than the male candidates. Figure 5.2 displays the proportion of participants who selected each candidate as likely to win the election. Across both the

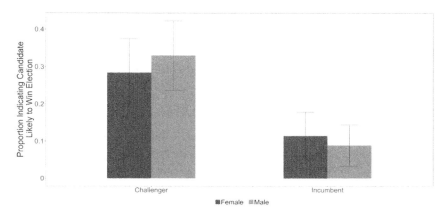

FIGURE 5.2 Candidate viability between female and male candidates.
Note: Each bar displays the proportion of participants indicating that each candidate was likely to win the general election. 95 percent confidence intervals displayed.

challenger and the incumbent conditions, there are no significant differences between the female and the male candidate conditions in the proportion of participants who thought Hartley was likely to win the election. These effects are most striking in the incumbent conditions, where participants rated the female incumbent as having 1.10 more skills relative to the male incumbent, but on viability participants were equally likely to think the female incumbent and the male incumbent would win the election.[7] Having more skills does not necessarily lead to the perception that the female candidate will win the election.

There are two key results from this first experiment. First, female candidates, especially female incumbents, receive more positive evaluations on minimum skill assessments relative to their male counterparts. The positive evaluations that female candidates receive on minimum skills are, I argue, due to the use of gender-typicality standards. Voters rate these female candidates positively because they are more highly skilled compared with a typical woman and not a typical leader. Second, these

---

[7] I also compared the female incumbent with the female challenger on the viability outcome. The earlier analyses showed that on minimum skills the female challenger had more skills than the female incumbent; according to my argument, this is due to the female politician standard. The effects of this unique female politician standard, which is made up of both feminine and masculine stereotypes, are evident on the viability outcome. The female challenger is thought, in fact, to be more electorally viable relative to the female incumbent, $p < 0.01$.

positive evaluations on minimum skills do not lead to increased electoral support for female candidates. The second experiment focuses more extensively on highlighting how role-typicality standards, shaped by masculine stereotypes, affect the broad inferences voters form of female candidates.

ROLE-TYPICALITY EXPERIMENT

I test how role-typicality standards create a high qualification bar for female candidates with a study that presented participants with two candidates, a male and a female candidate, running against one another for an open seat to Congress. Presenting participants with two candidates bolsters the external validity of the study as most female candidates run against male candidates (Palmer and Simon 2005). The manipulated candidate was either female or male and the second candidate was always male. I manipulated whether the candidate was female or male with the same names and photos from the first experiment: Carol or Chris Hartley; their opponent was always Tom Larson.

The manipulation included information about candidate partisanship, and Hartley and Larson always belonged to the same political party. I matched participants into conditions based on shared partisanship. This means Democratic participants received information about two Democratic candidates running for an open House seat, while Republican participants received information about two Republican candidates. I sorted participants identifying as Independent into partisan conditions based on the party they leaned most closely toward in a follow-up question about partisan identification.[8] With this design, I can be sure that any negative effects in the female candidate condition come from the candidate being a woman and not from inferred information about candidate partisanship. I pool together the partisan conditions.

Participants read a newspaper article about a primary election for an open seat to the US House of Representatives featuring two candidates. I used a primary election in the vignette because it allowed me to control for the partisanship of the two candidates so that any negative evaluations are not confounded by partisan affinity effects. The article described an upcoming primary election as a close race with Hartley and Larson evenly tied in the polls. The article always mentioned Hartley first and Larson second and stated that both candidates had prior experience serving in the

---

[8] Twenty percent of participants indicated they were a political independent on the first party identification question. All participants selected a party on the second question.

state legislature. Unlike in the first study, I hold information about candidate quality constant across the two conditions. The text of the news article is as follows:

Democratic/Republican candidates Carol/Chris Hartley and Tom Larson continued campaigning throughout the state as they seek the party's nomination for the open seat to the House of Representatives.

Carol/Chris Hartley just completed her/his first term in the state senate. Before serving in the senate, Carol/Chris worked in finance, and received her/his bachelor's degree from the State University.

Hartley's opponent is Tom Larson, who also has experience in the state senate. Larson is certainly a formidable opponent, and also held several major events and rallies throughout the state.

The two candidates are tied in the polls, and the race is expected to remain close right up until the day of the primary.

I asked two types of broad inference questions: vote choice and electoral viability. The vote choice question simply asked which candidate the participants preferred to vote for in a primary contest, Hartley or Larson. Support for the role-typicality prediction would emerge if the male Hartley receives a higher level of support relative to the female Hartley.

Participants rated the electoral viability of candidates in both the primary election and the general election. For viability, participants selected either Hartley or Larson as the likely winner. With both questions, the response options are either Hartley or Larson with the order randomized. I coded the viability variable as 1 if participants selected Hartley as the likely winner. A question about electoral viability leads participants to think about how well a candidate fits into the role of a political leader. Participants, when thinking about electoral viability, must think about who can actually win an election. The question on primary viability intentionally calls for an explicit comparison between the female and the male candidate running against one another. The comparison between the female candidate and a masculine standard of leadership should disadvantage the female candidate but advantage the male candidate. The general election vote choice question allows me to understand how role-typicality affects vote choice when there is not the same type of partisan control between the two choices. Here, voters are not necessarily thinking about whether they prefer Hartley to Larson. Because the question primes the general election, participants are likely thinking about how well Hartley or Larson will perform against an unknown opponent who is likely to be a male candidate belonging to the other political party. Again, this implicit comparison between a female candidate and an unknown male opponent should, if my argument is correct, benefit the male candidate and put the female candidate at a disadvantage.

Role-Typicality Results

If results follow the role-typicality prediction, then the female Hartley will not necessarily fare any better than the male Hartley over the male opponent, Tom Larson. Participants will think about who can best fill the masculine role of a political leader, and this will lead voters to default to the man as the best choice. On the vote choice outcome, there are no statistically significant differences in the percentage of participants who indicated vote support for the female Hartley (68 percent) relative to the male Hartley (61 percent). The female and male Hartley break even with one another – suggesting that role-typicality standards may not create an enormously larger advantage for a male candidate. While the female and male Hartley break even on vote choice, this does not necessarily undermine the role-typicality prediction nor does it mean that the process of campaigning for political office is a gender-neutral process. The premise of this book is that female candidates need to work harder just to achieve gender-neutral outcomes at the ballot. Recall from Chapter 4, for example, that female candidates need to work harder just to get information about their qualifications out to voters given the gendered information gap that appears in news coverage.

The primary and general election viability outcomes offer more insight about how participants think the candidates will fare on the campaign trail among other voters. The role-typicality prediction indicates that the female candidate should have no viability advantage over her male opponent. Figure 5.3 displays the proportion of participants who selected Hartley or Larson as very or somewhat likely to win the primary election or the general election. The left panel focuses on the primary viability results. This question more directly pits Hartley and Larson against one another because the treatment stated that the two candidates were running against each other for their respective party's nomination for a congressional seat.

In the female condition, 49 percent of participants selected Hartley as the likely winner of the primary, while 52 percent selected Larson as the primary winner. The 3 percent difference indicates that participants are split between the two candidates when Hartley is a woman, though the

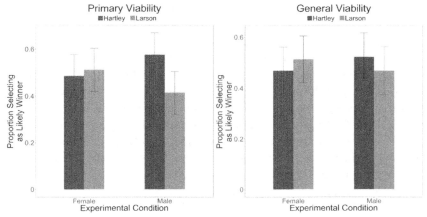

FIGURE 5.3 Differences in levels of perceived electoral viability.
Note: Each bar displays the proportion of participants who rated each candidate as the likely winner relative to Larson. 95 percent confidence intervals included.

difference in support does not reach statistical significance. In the female condition, participants are split as to whether the female Hartley has a shot at winning the election relative to her less qualified male opponent Larson. In the condition with two male candidates, approximately 58 percent of participants selected Hartley as the likely primary winner, while 42 percent selected Larson as the likely winner, and this difference is marginally significant at the $p < 0.10$ level. Focusing on just the female Hartley and the male Hartley shows a 10 percent gap in support between the two candidates, with the male Hartley having the advantage; this small male candidate advantage is in line with the role-typicality expectations. I compared whether the levels of perceived primary viability between the female and male Hartley were significant, and while the ten-point gap falls short of statistical significance using a two-tailed t-test, the difference is significant using a one-tailed test, $p < 0.10$, but a ten-point gap in perceived viability can certainly be substantial when it comes to electoral outcomes. These patterns fit with the expectations of the role-typicality prediction, which argued that any advantages the female candidate had on minimum skills would not appear on broad inference assessments.

The gender gaps on Hartley's margin of victory over Larson narrow slightly on the general election context question. The general election viability question asks participants to think about which candidate, Hartley or Larson, would be more likely to win against an unknown opponent belonging to the opposing political party. For most participants, this unknown opponent is probably going to be a male opponent. When Hartley is a woman, 47 percent selected her as the likely winner, while 51 percent selected Larson as the likely winner; this 4 percent difference in support is not statistically significant. Participants favored the male Hartley, with 52 percent selecting him as more likely to win a general election compared with Larson, and 47 percent of participants selecting him as the general election winner. This 5 percent difference in support is not statistically significant. Thinking about the likely victor in the context of the general election leaves participants evenly split about whether Hartley or Larson would be the better candidate to take on an opponent in the general election, even in the female Hartley condition. I compared the perceived general election viability between the female Hartley and the male Hartley, and the gender gaps in general election viability are statistically insignificant.

The key result from the role-typicality experiment illustrates that a female candidate only gets parity in general election outcomes, and a male candidate with the same qualification profile may have a slight advantage. The lack of a clear advantage for the female candidate is due, I argue, to masculine role-typicality standards. Pairing these results with the findings from the gender-typicality experiment shows that even if female candidates receive positive ratings on minimum skill metrics, these positive ratings are unlikely to carry over into electoral support. Positive minimum skill ratings are due to a gendered standard that creates a low qualification bar for women, but the qualification bar is raised when it comes to broad inference decisions.

ARE FEMALE CANDIDATES HELD TO A HIGHER (DIFFERENT) QUALIFICATION STANDARD?

The female senators and staff members who braved the snow, ice, and cold to come to work in the Capitol on January 27, 2016, may have done so due to gendered pressures. These gendered pressures create the perception that they will be judged more harshly for not making it into work than their male counterparts who stayed home for the snow day. It seems unlikely that Senators Murkowski and Collins would have faced career-ending blowback had they taken the day off. But this anecdotal example illustrates the internalized pressures that women feel to always perform at an exceptionally high level of excellence. And the results from this chapter suggest that voters do, in fact, hold female and male candidates to different sets of standards shaped by gender stereotypes.

The question posed at the onset of this chapter asked whether voters hold female candidates to a higher qualification standard relative to male candidates. This chapter illustrates that female candidates are, at times, held to a different qualification standard relative to male candidates, and voters rely on gendered standards to evaluate the qualifications of female and male candidates. The use of a "typical woman" and a "female politician" standard means that female candidates, as both challengers and incumbents, may appear to receive positive ratings for having more of the basic skills and qualities needed for political leadership. Indeed, the gender-typicality experiment showed that a female incumbent is rated as having 1.10 more skills than a male incumbent. The use of this gendered standard creates the illusion that female candidates have high levels of support among the public. These high levels of support may not always lead to more vote support at the polls. Vote choice decisions, and other types of broad inferences such as viability assessments, lead voters to shift to a role-typicality standard. Role-typicality standards lead voters to compare a female and a male candidate with a masculine standard of leadership. Female candidates, in general, must work harder to do more than break even with less qualified male opponents.

This chapter addressed two empirical puzzles in the literature. First, election polls and political science scholarship often find that voters rate female candidates as highly qualified for political office, but these evaluations do not always translate into vote support (see e.g., Hayes and Lawless 2016). These positive ratings stem from gender-typicality standards. Second, female candidates win elections at equal rates as male candidates (Seltzer, Newman, and Leighton 1997), but female candidates only get electoral parity in actual elections by being *more* qualified than those male opponents (Fulton 2012, Pearson and McGhee 2013). The use of role-typicality standards requires female candidates to have higher qualifications to win elections over male candidates. Role-typicality standards create an automatic advantage for male candidates and place female candidates at an automatic disadvantage. Pairing together the results of the gender-typicality and role-typicality experiments with the content analyses in the previous chapter suggests that voters need more evidence of a female candidate's ability compared with a male candidate, but this information is not necessarily available to voter. Voters have more than enough information about the political skills and abilities of a male candidate. Overcoming role-typicality expectations means that female candidates may need to be much more explicit when discussing their qualifications on the campaign trail.

An implication of the results from the two experiments discussed in this chapter is that gender stereotypes can subconsciously shape the way voters form impressions about candidates. The use of gender-typicality and role-typicality standards has negative implications for achieving gender parity, or even just more gains, in women's political representation. Gender-typicality standards can create a false sense of security for female candidates because the use of these standards creates the appearance of favorable attitudes among voters. Female candidates and their campaign strategists may decide that they do not need to highlight political experience or professional credentials in a campaign message if a majority of voters rate the candidate positively on qualifications. This strategic choice can undermine a woman's candidacy. Positive ratings on minimum skills do not necessarily mean that a voter thinks a woman will perform well in the role of a political leader. And getting these messages out to voters can be difficult given the disparities in news coverage, as noted in Chapter 4.

While role-typicality standards create a high bar for female candidates, these standards set a relatively low bar for male candidates. Fitting into a masculine standard of leadership is not as difficult for male candidates compared with female candidates because of the congruity between being male, being masculine, and being a leader. The boost that male candidates receive from masculine role-typicality standards means that voters might not be selecting the most qualified candidates to serve in political office, but that voters are simply selecting the most masculine political candidates. Voters may overlook female candidates with atypical perspectives and skill sets. These selection processes perpetuate the masculinity associated with political leadership but also affect how our democratic institutions function. Selecting candidates based on masculinity can lead to more aggressiveness, assertiveness, and gridlock in the legislative process. These are behaviors that can reduce trust in democratic institutions and can produce less favorable policy outcomes for citizens.

This chapter analyzed how feminine and masculine stereotypes shape the gender-typicality and role-typicality standards that voters use to evaluate the qualifications of political candidates. The use of these standards creates a high bar for women when it comes to securing electoral votes and a low bar for men, and the implication is that voters, in part, contribute to the observed gendered qualification gap where the women who win elections have better qualifications than the men who win elections. Feminine and masculine stereotypes affect how voters think about women, female candidates, and political leaders. These ideas also influence how voters think about the political parties. This chapter did not test whether Democrats and Republicans hold female candidates to different standards based on the way gender stereotypes map onto political parties. The next chapter turns to investigating whether the intersection of partisan and gender stereotypes gives rise to another standard, a partisan-typicality standard, that voters might use to evaluate female candidates.

6

Different Parties, Different Standards

I would think if I were a Republican candidate, I would not look forward to campaigning against Margaret Chase Smith in New Hampshire, or as a possible candidate for President. I think she is very formidable, if that is the appropriate word to use about a very fine lady. She is a very formidable political figure.

—President John Kennedy, commenting on the possible presidential candidacy of Republican Senator Margaret Chase Smith

Margaret Chase Smith served in the US House and the US Senate in an era of scarce political women in Washington, DC. For most of the near quarter-century Smith served in the Senate, she was the only woman in Washington's quintessential "good old boys' club." Smith first secured her place in Washington as a widow when appointed to fill her husband's seat in the House of Representatives after his death. Unlike some congressional widows, Smith had political ambitions and ran for the House in her own right. For nearly three decades, voters in Maine elected, and reelected, Smith to represent them – making her the first woman to serve in both legislative chambers. On the Hill, Smith earned a reputation for her grit, stamina, and willingness to stand up to party leaders on both sides of the political aisle. A key test of Smith's political will occurred when she dared to challenge fellow senator Joseph McCarthy at the height of the McCarthy hearings from a speech delivered on the floor of the Senate when she was still a freshman senator. Smith was certainly a woman not afraid to break the gender rules.

Smith's strong legislative record coupled with her popularity at home should have made her a formidable contender when she considered a presidential run in 1964. President Kennedy seems to be the only one who thought much of Smith's presidential ambitions. Smith's candidacy marked the first time a woman ran as a potentially serious presidential candidate in the post-suffrage era. Republicans, pundits, and most voters simply did not take her seriously. In fact, Smith received ample criticism based on her status as a woman and on her age. One newspaper columnist conceded that "Mrs. Smith has qualifications and experience for the Presidency no less than many men who have served in the office." Smith's age and being a woman automatically disqualified her because "the female of the species undergoes physical changes and emotional distress of varying severity and duration."[1] Smith was sixty-six years old at the time. Aside from implying that menopause made Smith unable to handle political office, this perspective reflects a classic stereotype of women as weak, infirm, and fragile – a characterization that contrasts with the expectation that leaders be physically and mentally tough, firm, and strong. Smith failed to win a single Republican primary. Even though Smith's resume, arguably, looked presidential, Smith, herself, by virtue of her sex and perceived feminine qualities, did not appear presidential.

Of course, in 1964 conditions were not exactly ripe for electing a Republican woman or a Democratic woman for the presidency. In that era, two noteworthy Democratic women ran for the party's nomination. Shirley Chisholm and Patsy Mink ran for the Democratic Party's nomination in 1972. Both women won election to their House seats as historic "female firsts." Patsy Mink was the first Asian American woman elected to the US House when she first won her seat in 1964, and Shirley Chisholm was the first black woman elected to the US House, winning her seat in 1968. The presidential candidacies of both women garnered few headlines with most of the news coverage relegated to the "Women's Pages" of newspapers. Neither woman won more than 1 percent or 2 percent of votes in a couple of primaries. Mink left the primary in May 1972, but Chisholm stayed in the race right up to the Democratic convention. Ultimately, the nomination went to George McGovern after a tumultuous convention. The Democratic Party was not quite ready to embrace a woman as the party's nominee for the presidency.[2]

---

[1] Quoted in Fitzpatrick (2016).
[2] It was not until 2000 that another woman of color ran for the Democratic Party's presidential nomination with Carol Mosley Braun's candidacy, and it was not until the lead-up to the 2020 presidential race that there were again multiple women of color running for the Democratic Party's nomination.

The candidacies of Margaret Chase Smith, Patsy Mink, Shirley Chisholm, and other female candidates in the historical record arguably failed to gain traction due to the perception of the presidency, and politics more generally, as a "man's game." Voters did not exactly hold gender egalitarian attitudes about women in leadership in the 1960s and the early 1970s. Conditions for Republican women have improved little since Smith's historic, but ultimately failed, presidential bid in 1964. Elizabeth Dole received little serious consideration as a presidential contender when she ran for the Republican nomination in 2000. One analysis found that the majority of news coverage surrounding Dole's campaign talked about her hair, shoes, and her husband, even when she led both George W. Bush and John McCain in the polls (Heldman, Carroll, and Olson 2005). More recently, the campaigns of Michele Bachman and Carly Fiorina never really gained traction in 2012 and 2016. As of the completion of this book, no woman ever won a state-level Republican presidential caucus or primary contest.

The climate for Democratic women pursuing the presidency is somewhat more positive. Women pursued the Democratic nomination in 2000 when former Illinois Senator Carol Mosley Braun entered the race, and Hillary Clinton ran for and lost the contest for the party's nomination in 2008. The Democratic Party nominated Hillary Clinton in 2016 to be the nominee – but it took a considerable amount of time for the Democratic Party to even get to nominating a woman, and Hillary Clinton is the only woman to win the Democratic Party's nomination. The prospect of nominating a Democratic woman to run for the presidency is certainly a distinct possibility in 2020, with at least six women, as of the writing of this book, pursuing the party's nomination.

Just looking at the challenges that faced Democratic and Republican women running for the presidency in the last twenty years suggests that the Democratic Party might be somewhat more receptive to having a female nominee, in the present, compared with the Republican Party. Do Democratic voters have a different set of gendered standards for female candidates relative to Republican voters? This chapter builds on the concept of gender-typicality and role-typicality standards developed in Chapter 5, which showed that gender stereotypes can serve as the comparative benchmark against which voters evaluate female and male candidates depending on the type of evaluation voters are forming about female candidates. Voters will use the more feminine stereotypic images of a "typical woman" to evaluate whether a female candidate has the minimum skills needed to serve in political office, but voters will shift to the more masculine stereotypic images of a "typical leader" to evaluate whether a woman can serve in political office. These masculine role-typicality standards can make it more difficult for women to win elections. Chapter 5 did not examine whether the use of these standards varies across candidate partisanship.

This chapter addresses the question: Do the political parties hold female and male candidates to different qualification standards? I argue that there is not just a gendered qualification gap, but a partisan qualification gap in the way Democrats and Republicans rate female candidate qualifications. There is a striking partisan imbalance in women's representation. Democratic women outnumber Republican women when it comes to candidates on the ballot and elected officeholders. Existing explanations for these partisan gender gaps focus on institutional barriers that vary across political party networks and the ideological impressions voters form of Democratic and Republican women. Missing from these existing accounts is whether gender stereotypes might affect the way voters evaluate Democratic and Republican female candidates.

I develop a theory of partisan-typicality standards in this chapter. I draw on research showing that voters hold distinctly gendered images of the political parties (Winter 2010). I merge this research with the theory of shifting standards developed in Chapter 5 to argue that Democratic voters use a partisan-typicality standard shaped by feminine stereotypes to evaluate candidates and that Republican voters have a partisan-typicality standard shaped by masculine stereotypes that they use to evaluate candidates. I argue that Democratic partisan-typicality standards, because they are shaped by feminine stereotypes, should create an advantage for Democratic female candidates running against Democratic male candidates in primary elections. Republican partisan-typicality standards, however, should create a disadvantage for Republican female candidates running against Republican male candidates in primary elections. I contend that voters will use these partisan-typicality standards most often in primary elections when choosing between two candidates of the same political party.

I test the use of these standards with an experiment that replicates the role-typicality experiment from Chapter 5, but breaks down the results by participant and candidate partisanship. The results find evidence of partisan-typicality standards, and uncover two key findings. First, the results show that feminine Democratic standards can erase any disadvantage posed by masculine role-typicality standards for Democratic female candidates. But feminine partisan-typicality standards do not necessarily provide female candidates with any advantages over Democratic male candidates. Second, masculine Republican standards create an exceptionally high qualification bar for Republican female candidates. Republican voters consistently rate the Republican female candidate as less electorally viable compared with the equally qualified Republican male candidate. These findings explain, in part, the role of voters in perpetuating the partisan gender gap, and the gendered qualification gap.

THE GENDERING OF THE POLITICAL PARTIES

The 2018 midterm elections illustrate the partisan gender gap in the present. This election cycle saw a record wave of women running for and winning political office. But to call this election cycle the "Year of the Woman" is not quite accurate. The 2018 election was really the "Year of the Democratic Woman" or the "Year of the Vanishing Republican Woman." Ileana Ros-Lehtinen, a Republican female member of the House who retired in 2018, declared Republican women an "endangered species." Organizations dedicated to electing more Republican women to political office actively discouraged Republican women from running. Megan Milloy, co-founder of Republican Women for Progress, stated, "We've told a lot of women, 'Don't run this year.' We've told them, 'You're a great candidate, if it were any other year you would win.' We don't want these women, who have such potential, to lose and get down and get out of politics."[3] How did this partisan gender gap emerge? In this section, I outline the process by which the Democratic Party became the more feminine political party and the Republican Party became the more masculine political party. The gender stereotypes associated with the political parties are important for explaining the gendered standards voters will use to evaluate Democratic and Republican women. Previous research identifies four central factors that contribute to the gender stereotypes associated with the political parties: patterns of issue ownership, the gender gap in voting, changing demographics in who runs for political office, and the visible representation of who is in political office.

In the nascent days of the modern women's movement, there was little divide or disagreement between the political parties on issues related to women. The dividing lines of the first wave of the women's movement

---

[3] Nancy LeTourneau, "Republicans to Women: Don't Run This Year," *Washington-Monthly.com*, August 16, 2018, https://washingtonmonthly.com/2018/08/16/republicans-to-women-dont-run-this-year/.

were not along partisan lines. There were some Democrats and some Republicans who supported granting women suffrage. Disagreements about suffrage tended to fall along lines about the appropriateness of granting women the right to participate in politics; whether women's participation in civic life would make a substantial difference in politics, with some arguing that it would just "double the vote" as women would vote as their husbands did; and whether one party would gain a strategic advantage over the other political party in a location (Banaszak 1996; Corder and Wolbrecht 2016; McConnaughy 2013; Teele 2019). Neither political party had a clear position, at the national level, as the pro-suffrage or anti-suffrage party.

In the early days of the second wave of the women's movement, during the 1950s through the late 1960s, issues affecting women still were not partisan issues. Both Democratic and Republican lawmakers supported the Equal Rights Amendment, equal pay legislation, Title IX, and reproductive autonomy (Freeman 1975; Wolbrecht 2002). This is not to say that legislation around women's issues was not a controversial issue (Evans 1979), but these issues found common ground for support among both Democrats and Republicans. Naturally, there were certainly Democrats and Republicans who did not support these issues. Wolbrecht (2000) explains that women's issues became more partisan issues as the coalitions of the parties shifted. The rise of the religious right in the 1970s and the 1980s had the effect of moving the Republican Party in a more conservative direction around social issues (Mansbridge 1986). The result is that women's issues became more divisive partisan issues. The two political parties, throughout the 1980s and 1990s, carved out distinct positions on a variety of issues that affected women's political, social, economic, and reproductive autonomy. The Democratic Party became the party more clearly associated with gender equity issue positions such as support for pay equity legislation and pro-choice positions (Petrocik 1996). In contrast, the Republican Party became the party more clearly associated with the more conservative position on gender equity issues, which included less support for pay equity and restrictive access to abortion (Kaufmann 2002).

A second factor that contributes to the gender stereotypes of the political parties is gendered patterns of voting among the electorate. The 1980 election was the first election for which the media noticed and reported on a gender gap, with more women voting for the Democratic candidate, Jimmy Carter, compared with men. In every election cycle since 1980, there is a gender gap that tends to follow a similar pattern, with a higher proportion of women voting for the Democratic candidate relative to the proportion of men voting for the Democratic candidate (Gilens 1988; Mansbridge 1985), though the size and significance of this gender gap can vary across each presidential election.[4] The existence of a gender gap led the news media to report more regularly on the voting preferences and patterns of female voters. Campaign strategists and consultants also began to develop campaign strategies designed to woo the female vote (Williams 1998). The result of these gendered patterns of voting is that women became associated more strongly with the Democratic Party.

As the political parties diverged on women's issues, the gendered demographics in those running for political office slowly shifted (Jennings and Farah 1981); this demographic shift contributes to the partisan gender gap, with women becoming more likely to support the Democratic Party (Ondercin 2017). Figure 6.1 traces the number of Democratic and Republican female Senate and House candidates from 1970 to the present. The top panel displays the Democratic and Republican female House candidates. Throughout the 1970s and the 1980s, the partisan gender gap in female House candidacies was quite small. In the mid-1980s Republican female candidates even outnumbered Democratic female candidates, though by a slim margin. A wide partisan gender gap in female House candidacies does not substantially emerge until 1992 – the first "Year of the Woman." The slowly growing partisan gender gap in House candidacies tracks with the gendered patterns of issue ownership. By 1992, the Republican Party had firmly positioned itself as the party of social conservatism, and this included opposing issues that sought to advance women's equality (Wolbrecht 2000).

Evidence of a partisan gender gap is not quite as clear in the Senate, as the bottom panel of Figure 6.1 illustrates. The two lines for the Democratic and Republican female candidates are both jumpy, and prior to 1992, there were several elections without a Democratic woman on the ballot and other years that did not have a Republican woman on the ballot. With the 1992 election, there is a spike in the number of Democratic women running for the Senate, but there is not as decisive a partisan gender gap that persists up to the present. There are many fewer

---

[4] More recent analyses of the gender gap show that this gap is more accurately a racialized-gender gap with women of color, especially black women, being much more consistent and reliable supporters of Democratic candidates compared with white women and men (Junn 2017).

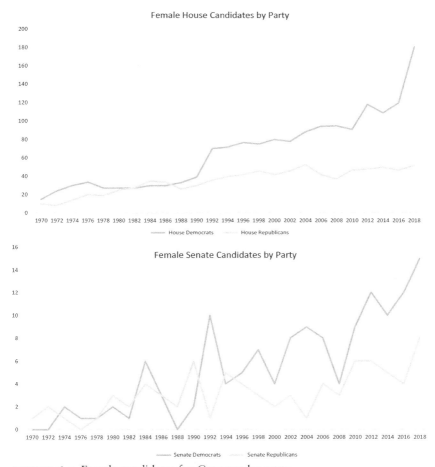

FIGURE 6.1 Female candidates for Congress by party

opportunities for women to enter into the Senate given that there are only 100 seats; only one-third of the body is up for election at any given time; and the incumbency advantage can deter a woman from running given that women prefer to run in open-seat elections (Maestas et al. 2006). The changes over time in the number of Democratic women running and the number of Republican women running for the Senate do show striking differences. In the 1970s, both parties had about two to four candidates running in any given election. Between 2008 and 2018, the Democratic Party fielded, on average, ten women in each election cycle. The Republican Party fielded, in those same ten years, five women, on average, in each election cycle.

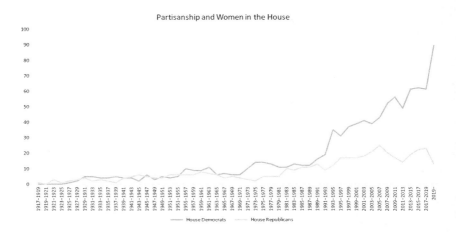

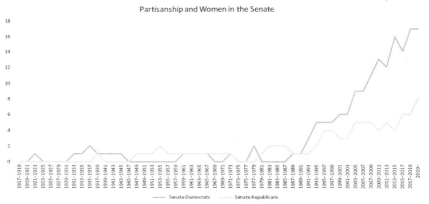

FIGURE 6.2 Partisan gaps in women's representation

More women running for political office under the umbrella of one political party leads voters to see that party as having more of the stereotypic qualities associated with women. A partisan gender gap in women's candidacies also contributes to a partisan gender gap in women's representation. Figure 6.2 breaks down the number of women elected to the House and the Senate based on partisanship. Most of the women serving in elected office do so as Democrats. The top panel displays the number of women in the US House by partisanship. Before the 1960s and 1970s, there was no discernible gap in the numbers of Democratic and Republican women in the chamber. A small partisan gender gap emerges in the 1970s, but a decisive and wide partisan gender

gap does not emerge until the late 1980s and the early 1990s. The gap
reaches its widest point in the most recent congressional term. Republican
women in the House, post-2018, lost half their caucus.

The bottom panel of Figure 6.2 displays the partisan gender gap in the
Senate. The narrower partisan gap in the Senate did not begin until the
early to mid-1990s, but this is a gap that holds up to the present even with
the current record-high number of eight Republican women elected to the
Senate. The considerably smaller numbers of women, overall, reflect the
small pool of candidates pursuing these seats in any given election year,
and reinforces the masculinity of this office. These patterns of women's
representation, and women's candidacies, roughly track with the gendering of the political parties along women's issues. As the Democratic Party
took more liberal positions on women's equity issues, the party also
attracted and strategically recruited and supported women running for
office (Sanbonmatsu 2006). As the Republican Party took opposing positions on women's issues, the party failed, intentionally or not, to attract
more female candidates (Crowder-Meyer 2013).

The result of these combined forces is a gendered construction of the
parties that created and cemented the gendered images of the political
parties that exist in the present. Indeed, voters see the Democratic Party as
the more feminine party and Republicans as the more masculine party.
Voters associate many Democratic candidates with feminine traits such as
being more warm, compassionate, and caring; likewise, voters associate
many Republican candidates with masculine traits such as being more
stern, aggressive, and decisive (Hayes 2005, 2011; Rahn 1993; Winter
2010). I argue that the gender stereotypes associated with the political
parties contribute to, and indeed exacerbate, the partisan gender gap.
Before developing the different standards, I outline the existing explanations for the partisan gender gaps in the literature, and how these current
explanations do not account for the use of gendered qualification standards to evaluate female and male candidates.

EXPLANATIONS FOR THE CONTEMPORARY
PARTISAN GENDER GAP

There are two dominant accounts in the literature to explain why the
partisan gender gap continues to persist in the modern era. First, the
parties engage in different recruitment patterns. Second, there is a perception that Republican women do not fit ideologically with their political
party. These two forces offer insight into differences in the recruitment of

Democratic and Republican women to pursue political office; recruitment affects the number of women who get elected to political office. Neither of these explanations, however, accounts for how voters evaluate the qualifications of political candidates through a gendered partisan lens.

First, the Democratic Party is more likely to recruit and field female candidates compared with the Republican Party (Crowder-Meyer and Cooperman 2018). Women are more likely to commit to running for political office when recruited and supported by local party networks (Sanbonmatsu 2002b), and when women have support from their family, friends, and professional networks (Carroll and Sanbonmatsu 2013). The Democratic Party is more likely to have strong local party networks that actively seek out female candidates to fill open slots on ballots. The Republican Party, when it does have strong local party networks, does not always prioritize the recruitment of women (Crowder-Meyer 2013). Local Republican Party networks may not prioritize candidate recruitment due to limited resources and the availability of male candidates who self-select into the candidate pool.

The gendered self-selection problem does not entirely explain the dearth of Republican women on the ballot. Deckman (2016) conducted an extensive study of conservative women embedded in the Tea Party. She found no shortage of conservative women looking for avenues to actively participate in local, state, and national Republican Party networks. Partisan elites stymied the participation of these women in Republican Party politics by simply ignoring or marginalizing these women. The Republican Party has the potential to change the partisan gender gap. Karpowitz, Monson, and Preece (2017) found that when local Republican Party leaders prioritized the selection of women to run for political office, more women volunteered to run and received support from party members.

Second, there is a perception that Republican women do not ideologically fit with the Republican Party (Thomsen 2015). Voters rate Republican female candidates as more ideologically liberal relative to Republican male candidates (Koch 2000; McDermott 1997). The move of the Republican Party further to the right of the ideological spectrum means that Republican female candidates may not be perceived as conservative enough for the party. Stereotypes of women as more compassionate and more focused on social issues drives the classification of Republican women as more moderate relative to Republican men (Sanbonmatsu and Dolan 2009). Parties prioritize selecting candidates who ideologically fit with the political party. Given the choice between a Republican man and a Republican woman in a primary, Republican voters tend to default toward selecting the man (Lawless and Pearson 2008) because voters will stereotype him as more conservative (McDermott 1997). Ideological perceptions of women appear to work to the detriment of Republican women but benefit Democratic women. Voters rate Democratic female candidates as more liberal than their male counterparts, and these candidates have a clear ideological home within the Democratic Party. The ideological fit explanation for the partisan gender gap hints at but does not fully explain the role that gender stereotypes play in shaping how voters think about the ideological fit of female candidates.

Perceptions of ideological fit are related to but distinct from perceptions of candidate qualifications. The ideological fit approach looks at how ratings of candidates on the ideological spectrum affect how potential candidates select into, or out of, the candidate pool (Thomsen 2015). Thomsen (2018), relying on data about primary elections from 1980 until 2012, found that there was no statistically significant negative relationship between the ideological ratings of Republican female candidates and their probability of winning a primary or a general election. This finding does not mean that Republican women win primary elections, just that ideological perceptions did not explain the loss in a statistically significant way. Across the partisan aisle, the perception of Democratic woman as ideologically liberal gave them a boost in primaries that Republican female candidates did not get. This research shows that the ideological explanation does not entirely account for why Republican women have a lower probability of winning primaries relative to Republican men (Barnes, Branton, and Cassese 2017; Lawless and Pearson 2008). Thus, in the case of Republican female candidates, voters in primary elections may not be relying strictly on cues about ideology.

Current scholarship also measures how the relationship between gender and party affects the traits and issues ascribed to Republican female relative to Republican male candidates (Bauer 2018; Hayes 2011; Sanbonmatsu and Dolan 2009; Schneider and Bos 2016). It is not clear how these stereotypic images of Republican and Democratic women affect perceptions of candidate qualifications and how assessments of candidate qualifications map onto voter decision-making. For instance, the ideological fit model does not explain whether co-partisan voters see Republican female candidates as less experienced, knowledgeable, or qualified relative to a comparably qualified Republican male candidate. Perceptions of candidate qualifications are distinct from perceptions of ideological fit where voters will form assessments about where the candidate falls along the ideological spectrum based on assessments, accurate or not, of the issue positions of candidates.

Party recruitment patterns explain, in part, the scarcity of women in Republican and, often, Democratic Party politics. If party leaders do not prioritize recruiting women to pursue political office, women are less likely to run for political office (Carroll and Sanbonmatsu 2013). Perceptions of ideological fit can also affect whom party leaders see as the best candidates to recruit under the party banner. Missing from these explanations is the role that voters play when they consider the qualifications of Democratic and Republican female candidates, especially when voters must choose between two candidates of the same political party. I argue that the gender stereotypes voters hold of the political parties affects how voters evaluate the qualifications of both Democratic and Republican female candidates. The intersection between partisan and gender stereotypes can affect how voters consider female candidates, and can create unique obstacles for female candidates based on partisanship (Bauer 2019; Cassese and Holman 2018). This chapter elaborates the partisan-typicality standard that co-partisan voters will use when selecting one of two candidates belonging to the same political party.

PARTISAN-TYPICALITY STANDARDS

Gender-typicality and role-typicality standards explain how voters consider whether a female candidate has the minimum qualifications needed for politics and how stereotypic ideas about political leadership affect vote choice decisions. These two standards explain why female candidates often receive positive qualification ratings that do not translate into electoral support. Not accounted for in the previous chapter is the intersection between gender stereotypes and partisan stereotypes, which can, under some conditions, lead voters to shift to another gendered standard to evaluate candidate qualifications. Voters see the parties through a distinctly gendered lens. Using partisan standards leads voters to compare how close a typical female or a typical male candidate is to a "typical Democrat" or the "typical Republican." I argue that partisan-typicality standards lead to differences in how voters evaluate the qualifications of Democratic and Republican female candidates.

Voters will use partisan-typicality standards when partisan cues are equitable across two candidates. The most obvious context where the candidate's status as a woman or a man will matter more than party is a primary election. Primary elections represent a case where the two candidates belong to the same political party, and this means voters will pay more attention to whether the candidate is female or male. I argue that in a primary election, voters will not draw on role-typicality standards because voters are not thinking, yet, about how well a candidate can fit into a masculine leadership role. Primary voters think about how well a candidate can fit into the role of being the party's nominee. It is likely that primary voters will evaluate how well Democratic female candidates fit into the feminine stereotypes associated with Democrats and how well Republican female candidates fit into the masculine stereotypes associated with Republicans.

Stereotypes about the Democratic Party are the basis of the partisan-typicality standards voters will use when choosing between two Democratic candidates. Voters will look for a candidate that fits the typical Democrat. A "typical Democrat" has many qualities that reinforce feminine stereotypes, and this should, I argue, create a baseline advantage for a Democratic female candidate relative to a Democratic male candidate. Voters will assume, based on the candidate's status as female and candidate party, that a Democratic woman has the feminine traits that match the traits associated with a "typical Democrat." This means that the Democratic female candidate should have an advantage over Democratic male candidates. A Democratic male candidate should have a more difficult time convincing voters he has the feminine traits voters look for in Democrats because stereotypes about men do not fit with stereotypes about Democrats.

Democratic Partisan-Typicality Prediction: Democratic female candidates will receive more positive evaluations relative to Democratic male candidates.

There is certainly evidence of the Democratic typicality prediction in the 2018 midterm primary elections. Partisan-typicality standards may have advantaged candidates such as Ayanna Pressley and Alexandria Ocasio-Cortez. Pressley challenged entrenched Democratic incumbent Mike Capuana in Massachusetts's Seventh Congressional District, and became the first black woman to represent Massachusetts in Washington, DC. Ocasio-Cortez, a twenty-nine-year-old self-described Democratic socialist, defeated a Democratic male incumbent, Joe Crowley, in New York's Fourteenth District. Stereotypes about women helped to distinguish Pressley and Ocasio-Cortez from their male opponents and may have led voters to see these women as a better fit for the Democratic Party.

Partisan-typicality standards will, according to my theory, create obstacles for Republican women. Stereotypes about the Republican Party will be the partisan-typicality standards voters will use to evaluate Republican female and male candidates. Voters associate the Republican Party with masculine issues and masculine traits. The masculinity associated with the Republican Party will benefit Republican male candidates but will disadvantage Republican female candidates. Republican female candidates will have difficulty fitting into the stereotypes of the Republican Party because of mismatched feminine stereotypes.

Republican Partisan-Typicality Prediction: Republican female candidates will receive more negative evaluations relative to Republican male candidates.

Republican women, in general, battle to win support from within their political party in primary elections (Barnes, Branton, and Cassese 2017; Lawless and Pearson 2008). House Republican Martha Roby of Alabama, a four-term incumbent, failed to secure enough votes in her Republican primary to guarantee her a spot in the 2018 general elections, forcing her into a runoff election. Roby's male opponent, Bobby Bright, became a Republican only shortly before the 2018 primary election filing deadline. Bright previously won this House seat in 2008 as a Democrat, and lost to Republican Martha Roby in 2010. Roby is a conservative member of the House in a conservative district running against an opponent with questionable Republican credentials – securing the Republican primary runoff should have been easy. Ultimately, Roby won the runoff. Of course, there were many other dynamics at play in this race that could account for Roby's near-loss, including her defiance toward Trump after the infamous *Access Hollywood* tape. But the challenge from a male candidate with questionable Republican credentials suggests that masculine typicality standards could have affected the choices some voters made.

When voters choose between two candidates who belong to the same political party, partisan-typicality standards will come into play over gender-typicality and role-typicality standards. I argue that voters will use partisan-typicality standards to form broad inferences about which candidate best fits into partisan stereotypes. Partisan-typicality standards mean that Democratic female candidates should receive *more favorable* evaluations relative to a Democratic male candidate. Republican female candidates will not benefit from partisan-typicality standards. Rather, partisan-typicality standards should lead voters to rate Republican female candidates *less favorably* relative to Republican male candidates.

EVIDENCE FOR PARTISAN-TYPICALITY

The partisan-typicality experiment uses the same design as the role-typicality study from the previous chapter. The only difference is that this experiment has higher levels of statistical power and more balance across the conditions to separate the comparisons out by partisanship. As with the role-typicality experiment, I sorted participants into conditions where they evaluated candidates with whom they shared partisanship. Shared partisanship is key for testing the use of partisan-typicality standards. Partisan voters will look for candidates who best fit the gendered image of each political party. The experimental design replicates a primary election contest where voters will most likely use partisan-typicality standards.

I asked questions about candidate qualifications as well as questions about electoral viability to assess the use of partisan-typicality standards. Participants rated each candidate's level of experience and knowledge, two more conventional metrics of candidate evaluations (see, e.g., Bauer 2017). Participants compared Hartley and Larson's levels of experience and knowledge with one another, with response options including Hartley is more experienced/knowledgeable than Larson and Hartley is somewhat more experienced/knowledgeable than Larson, and comparable categories with Larson as the more experienced or knowledgeable candidate.[5] Experience and knowledge are useful assessments of candidate qualification because these are two characteristics that voters place a high level of importance on in leadership evaluations (Funk 1999; Huddy and Terkildsen 1993; Miller, Wattenberg, and Malanchuk 1986). Experience and knowledge are dimensions where voters often perceive female candidates to be at a deficit (Schneider and Bos 2014). I recoded both variables to range from 0 to 1, with higher values indicating more positive evaluations. If participants use partisan-typicality standards, then the Democratic female candidate will have an advantage over the Democratic male candidate, but the Republican female candidate will have no such advantage over the Republican male candidate.

I measured the effects of partisan-typicality standards using the same viability questions noted in Chapter 5. The primary election viability question asks voters to directly choose whether Hartley or Larson will be more likely to win the election, but the general election viability question does not specify the opponent. On general election viability,

---

[5] See the Appendix to Chapter 6 for more details on the experimental design.

participants must consider the hypothetical opponent who belongs to the other political party, and this hypothetical opponent, for many participants, is likely to be a male candidate. Both viability questions ask participants to indirectly think about how much bias the candidates will face among other voters, and participants who are less likely to select the female Hartley may anticipate high levels of gender bias among other voters – whether or not this bias exists (Lawless and Fox 2010). This variable is coded 1 if participants selected Hartley as the likely winner and 0 for Larson as the likely winner. The Democratic-typicality prediction argues that female candidates will have an advantage over male candidates, while the Republican-typicality prediction suggests a female candidate disadvantage. The primary viability question is where the use of partisan-typicality standards should be most prominent, if results follow expectations.

Figure 6.3 shows the difference in the experience and knowledge ratings for the female compared with the male Hartley. Positive values indicate the female Hartley received a more positive evaluation than the male Hartley, while negative values indicate the female Hartley received more negative evaluations compared with her male counterpart. Comparing the bar and the confidence interval for the Carol condition to the Chris condition offers insight into whether the female candidate has an advantage or a disadvantage from partisan-typicality standards. If the

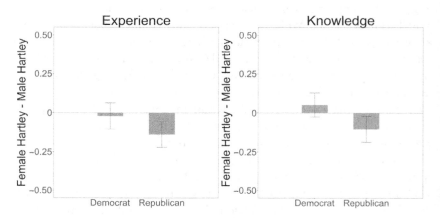

FIGURE 6.3 Partisan differences experiment: differences in experience and knowledge ratings.
Note: Each bar displays the difference in the average evaluation for the female Hartley relative to the male Hartley broken down by partisanship. 95 percent confidence intervals included.

confidence intervals for the female and the male conditions overlap, this suggests there is no significant differences between the female and male candidates, but a wide gap on the confidence intervals suggests a significant difference due to Hartley's status as female.

On both measures, there are no statistically significant differences in how Democrats rate Hartley between the female and male candidate conditions. This finding offers mixed support for the Democratic partisan-typicality prediction. At first glance, these results suggest that Democratic voters do not exhibit bias toward Democratic female candidates. An outcome that produces no differences between female and male candidates is not necessarily evidence of a voter decision-making process free of gender bias. Partisan-typicality standards, in the context of Democratic candidates, should create an advantage for Democratic female candidates over Democratic male candidates. Instead, the Democratic female candidate breaks even with her male opponent. These comparisons suggest that partisan-typicality standards, for Democrats, may neutralize the high bar set by masculine partisan-typicality standards but do not necessarily create a baseline advantage for Democratic women over their co-partisan male counterparts.

The gap in evaluations is significantly wider among Republicans, a finding in line with the Republican partisan-typicality prediction. The Republican female Hartley received a significantly lower rating on experience, $p < 0.01$, and knowledge, $p < 0.05$, relative to the Republican male Hartley with the same qualifications running against the same male opponent. Republican participants consistently rated Hartley as less qualified relative to her male opponent, Larson, when she is female; but when Hartley is male, Republican participants rate him much more positively. These results fit with the expectations of Republican partisan-typicality standards. A Republican partisan-typicality standard consists of masculine standards, and this creates a barrier for Republican female candidates while giving Republican male candidates an automatic advantage.

Figure 6.4 graphs the margin of victory or the gap in the percentage of participants selecting Hartley as the likely winner over Larson based on Hartley's status as a woman and partisanship. Positive values indicate that Hartley has the electoral advantage, and negative values indicate greater vote support for Larson. In the Democratic conditions, there are no differences in the perceived viability of the female Hartley relative to the male Hartley at the primary or the general election level. Between female and male candidates, more participants perceive Hartley as more

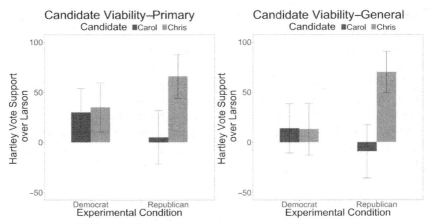

FIGURE 6.4 Differences in perceptions of electoral viability.
Note: Each bar displays the difference in the percentage of participants selecting Hartley over Larson as the likely winner across the partisan conditions. Each bar represents Hartley's margin of perceived electoral victory. 95 percent confidence intervals included.

likely to win the primary and general election compared with Larson. Again, these results match the comparisons from the experience and knowledge ratings. Democratic female candidates do not have a disadvantage in Democratic primary elections, but stereotypes about women and stereotypes about parties do not give Democratic women an advantage over male candidates. These outcomes illustrating no differences for Democratic female and Democratic male candidates do not necessarily mean that bias does not affect how Democrats evaluate female candidates of their own political party. The feminine stereotypes that color how voters view the Democratic Party do not provide a boost to Democratic female candidates.

The comparisons in the Republican partisan conditions are striking. These findings suggest that Republican female candidates will face a tough time securing support from within their own party – a result in line with the Republican-typicality prediction. On the primary election question, the female Hartley has a narrow five-point margin of victory over Larson, her male opponent. When Hartley is male, he has an enormous sixty-six-point margin of victory over Larson, p < 0.01. At the general election level, the *negative nine-point* value indicates that Republican participants thought the Republican female Hartley was unlikely to win the election. In other words, participants defaulted to Larson, the male opponent, as the likely winner in a general election contest. When Hartley is male, the candidate has a large, seventy-point advantage over Larson in the general election, $p < 0.01$. Recall that the only difference between the two Hartley conditions is that one is a female candidate and one is a male candidate – the two candidates had the same set of qualifications and faced off against the same male opponent. Republicans do not see a Republican female candidate as electorally viable. This wide gap suggests that a combination of masculine partisan-typicality standards negatively affects Republican female candidates but gives a large boost to Republican male candidates, and this negative finding for Republican women confirms the Republican partisan-typicality prediction.

The primary and general election viability outcomes for the Republican conditions show vast disparities between the Republican female Hartley and the Republican male Hartley. I argue that these gaps come from the masculine standards Republican voters use to evaluate the Republican candidates. A competing explanation, especially for the primary viability outcome, is the lack of ideological fit explanation. The experiment, in the post-test, asked participants to rate the perceived ideology of each candidate. In the Democratic conditions, participants rated the female Hartley's rating as more ideologically liberal than the Democratic male candidate's – and this finding is in line with past research (Koch 2000; McDermott 1997). In the Republican conditions, there are no statistically significant differences in the ideologically conservative rating of the female Hartley relative to the male Hartley and relative to her male opponent, Larson. In other words, the Republican female Hartley is seen as just as conservative as her male contenders. The ideological fit explanation cannot account for the poor performance of the Republican female Hartley.

To summarize, Republican partisan-typicality standards place Republican female candidates at a distinct electoral disadvantage. Republican voters will view a Republican male candidate as having more of the minimum qualifications needed for political office and will view the Republican male as better able to fill leadership roles. The results were not quite as bleak for the Democratic female candidate, but the findings certainly suggest that Democratic women can face subtle biases from within their own partisan networks. If partisan stereotypes affected the way voters viewed the qualifications of Democratic female candidates, then Democratic women should have an advantage over Democratic men. Instead, Democratic female candidates manage only to break even with their male counterparts. Not only does the gendered qualification gap occur between women and men, but there is a partisan dimension as well between Democratic and Republican women.

DO VOTERS HOLD DEMOCRATIC AND REPUBLICAN FEMALE CANDIDATES TO DIFFERENT STANDARDS?

In 1964, neither Republicans nor Democrats were ready to consider nominating a woman to run for the presidency. But, fifty-five years later, the Democratic Party has become more open not only to electing a woman to the presidency but also to electing women at all levels of political office. The Republican Party, however, exhibits more resistance toward women in leadership at both the presidential and congressional levels. This partisan gender gap is due not only to the different demographic characteristics of the political parties and the divergent policy preferences of the parties around issues affecting women but also to the distinctly gendered images voters hold of the political parties. The masculine stereotypes voters hold of the Republican Party, more generally, are barriers for Republican women, while the feminine stereotypes voters broadly hold of the Democratic Party open doors for electing more women. This is evident just looking at the partisan makeup of the women in Congress.

This chapter continued to answer the question about whether voters hold female candidates to different standards relative to male candidates. Not only do voters hold female and male candidates to different standards, but voters within each political party hold co-partisan female and male candidates to different standards. I developed the concept of partisan-typicality standards to explain the role voters play in contributing to the partisan gender gap. The gendering of the political parties affects the assessments voters form of candidate qualifications. I integrated the psychological theory of shifting standards with research documenting how voters hold distinctly gendered images of the political parties. The gender stereotypes voters hold of Democrats and Republicans affect the qualification standards partisans use to evaluate co-partisan candidates. These gendered images can close the qualification gap for Democratic female candidates but widen the gap for Republican female candidates. The use of Democratic partisan-typicality standards means that voters will use a feminine qualification standard to evaluate Democratic candidates; this feminine standard comes from the feminine stereotypic images voters hold of the Democratic Party. The use of Republican partisan-typicality standards means that voters will use a masculine qualification standard to evaluate Republican candidates; this masculine standard comes from the masculine stereotypic images voters hold of the Republican Party.

The consequences of the gendered qualification gap that occurs among partisans are more damaging for the Republican Party. The Republican female candidate consistently received more negative evaluations relative to the comparable Republican male candidate. Indeed, the experiment illustrated the steep obstacles facing Republican women on evaluations of experience and knowledge as well as viability assessments. These patterns mirror the demographic characteristics of the Republican Party outside the experimental context. Republican women lost seats in Congress in 2018. The Republican women who do run for political office have difficulty establishing the same networks of support available to Democratic women, especially donor and fundraising networks (Crowder-Meyer and Cooperman 2018). Part of the problem with the partisan gender gap is that Republican voters look for and prioritize masculinity and maleness in political candidates. Meeting standards of masculinity is easier for candidates who are male.

Partisan-typicality standards did not produce quite such glaring gaps and differences between Democratic female and male candidates. In fact, the results of the experiment in this chapter show parity between the Democratic female and Democratic male candidates. But the use of feminine partisan-typicality standards should *advantage* a female candidate over a male candidate in the same way that masculine typicality standards advantage a male candidate over a female candidate. Feminine typicality standards among Democrats do not give Democratic female candidates an edge over their co-partisan male counterparts. The congruity between being male and being a leader will always provide a little bit of a boost for male candidates, and this will wash out any benefit a Democratic female candidate might accrue from the alignment between feminine stereotypes and partisan stereotypes.

Partisan-typicality standards will likely matter the most in primary elections. Primary elections determine the set of candidates from which voters get to select an officeholder in the general election. Partisan voters in primaries look for Democratic and Republican female candidates who best fit the image of a partisan, but this is not necessarily what voters look for or want in a representative. The use of gendered standards to select candidates in primaries disadvantages female candidates and limits the pool of candidates that advance to the general election ballot. The dynamic is such that male candidates, especially Republican male candidates, have a baseline advantage in primary elections even if these male candidates are not the most qualified political candidates in the primary. Primaries may give voters the worst rather than the best set of candidates from which to choose on Election Day.

If a political party systematically excludes one gender from running for political office, then that party is limiting the ability of women to share their talents, skills, and abilities with others. The underrepresentation of women, especially among the Republican Party, has consequences for how voters perceive the legitimacy of the democratic process (Clayton, O'Brien, and Piscopo 2019). Voters, both female and male, see decision-making institutions that exclude women as less legitimate and less valid institutions compared with institutions that include both women and men in the decision-making process. It is not hard to find examples of all-male decision-making bodies in the US government. In 2017, the Republican-controlled government put together a thirteen-member task force to develop a set of reforms to the Affordable Care Act. Not a single member appointed to the committee was female. The photo of the all-male decision-making body became an internet meme overnight. During the Kavanaugh confirmation hearings, the Republican-controlled judiciary committee worried about showing only Republican men questioning a female survivor of sexual assault. The party, rather than appointing one of the then five Republican women in the Senate to the committee, hired a woman to question the survivor. The problems of all-male panels are not unique to Republicans. Democrats contended with the backlash of an all-male panel twenty-five years ago when the all-male judiciary committee questioned Anita Hill about her experiences of sexual harassment at the hands of a Supreme Court nominee. Partisan-typicality standards not only are a problem for Democrats or for Republicans but are a problem for democratic institutions.

From a normative perspective, the partisan gender gap in representation is problematic. But recent survey research suggests that the Republican Party may not have much motivation among the electorate to change or adjust the biased standards that keep women from succeeding in politics. A 2018 Pew study found that while a majority of Democratic voters want and believe a woman will win the presidency in their lifetime and want to increase women's representation, the same is not true of Republican voters. Among Democrats, 80 percent of women and men personally hope a woman will win the presidency in their lifetime. Among Republicans, that number plummets to 22 percent of men and 26 percent of women. The partisan-typicality standards voters use to keep Republican women out of politics contribute, in part, to these dynamics.

Excluding women from the policy-making process, among both Democrats and Republicans, affects the way that our political institutions function. The lack of women in the Republican Party pushes the party, overall, far to the right of the ideological spectrum and leaves little room for the more moderate voices of female candidates (Thomsen 2015). More broadly, the scarcity of both Democratic and Republican women in office can contribute to the diminished productivity and increased gridlock of political institutions. Women in political office, of both political parties, are more likely to compromise and build consensus with one another, often based on whether they are part of the party in power or out of power in the legislature (Dittmar, Sanbonmatsu, and Carroll 2018; Volden, Wiseman, and Wittmer 2013). But fewer women in office diminishes the opportunities for women to broker compromise with one another and with other male lawmakers. The next chapter turns to examining whether it is possible to close the gendered qualification gap at the level of the individual voter.

7

Gender Bias, Disrupted

A possible turning point in the 2016 presidential election came just a month before Election Day when a tape of old footage from the *Access Hollywood* television show featuring presidential candidate Donald Trump (though at the time of the tape's creation he was a television star) explaining his approach to pursuing women. Trump told the interviewer that when you are famous you can simply "grab them by the pussy." The tape was jarring. A presidential candidate, as it appeared from the video, admitted to committing sexual assault. For weeks, Democrats and Republicans decried Trump's comments, but the video did not appear to dent the president's base of support. Fast-forward to the summer of 2017, and the issue of sexual assault had not receded from public discourse. A series of news articles reported accounts of high-profile men sexually assaulting women, including Harvey Weinstein, Charlie Rose, and Matt Lauer – among many others. The reports illustrated that Trump's violent approach to pursuing the opposite sex was seemingly normal behavior for a surprisingly large number of influential men. These revelations of sexual harassment and assault instigated a broader #MeToo movement, sparking public discourse about how some men abuse power.

Congress was not immune from the power of the #MeToo movement. Reports emerged throughout the summer of 2017 of lawmakers sexually harassing and assaulting female staff members. By the end of the summer of 2018, nine members of Congress resigned over reports of sexual harassment. The stories of what female congressional staff members experienced daily were shocking. House Representative Pat Meehan wrote love letters to a female staffer, and when asked about these notes by the press, he justified the behavior by explaining that the woman was his "soul mate." The woman disagreed. Reports of sexual harassment and assault not only plague male lawmakers but affected some female lawmakers who allowed male staff members to keep their jobs after abusing female coworkers. Representative Elizabeth Esty came under fire for permitting a male staffer member to keep his job after he threatened to murder a female colleague with whom he previously had a romantic relationship. If there was any doubt before about politics as a masculinized institution, the #MeToo movement left little speculation that masculinity, some would say toxic masculinity, infects American political institutions.

These accounts suggest that Congress has an institutional problem with how some men, and even women, in positions of power view the appropriate role of women in the workplace. Remedying the culture of assault and harassment requires not only institutional reforms but broader reforms about what constitutes biased and discriminatory behavior toward women. Congress started taking small steps in this direction. Members of Congress can no longer use public funds to provide restitution to sexual harassment and assault survivors; instead, members of Congress must use personal funds for these expenses. Congress also changed the reporting procedures for sexual harassment. Previously, Congress mandated that women who filed reports of sexual harassment undergo counseling before launching an investigation into the allegations, the implication being that the survivor rather than the abuser might be in the wrong. This requirement no longer exists. While important, these changes do not address the biases that affect how some within the institution perceive the role of women in the workplace.

One suggested solution to creating institutional change for Congress is to mandate that members undergo implicit bias training designed to limit biased behavior toward women. The goal of implicit bias training is to teach individuals to recognize the subtle, unconscious, and automatic biases that affect how they judge and interact with members of stereotyped and marginalized groups (Bargh 1989; Devine 1989). Learning about these subtle biases gives individuals the tools needed to keep those biases in check. So, you must teach members of Congress that it is inappropriate to offer a female staff member $5 million to carry one's child because this request devalues the professional accomplishments of women and reduces women to their biological capacities. Following training, a baby-seeking member of Congress would, ideally, think twice before making such a request of a female staffer.

As these accounts illustrate, women not infrequently face hostility, harassment, and violence when entering public institutions traditionally dominated by men (Jane 2014a, 2014b), and this can happen to women in politics (Biroli 2018; Kuperberg 2018; Rheault, Rayment, and Musulan 2019). This hostility comes from the perceived threat to the dominant masculine power structure that occurs when women occupy a social role conventionally occupied by men (MacKinnon 1979; Manne 2018). If women enter political roles, some men and women worry that they will lose their power, status, and social roles (Cassese and Barnes 2019). Evidence of this perceived threat comes from the pushback female presidential candidates pursuing the 2020 Democratic nomination receive when they prioritize women as a group and women's issues. For example, during a Fox News town hall forum, presidential candidate Kirsten Gillibrand explained that "we want women to have a seat at the table" when asked about her campaign's emphasis on women and their role in the political system. The host immediately countered with the question, "What about men?" The premise of the question ignores the fact that men, historically and contemporaneously, occupy most seats across all levels of political office in the United States, and in nearly every country worldwide. Gillibrand's response, somewhat humorously, challenged the host on the premise of this question, "They're already there – do you not know?" The host backed down, stating "All right, we're not threatened." The exchange acknowledges the implicit threat felt by some about putting women in positions of power.

Much of the research and public discourse surrounding implicit bias training focuses on racial bias. In May 2018 Starbucks closed its stores in the United States for a day so that employees could undergo training to reduce implicit racial bias. The move came after an incident in a Philadelphia Starbucks when a store manager called the police after two black men sat down at a table in the store and did not immediately order food or beverage. The idea behind implicit bias training is well intentioned. Calling attention to the fact that nobody calls the police when white people sit at a Starbucks table without ordering a pastry or beverage shows how individuals form assumptions about black men based on negative racial stereotypes. Gender bias, like racial bias, can be subtle, automatic, and frequently unconscious (Blair 2002), but this bias contributes to the gendered qualification gap in politics because it leads voters to hold female candidates to a higher qualification standard relative to male candidates. Teaching voters about feminine stereotypes and implicit bias and how these concepts affect voter decision-making has the potential to close the gendered qualification gap.

This chapter turns to the final critical question guiding this book: How can female candidates overcome the gendered qualification gap? I draw on theories of implicit bias reduction from social psychology research to develop methods for overturning the use of gender stereotypes to evaluate the qualifications of female candidates. Implicit bias affects the judgments individuals form of others because it is automatic; in short, individuals are not often aware they are engaging in stereotyping. The use of stereotypes in judgment often increases when individuals do not have enough individuating information about a member of a stereotyped group. Theories of implicit bias reduction suggest that strategies such as providing counter-stereotypic information of members of stereotyped groups can reduce the extent to which others rely on stereotypes to form judgments about others. I apply theories of stereotype reduction to the gendered qualification gap to test which strategies can disrupt the use of stereotypes and which strategies might not be as effective. While a vast body of research documents the challenges female candidates face when it comes to winning over voters, there are fewer studies that chart out strategies female candidates can use successfully to overturn biases among voters. This chapter starts to develop strategies aimed at limiting the gender biases identified in the earlier chapters of the book.

I developed three different ways to train voters to form objective and less biased evaluations about the qualifications of female political candidates. The three tests each speak to the different facets of the gendered qualification gap uncovered in the previous chapters. First, I test whether providing voters with information about the success of female candidates in political office improves their qualification ratings. The information experiment investigates whether closing the information gap that occurs in news coverage, highlighted in Chapter 4, will benefit female candidates. The second experiment addresses whether it is possible to shift the standards voters use away from the masculine role-typicality standards that disadvantage female candidates. This experiment uses the premise from the shifting standards framework that individuals need a comparative anchor when evaluating others, and in broad inference decisions masculine role-typicality standards provide that comparative anchor. The third experiment I test in this chapter addresses whether female candidates can benefit from self-promotion. Chapter 4 found that female candidates do not demur from self-promotion when it comes to the way they present themselves on their campaign websites. In this chapter, I test whether female candidates face a backlash for engaging in self-promotion strategies or whether behaving counter-stereotypically can benefit female candidates.

The three experiments offer mixed support about whether it is possible to shift the standards voters use to evaluate female candidates away from gender stereotypes. Simply providing information about the accomplishments of female candidates is not enough to close the gendered qualification gap. Self-promotion strategies also do little to close the gendered qualification gap. Providing an alternative comparative context, in my second experiment, does appear to close the gendered qualification gap in a way that benefits female candidates. Telling voters that women in Congress are, on average, more productive than men in Congress improves evaluations of female candidates and reduces evaluations of male candidates. These findings suggest that providing voters with contextual information about *how* to evaluate the accomplishments of female candidates can help voters interpret and make sense of this information. This finding, while preliminary, is consequential because it offers a simple strategy for shifting the comparative metric voters use to evaluate candidates. This chapter starts by reviewing social psychology research on eradicating implicit bias in decision-making. Next, I present the three experiments; each one speaks to a specific aspect of the gendered qualification gap uncovered in the previous chapters. Finally, I discuss several broad implications about what these results mean for the campaign landscape facing female candidates.

THE LOGIC OF REDUCING BIAS

Eradicating implicit bias toward women in politics requires preventing individuals from accessing and applying the conventional stereotypes of women as ineffective leaders. Disrupting implicit bias starts by altering the process of stereotype reliance. Stereotype reliance is a two-step process (Devine 1989). Step one is the automatic association individuals form between a member of a stereotyped group and the broader group stereotype (Bargh 1994). Stereotypes about women are ubiquitous concepts with a shared cultural meaning (Glick et al. 2004; Prentice and Carranza 2002), and this cultural knowledge about the content of gender stereotypes makes it easy for these ideas to affect the way individuals automatically and subconsciously form impressions of others. For example, an individual might see a woman walking to work and wonder who is taking care of her children if she has no children in tow. In this example, an individual forms an automatic and unconscious association between a specific woman and stereotypes of women as mothers and caregivers. The key to this automatic association is that the individual is not necessarily aware that they are relying on feminine stereotypes to form an assumption about a woman.

The first stage of stereotyping is subtle, unconscious, and automatic. The second stage of the stereotype process involves the controlled processing of stereotypic information (Blair 2002). Step two occurs when an individual actively uses the stereotype to form judgments about a member of the stereotyped group (Blair and Banaji 1996). An individual might pass a woman on the street and assume that she is a mother based on her sex, but in this example, it is unlikely an individual would use feminine stereotypes to actively form judgments of this particular woman. Simply walking by a woman does not require individuals to evaluate that woman. If a woman arrives at a job interview, feminine stereotypes could automatically affect the first impressions formed of her. A hiring manager might automatically assume the woman is a mother. The controlled stage of stereotype reliance occurs if the interviewer uses stereotypes to assume the female job applicant will always arrive late due to the demands of raising children and working, and decide not to hire her based on this stereotypic inference.

It is also possible that the interviewer will form the automatic association between the woman and stereotypes but then will not use the stereotype to form judgments about this particular woman because the interviewer is aware that this is a stereotype-based judgment that might not be accurate (Devine 1989). The female job applicant might discuss experiences that have nothing to do with feminine stereotypes and might not behave in ways that affirm stereotypes about women. In this case, the automatic stereotype association does not affect decision-making. It is at the controlled processing stage of stereotype reliance when it is possible to alter the way individuals use stereotypes to evaluate the qualifications of political candidates. Disrupting the automatic processing of stereotypes requires providing individuals with information that directly overturns the negative stereotypes individuals hold about female candidates. The three experiments I present in the rest of this chapter test different ways of disrupting the automatic process of stereotyping so that voters actively avoid the use of stereotypes in the controlled stage of impression formation.

PROVIDING QUALIFICATION INFORMATION

The idea of just telling people about a female candidate's qualifications seems simple. Anecdotal evidence suggests information can help. Take, for example, MJ Hegar. Hegar ran for the House in a very conservative congressional district in Texas in the 2018 midterms. She was one of fourteen female veterans running for political office. Hegar not only is a veteran of the war in Afghanistan but also received a Purple Heart for her service in combat and the Distinguished Flying Cross for heroism in aerial flight.[1] A poll conducted in August 2018 asked voters two questions about their support for Hegar against the Republican incumbent John Carter. The first question simply asked about support for the candidates and only mentioned candidate names and party affiliations. Forty percent of voters expressed support for Hegar, with 46 percent supporting Carter. The second question provided information about Hegar's three tours of service in Afghanistan, her military awards, and her role as a small business-owner – information about the, arguably, impressive qualifications that Hegar brings to politics. More importantly, these are examples of how Hegar excelled in stereotypically masculine roles. The question also told voters that Carter, her male opponent, first won election in 2002 and previously served as a district court judge. Support for Hegar increased to 46 percent and support for Carter dropped to 44 percent. These shifts are small, but suggest that telling voters about the qualifications of female candidates can change levels of support for female candidates.

Chapter 4 showed that female candidates, at least on their websites, provide voters with just as much, if not more, qualification information compared with male candidates. But this information does not always make it through to voters via news coverage. The first strategy for closing the qualification gap that I test in this chapter examines whether simply providing voters with more information about the success of women in masculine, counter-stereotypic roles boosts evaluations. The logic of providing information is that it should disrupt the automatic stage of stereotype processing. The automatic stage of stereotype processing is where an individual sees a woman and immediately, and subconsciously, starts to associate that specific woman with feminine

---

[1] Hegar is only the second woman to ever receive the Air Force's Flying Cross Award, after Amelia Earhart. Hegar is also the woman whose lawsuit against the Pentagon in *Hegar v. Panetta* eventually led to the Pentagon removing the ban on woman's service in military combat roles.

stereotypes. A lack of information or ambiguous information can trigger stereotyping, especially in a political context (Krupnikov and Ryan 2017; Milita et al. 2017; Piston et al. 2018). Individuating information about a specific woman that counters stereotypes should disrupt the automatic stage of stereotypic processing (Bargh 1994; Blair and Banaji 1996; Fiske and Neuberg 1990). And, in general, information reduces heuristic reliance (Bernhard and Freeder 2018). Applying this logic to candidate qualifications means that providing voters with information about the success of female candidates in politics should disrupt the automatic association voters might form that a woman does not fit into the stereotypic image of a political leader. Thus, information should boost a female candidate's qualification ratings.

Information Prediction: Female candidates will receive more positive evaluations in the information condition relative to the control condition.

In this first experiment, I presented participants with female and male candidates. I either provided information about the candidate's success as a legislator or provided no such information.[2] The information provided in the treatments was very specific about what each candidate did while in political office. The text read:

Congresswoman Diane (David) Bailey, a two-term Democrat (Republican) in the House is running for reelection. This legislative session, Bailey sponsored 21 bills and co-sponsored 26 bills with colleagues – three of these bills were passed into law. Bailey also chaired a major committee and secured $50 million in federal funding for projects in her (his) district.

Using information about productivity and experience directly overturns stereotypes about women as lacking experience, and providing this counter-stereotypic information is critical to disrupting bias (Holman, Merolla, and Zechmeister 2017). The information about the female and male candidates was exactly the same. Holding the information constant between the female and male candidate conditions isolates the role of gender bias, or the lack thereof, in voter evaluations. I used productivity information because the content analysis of news coverage from Chapter 4 showed that the qualification gap in news coverage was likely to disadvantage female candidates the most. The control condition simply stated that the candidate was running for reelection to the House and included the name and partisan affiliation of the candidate and said nothing about

---

[2] The Appendix to Chapter 7 include more details about the experimental design.

what the legislator did while in office. The experiment presented each participant with only one candidate and matched participants into shared partisan conditions.

The study asked participants to rate the effectiveness, experience, knowledge, and strong leadership of the female and the male candidates. The key comparisons here are the shifts in the ratings of the female candidate in the information condition compared with the control condition. I include the male conditions to test whether the male candidate is disproportionately rewarded for his high level of legislative performance relative to a female candidate. If providing information shifts the gendered standards used to evaluate female candidates, then the female candidate should receive *more positive* evaluations in the information condition relative to the control condition.

Figure 7.1 displays the difference in candidate ratings from the information condition relative to the control condition. I scaled each variable to range from 0 to 1 so that each bar can be interpreted as the proportion by which the candidate's evaluation changes from the control condition relative to the information condition. Information does not hurt a female candidate but also does not really help the female candidate. Providing more information simply might have no discernible effect on perceptions of the female candidate's effectiveness, experience, knowledge, and strength – showing no support for the information prediction. The male candidate, however, receives significantly large boosts on the four outcomes when voters have more information about his legislative performance. The male

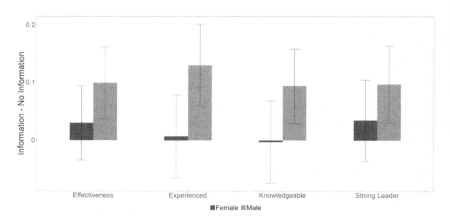

FIGURE 7.1 Effects of information.
Note: 95 percent confidence intervals displayed. Each bar displays the difference in the candidate's rating from the information condition to the no information condition.

candidate's ratings increase by approximately 9 percent on effectiveness, experience, knowledge, and strength, each significant at $p < 0.01$.

To further examine the extent to which the female candidate has a higher bar to meet than the male candidate, I conducted two additional comparisons. First, I compared the difference in differences between female and male candidates. Second, I compared directly across the treatment conditions. Comparing the difference in differences between the female condition and the male condition shows no significant differences. The size of the effect in the male condition from the treatment to the control is not statistically different from the size of the effect in the female condition from the treatment to the control. I also directly compared female and male candidates in the two treatment conditions, thereby leaving the control condition ratings out of the analysis. The only significant difference is on experience, where the male candidate has the more positive rating. The extent to which the male candidate benefits more than the female candidate may not be that great. Nevertheless, the information prediction does not bear out. This study only provided participants with a list of what the candidate accomplished in political office, and the study did not tell voters that, on average, female lawmakers outperform male candidates in terms of legislative productivity. The next experiment examines what happens when a different comparative context is added about just how qualified and productive female lawmakers are relative to their male colleagues.

SHIFTING THE COMPARATIVE CONTEXT

Simply telling voters about the accomplishments of female candidates is not enough to close the gendered qualification gap. One reason why information has no discernible effect on support for female candidates is that voters do not necessarily know how to interpret the information about the productivity of the candidates. Telling voters about the number of bills sponsored and the federal dollars secured by a female candidate is very precise information, but most voters do not know whether the number of bills supported by a candidate is a high or a low number of bills for a typical female lawmaker, or just a lawmaker in general. The lack of information that voters have about how Congress functions coupled with news coverage that focuses more on congressional gridlock rather than on congressional productivity makes it unlikely the average voter will have the tools needed to evaluate the qualification information (Hibbing and Theiss-Morse 2002). This next experiment investigates whether shifting the comparative metric voters use to evaluate candidate qualifications can close the gendered qualification gap.

This experiment still builds on the logic that overturning implicit bias requires providing individuating information that is counter-stereotypic about women but also requires providing individuals with the tools needed to make the appropriate comparison. Individuals need a comparative anchor when forming impressions of other individuals because such comparative anchors ease the task of decision-making (Campbell, Lewis, and Hunt 1958; Postman and Miller 1945). Chapter 5 showed that gender stereotypes provide individuals with an easy and accessible comparative metric they can use to evaluate the qualities of an individual woman or a man (Biernat and Manis 1994). Providing an alternative comparative anchor can disrupt the process of using gender stereotypes as the anchor. In this experiment, the comparative anchor I provide in the vignette is actual information about the performance of women and men, in general, in Congress. This is where I draw on the research showing that female legislators, on average, outperform male legislators (Anzia and Berry 2011). The logic is that telling voters that women, on average, are better than men will lead voters to evaluate the qualifications of a specific woman more positively. Conversely, telling voters than men, on average, are not as high-performing as women should lead voters to rate men less positively.

Comparative Context Prediction: Participants will rate the female candidate more positively when provided an alternative comparative context about the overall performance of women in Congress relative to when there is no alternative comparative context provided.

The comparative experiment builds on the design of the information experiment.[3] The study included female and male candidate conditions, and I provided the same qualification information about the female and male candidates. The text read:

Congresswoman Diane/Congressman David Bailey, a two-term Democrat in the House, is running for reelection. This legislative session, Bailey sponsored 21 bills and co-sponsored 26 bills with colleagues – three of these bills were passed into law. Bailey also chaired a major committee and secured $50 million in federal funding for projects in her/his district.

I again matched participants into shared partisan groups so that each participant always saw a candidate with whom they shared partisanship.

---

[3] See the Appendix to Chapter 7 for more details on the context experimental design.

I included the same four outcome questions from the first experiment. The key difference in this study is that I added a comparative context condition for the female and male candidates. The comparative context conditions provided information about the average performance of women and men in Congress. The comparative information for the female condition reads:

Bailey ranks far ahead of her male colleagues in terms of productivity. Research shows that, on average, female lawmakers in the US Congress have higher levels of productivity than male lawmakers. Female members of Congress, in both the House and the Senate, sponsor and co-sponsor more legislation than male members of Congress. Women in Congress pass, on average, three more pieces of legislation into law and bring home 9 percent more in federal dollars to their districts compared with their male counterparts.

This information appeared after the text documenting the number of bills sponsored, co-sponsored, or passed into law by the candidate along with the other productivity information about the candidate. I provided the same information about the male candidate, but I changed the line that reads, "Bailey ranks far ahead of her male colleagues in terms of productivity" to read, "Bailey lags far behind his female colleagues in terms of productivity." This information deliberately frames the male Bailey's legislative productivity to be less positive relative to the female Bailey's legislative productivity. Again, this setup is deliberate to reflect the fact that male legislators are, in fact, less productive than their female colleagues.[4]

The comparative information should disrupt implicit bias by telling participants how to interpret the qualification information in the female condition. The goal of the comparative information is to allow people to overcome the shifting standards dynamic uncovered in Chapter 5. If the results follow from my expectations, then the female Bailey's evaluations should *improve* in the comparative condition relative to the condition that lacks an explicit comparative context. Figure 7.2 shows the effects of providing an alternative point of comparison as a strategy for disrupting implicit bias. Each bar shows the change in the candidate's evaluation from the condition with just the productivity information compared with the condition with the added comparison. Providing the comparison information benefits female candidates and offers support for the comparative context prediction. The evaluations of the female candidate

---

[4] I did not include a condition where the comparative context stated that male legislators are more productive than female legislators because the empirical evidence suggests this is not the case in practice (see, e.g., Anzia and Berry 2011; Lowande, Ritchie, and Lauterbach 2019).

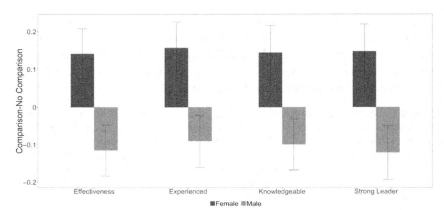

FIGURE 7.2 Shifting the comparative context.
Note: 95 percent confidence intervals displayed. Each bar displays the difference in the candidate's rating from the information condition to the no information condition.

improve by 14–15 percent on each evaluation metric. Telling participants about the overall high levels of productivity among female candidates appears to prevent voters from holding female candidates to a high bar set by masculine role-typicality standards.

It is possible that the female candidate's boost in the treatment condition is motivated by other factors. Her reward could be a group solidarity effect where she is rewarded not necessarily for being productive but for behaving like other female lawmakers. Looking at the effects for the male candidate is helpful for determining whether the female candidate reward is due to a group solidarity effect. If participants reward the woman for behaving like other women, then participants should not necessarily punish the male candidate for failing to behave like other women. The information about women's performance in Congress hurts the male candidate on the four evaluative outcomes. The male candidate's ratings *drop* by 12–15 percent on effectiveness, experience, knowledge, and strong leadership in the comparison condition relative to the conditions that lacked the explicit comparative context.

A limitation of the design is that it does introduce an element of gender competition comparing the performance of a female lawmaker with male lawmakers, and vice versa. Future work should test the effect of other forms of comparative context information. For example, comparing the performance of a specific female lawmaker with the overall performance of Congress as an institution is a way to provide a comparative anchor that does not necessarily introduce an element of gender group competition. Providing voters with information about the qualifications of female candidates and putting that information into a broader narrative about the qualifications of female candidates overall appears to be a possible strategy for closing the gendered qualification gap. *Does this strategy close the partisan gendered gap?* The partisan gender gap, uncovered in Chapter 6, shows that Republican female candidates have a much higher qualification bar to meet relative to Democratic female candidates. I conducted another set of analyses to see if the Democratic and Republican female candidates benefit similarly from the shift in comparison. For these next analyses, I focus on comparisons just in the treatment conditions. First, I compared the Democratic female candidate with the Republican female candidate. Second, I compared the Democratic female candidate with the Democratic male candidate, and then I separately compare the Republican female candidate with the Republican male candidate. These analyses are from the same comparative context experiment.

Figure 7.3 displays the average ratings of each candidate broken down by Democratic and Republican female and male candidates in the treatment condition. Comparing the ratings of the Democratic and Republican female candidates to one another shows no significant differences across female candidate partisanship. The lack of partisan differences in the comparison information conditions suggests that being female is not creating different standards for Democratic and Republican women.

The next key test is to compare within candidate partisanship and between female and male candidates to test whether there are any differences in candidate evaluations. The main results of the comparative

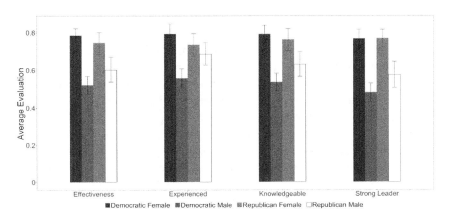

FIGURE 7.3 Partisan differences.
Note: 95 percent confidence intervals displayed.

context study showed that female candidates gained an advantage over male candidates. If the comparison strategy closes the partisan gap, then the Democratic female candidate should receive more positive evaluations than the Democratic male candidate, and the Republican female candidate should also receive more positive evaluations than the Republican male candidate. Within the Democratic conditions, the female candidate consistently receives more positive evaluations compared with the male candidate on all four outcomes. In the Republican conditions, the female candidate also receives more positive evaluations relative to the male candidate on three out of the four outcomes. The only outcome where the Republican female candidate does not close the qualification gap is on experience. The Republican female candidate has wide advantages in effectiveness, knowledge, and strong leadership.

Closing the qualification gap not only requires telling voters about the accomplishments of female candidates but also requires explicitly telling voters how to evaluate these accomplishments. Voters need information that female candidates have better qualifications than their male counterparts. Without that explicit comparison, voters do not know whether a female candidate is poorly qualified, well qualified, or just adequately qualified. The two experiments presented so far provided information to voters as though it were embedded in a news article. The third experiment investigates what happens when candidates explicitly brag about themselves to voters.

SELF-PROMOTION STRATEGIES

The third strategy for closing the gendered qualification gap tests whether female candidates benefit from self-promotion. A self-promotion strategy draws on classic congressional research about how lawmakers secure election and reelection. Candidates self-promote as a way to share legislative successes (Mayhew 1974). Self-promotion allows candidates to demonstrate to voters that they are productive lawmakers, but also sends the message that a lawmaker is responsible for producing a desirable outcome from government. Self-promotion is a behavior that reinforces agency and power – an approach that harkens to masculine stereotypes. Chapter 4 found that, when it comes to using campaign websites, female candidates self-promote just as much as male candidates. This final experiment tests how voters respond to such messages.

Self-promotion has the potential to close the gendered qualification gap because these messages provide voters with information that counters the baseline stereotypes voters hold of women. A self-promoting female candidate breaks with the perception that women lack the ability to fill a masculine leadership role, and engaging in counter-stereotypic behaviors can reduce reliance on feminine stereotypes (Blair 2002). A self-promotion strategy may be effective because these messages provide voters with individuating information about a specific woman. When voters have more information about the policy positions of a specific woman in politics, the use of feminine stereotypes to form judgments decreases.

Self-Promotion Benefit Prediction: Self-promotion will improve evaluations of the female candidate relative to when she does not engage in self-promotion.

Self-promotion can have unintended consequences for women. Bragging about one's accomplishments breaks with feminine expectations that women be meek and humble (Prentice and Carranza 2002). Women who break with feminine norms can face a gendered penalty (Rudman 1998), and the self-promotion penalty can be especially harsh for women operating in masculine institutions (Rudman 1998). The logic behind this gendered penalty is the same type of logic that had the potential to deter female candidates from self-promotion on their campaign websites, as explicated in Chapter 4. Women on job interviews who talk about their qualifications or female managers who highlight how they led their staff to success receive negative evaluations for not being humble (Heilman and Okimoto 2007). Voters may ignore the information provided by a self-promotion behavior and, instead, focus on the woman's break with stereotypic norms. This perspective suggests a conflicting expectation that female candidates will not benefit from self-promotion.

Self-Promotion Backlash Prediction: Female candidates who self-promote may suffer a penalty from engaging in a strategy that breaks with feminine stereotypes relative to a male candidate who also self-promotes.

I tested whether self-promotion closes the gendered qualification gap with a final experiment.[5] The experiment, similar to the previous two studies, manipulated whether the candidate was a man or a woman and whether the candidate engaged in self-promotion or did not engage in self-promotion. I presented participants with a brief news article covering a rally at a female or a male incumbent candidate's campaign for

---

[5] See the Appendix to Chapter 7 for more information on the details of the self-promotion experiment.

reelection. The article included a quotation from a speech delivered by the candidate at the rally, and stated:

I, alone, passed legislation to build a new community center, repair the roads in the state, and provide support for our veterans. I am single-handedly responsible for attracting new businesses and thousands of jobs in our state. Many of the bills I introduced became law because I secured the support of my colleagues. Through my determination, I single-handedly improved the lives of people in our state.

The self-promotion condition listed the accomplishments, including passing legislation to build a community center, repairing roads, supporting veterans, and creating jobs in the district. The self-promotion quotation uses agentic language such as "I, alone, passed legislation" or "I am single-handedly responsible." The control condition included no information about the legislator's accomplishments and simply stated that the candidate attended a rally and was embattled in a close race for reelection. I asked participants the same four outcome questions from the first two studies. Support for the benefit prediction would occur if the female candidate receives a more positive evaluation in the self-promotion prediction relative to the control condition. Support for the backlash prediction would occur if the female candidate receives a more negative evaluation in the self-promotion condition relative to the control condition and if the male candidate does not receive a punishment. The male candidate not receiving a punishment but the female candidate receiving a punishment suggests a gendered tinge to any backlash the female candidate might receive, whereas if both candidates receive a punishment, the mechanism of this punishment might be related to a factor beyond gendered dynamics.

Figure 7.4 displays the difference in the candidate's rating from the treatment to the control condition on effectiveness, experience, knowledge, or strong leadership. Self-promotion does not benefit either female or male candidates. The female candidate does not receive a gendered penalty, because these messages have no statistically significant effect on her evaluations. This does not necessarily mean that self-promotion will never be effective for candidates, but that candidates need to develop more innovative strategies for touting their successes on the campaign trail.

Together, the three experiments in this chapter suggest that it is difficult but possible to disrupt the biased patterns of evaluations exhibited by voters, as discussed in Chapters 5 and 6. Simply telling voters about the accomplishments of female candidates is not enough to overcome the biases female candidates face at the polls. Voters will assume that female

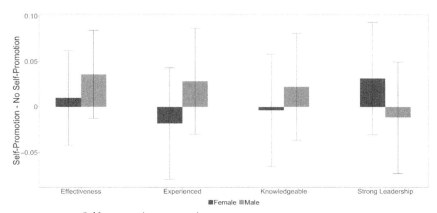

FIGURE 7.4 Self-promotion strategies.
Note: 95 percent confidence intervals displayed. Each bar displays the difference in the candidate's rating from the information condition to the no information condition.

candidates lack the qualifications needed to serve in high-profile and high-power leadership roles. Providing an explicit point of comparison and telling voters that women in politics, overall, have far better qualifications relative to men in politics can disrupt the biased evaluations voters form of female political candidates.

IS IT POSSIBLE TO CLOSE THE GENDERED QUALIFICATION GAP?

The idea of implicit bias training is intuitively appealing. If people are taught about the subtle biases they hold, these biases will be less likely to affect the way they treat members of stereotyped and marginalized groups. Leveraging this logic to the setting of a political campaign and voter decision-making is somewhat more difficult. It is not exactly practical or possible to have the American public all attend an implicit bias training designed to overturn the biases that affect the impressions voters form of female candidates. Indeed, when Congress passed its series of reforms designed to create an improved system for addressing sexual assault and harassment, the proposal for implicit bias training did not make it into the final bill. Studies conducted in the workplace suggest that individuals learn and can identify appropriate and inappropriate behaviors regarding the treatment of women, but individuals do not always put this knowledge into practice (Chang et al. 2019).

This chapter addressed the final core question guiding this book: How can female candidates overcome the gendered qualification gap? Adapting the logic of implicit bias reduction, this chapter tested three specific strategies for closing the gendered qualification gap: providing counter-stereotypic information about female candidates, shifting the comparative anchor that individuals use to evaluate that counter-stereotypic information, and self-promotion. Not all these strategies were successful. Simply providing counter-stereotypic information did little to shift the initial impressions voters formed of the female candidate. And self-promotion strategies also had no effect on the impressions voters formed about the success of female and male political candidates. The strategy with the most potential to close the qualification gap is to shift the comparative anchor voters use away from masculine role-typicality standards. Providing a comparison reduces the likelihood voters will use gender-typicality, role-typicality, or partisan-typicality standards to evaluate candidates. Voters need a comparative anchor when forming impressions of other voters because such comparative anchors ease the task of decision-making (Campbell, Lewis, and Hunt 1958, Postman and Miller 1945). The treatment information adds the comparison voters need so they can more accurately assess whether a female candidate is highly qualified or not.

A critical question about how to apply the results from the studies I conducted here to the context of real-world elections is: Who can best deliver this information to voters? The self-promotion study provides evidence that female candidates may not be their own best messengers. Self-promotion is relatively unavoidable in running for political office. Most successful candidates generally ask voters for their support and explain why they are the best person for the job. This task is fraught with gendered challenges. Using "I" statements to highlight accomplishments can leave listeners thinking that a female candidate is boasting just a little bit too much. Using "we" statements reflects a more communal and feminine style of leadership but can minimize the accomplishments of women. Clinton frequently received criticism when she highlighted her accomplishments using "I" statements, and she still received criticism when she used "we" statements.

Outsourcing self-promotion, with campaign proxies, may be a way for female candidates to promote without falling into a gendered bind. I did not test whether female candidates can outsource the task of selling their qualifications to voters. At the July 2016 Democratic National Convention, Barack Obama gave a resounding endorsement of Hillary Clinton where he asserted, "I can say with confidence there has never been a man or a woman more qualified than Hillary Clinton to serve as President of the United States of America." The tactic of having high-profile and popular political leaders serve as surrogates for candidates is not novel – candidates do this frequently – but this tactic may help female candidates who do not benefit from self-promotion. If female candidates have high-profile and trusted messengers touting their qualifications, they may have more success with self-promotion strategies.

While female candidates may not be able to tout their own accomplishments, this does not necessarily mean they will not be good proxies for other candidates. During the 2016 election, Clinton frequently used First Lady Michelle Obama and Senator Elizabeth Warren to campaign on her behalf – both women. Women may be more effective when they promote the qualifications of others rather than themselves. Psychology research shows that women who ask for a pay raise during job negotiations face a backlash, but women who negotiate on behalf of *other* women do not face a punishment (Smith and Huntoon 2014). Women can promote the accomplishments of other women without fear of a gendered penalty. And, of course, men can also promote the accomplishments of women. A key way to follow up on this research is to test whether and among which types of voters messages from female and male campaign proxies are most effective for female candidates.

Overturning long-held biases about the inability of women to fit into positions of political leadership long associated with masculinity is not an impossible task, but it is certainly a difficult one. The information strategies tested in this chapter focus on communicating to voters that female candidates have the qualifications needed for political office. I did not test whether it is possible to change the masculine stereotypes voters associate with political leadership and the feminine stereotypes voters associate with women more generally. The association between leadership and masculinity is strong. Voters associate masculinity with leadership, but being an effective leader and an effective legislator frequently require feminine qualities and not masculine qualities. The campaign process conditions voters to look for the most aggressive, most tough, and most masculine political candidate. This is a fundamental tension in the American democratic system. The key might not necessarily be training voters to evaluate candidate qualifications objectively but training voters to radically rethink political leadership.

8

The Future Is Female

If they don't give you a seat at the table, bring a folding chair.
—Shirley Chisholm

It is tempting to conclude from the successes of female candidates in 2018, coupled with the record-setting six women vying for the Democratic presidential nomination for 2020, that gender bias may not pose an insurmountable barrier for women when they run for political office. However, this conclusion would not be entirely accurate. Examining only the positive outcomes from elections obfuscates the challenges many female candidates face along the campaign trail. Looking at the women who ran for Congress in 2018, for example, there were 4,193 women who put their name on the ballot, knocked on doors, and made a case to voters about why they should represent them in government. Of these women, about half, or 2,178 to be more precise, lost their races. Many of these unsuccessful female candidates had the right qualifications for the job.

For female candidates, simply being able to check off all the right boxes on their resumes is not enough to guarantee victory. Electorally viable female candidates must, on average, look like male candidates but be better than male candidates. Perceptions of who is qualified to be a political leader are intrinsically linked to perceptions of masculinity. This attachment between masculinity and serving in political leadership poses an inherent obstacle for female candidates. Women, based on their sex, do not fit into traditional perceptions of masculinity. Take, for example, Gina Ortiz Jones, a veteran of the Iraq War and former intelligence officer. Ortiz Jones ran for the House to represent Texas's Twenty-third

Congressional District in 2018, and few would argue that she lacked the masculine qualifications needs for political office. Despite impressive qualifications that certainly fit a "masculine profile," Ortiz Jones narrowly lost to the incumbent Will Hurd, who also had a background in intelligence. Even though Ortiz Jones had the right masculine profile, she could not necessarily "out-masculine" her male opponent. Of course, other factors beyond qualifications affected Ortiz Jones's very narrow loss, including the partisan dynamics of the district and the difficulty of defeating an incumbent. But Ortiz Jones was only one of many highly qualified women who lost in 2018.[1]

Despite the losses of women in 2018, the United States is, possibly, on the cusp of a new era of women's political power. Six women, as of the summer of 2019, declared candidacies for the Democratic presidential nomination in 2020, including Elizabeth Warren, Kirsten Gillibrand, Kamala Harris, Amy Klobuchar, Tulsi Gabbard, and Marianne Williamson. Looking forward to 2024, there are Republican women emerging as leaders within the party, including Nikki Haley, Marsha Blackburn, Joni Ernst, and Martha McSally. The ability of female candidates to maintain the momentum started after Hillary Clinton's historical race in 2016 depends on the ability of women to overcome the challenges of the gendered qualification gap. While 2018 was a good year for women at the ballot, the road to parity in representation is a long one. Men still hold most of the political power. It will take more than one "pink wave" to reach parity. The research presented in this book shows how gendered notions of political qualifications pose a barrier for female candidates. These barriers limit the success of women at the polls, perpetuate women's underrepresentation in elected office, and marginalize the voice of women across the electorate. The consequences of the gendered qualification gap are far reaching.

In this final chapter, I start by reviewing the main findings from the multiple empirical tests conducted in the previous chapters. Following this brief review, I then discuss why closing this gap matters for the health of American democratic institutions. Next, I outline how future scholarship can build on the research presented in this book. Finally, I place the concept of the gendered qualification gap into a broader context beyond politics. Women, whenever they enter into any institution traditionally dominated by men, will likely be held to higher standards shaped by stereotypes.

---

[1] Gina Ortiz Jones is running again in 2020 for the Texas twenty-third House seat.

SUMMARY OF MAIN ARGUMENT AND FINDINGS

The central puzzle motivating the research in this book is that the female candidates who win elections have better qualifications than the male candidates who win elections, but these women win elections by smaller electoral margins than their male counterparts. Existing accounts of this gendered qualification gap center on the gendered socialization processes that affect women's political careers and the institutional barriers that make it more difficult for women to enter the political pipeline. This previous body of scholarship has yet to consider the role of gender stereotypes in how voters evaluate the qualifications of female candidates. The research in this book fills that gap, and does so by addressing four major questions about the gendered qualification gap. First, how do ideas about gender affect what it means to be qualified for political office? Second, what information do voters have about candidate qualifications? Third, do voters think differently about the qualifications of female candidates and male candidates? Finally, how can female candidates overcome the gendered qualification gap? In each chapter, I draw on theoretical insights from social psychology and voter decision-making to develop a series of empirical tests designed to answer these critical questions.

Chapter 1 defined the gendered qualification gap, which is a phenomenon where the women who run for and win political office have, on average, more impressive resumes relative to the men who run for and win political office. Being better than a man only gets a female candidate to electoral parity. This book examines why, from the voters' perspective, highly qualified female candidates do not win elections at higher rates and by larger margins of victory compared with male candidates. I argue that voters hold female candidates to higher qualification standards compared with male candidates, and these higher standards originate from the intrinsic link between masculinity and political leadership. Conventional explanations for the gendered qualification gap fail to account for how stereotypes about women and gender stereotypes about political roles factor into the voter decision-making process. This book fills a major gap in scholarship documenting how voters evaluate both male and female political candidates. Ideas about gender are often at play in how voters see political candidates, even if their influence is subtle and subconscious.

Chapter 2 took a historic perspective on the status of women in American political life. Hillary Clinton received ample attention for her glass-shattering presidential campaigns, but she was not the first woman to pursue the presidency. Women sought a voice in masculine political institutions in the United States at the founding, when Abigail Adams pleaded with her husband to "remember the ladies." As candidates for political office, much of women's success occurred only in the last half-century. Part of the problem in women's representation is that it is not clear whether the public supports female political candidates, especially at the highest levels of political leadership. Public opinion polls that simply ask about support for a "qualified" woman for the presidency suggest that women should have no problem winning an election. These types of polling data do not offer any insight into who is a qualified woman or what constitutes "qualified" for a woman.

Ideas about femininity and masculinity shape how voters think about political leadership. A central argument of this book is that voters associate political qualifications with masculinity. Chapter 3 draws on social role theory to develop a framework to understand the association between masculinity and leadership. Leadership, in early communities, required physical strength and protection. The biological capacities of men made them better fit to serve in these leadership roles, while the reproductive capacities of women limited their ability to take on roles that required physical strength. Political leadership no longer requires physical strength, but the association between masculinity and leadership persists. The historical dominance of men in positions of political leadership further reinforces a "think leader, think male" paradigm. The masculinity of leadership poses a qualification barrier for women simply because they are not men.

Chapter 4 focused on whether there is a gendered information gap. A gendered information gap can widen the gendered qualification gap because if voters lack information about a woman's qualifications, they will assume she lacks the appropriate qualifications. The roots of this assumption rest with the separate social roles occupied by women and men. The first half of the analyses examined the content of campaign websites to test whether female candidates engage in different patterns of self-promotion compared with male candidates. Female and male candidates do not engage in different self-promotion patterns. Through analyses of campaign news coverage, I found that the news media are less likely to provide information about the political and professional experiences of female candidates compared with male candidates. Instead, the news media are more likely to highlight the families of female candidates compared with male candidates. These gendered information gaps reinforce stereotypes of women as not fitting into the masculine image voters have of a political leader.

Chapter 5 relied on a series of survey experiments to determine if voters hold female candidates to a gender-based qualification standard. I illustrated how voters use gender-typicality and role-typicality standards to evaluate both female and male candidates. Gender-typicality standards create the illusion that voters see female candidates as highly qualified for political office, but these seemingly positive evaluations occur because voters compare a female candidate's experience or knowledge with that of a typical woman. When it comes to more consequential electoral choice decisions, voters fall back on masculine role-typicality standards that create a high bar for female candidates. Masculine role-typicality standards also create a lower bar for male candidates. Voters hold female candidates to these higher qualification standards regardless of whether the woman is a well-seasoned political veteran or an up-and-coming challenger. For female incumbents, voters use a gendered standard that I call the female politician standard, which is a mix of feminine and masculine qualities. Gender-typicality standards explain how outcomes that appear neutral between female and male candidates are not, in fact, the result of a gender-neutral decision-making process.

Chapter 6 turned to investigating whether there is a partisan gap in the way voters evaluate the qualifications of female candidates. Voters apply stereotypes about women and men to the political parties such that voters see Democrats as the more feminine party and Republicans as the more masculine party. Voters use these gendered partisan stereotypes to develop standards about which candidates have the best qualities to lead their political parties. Republican voters hold Republican female candidates to exceptionally higher standards relative to Republican male candidates. If given the choice between a Republican woman and a Republican man, fellow Republican voters will choose the man over the woman. There is more parity between Democratic female and Democrat male candidates when faced with co-partisan voters. These findings track with the status of women in politics, as Democratic women far outnumber Republican women in politics.

Chapter 7, the final empirical chapter, tested strategies designed to disrupt the use of stereotypes to evaluate female candidates. The results show that not all messages bolster the success of female candidates. Voters are most responsive to information about the qualifications of female candidates that is put into a comparative context. Voters need to be provided with an alternative comparative context telling them whether this candidate is highly qualified or not. Messages that simply list the accomplishments of female candidates do not close the gendered qualification gap. Self-promotion messages, based on the initial test conducted in that chapter, also did not shift the impressions voters formed of female or male candidates. This chapter points to the need for more research identifying strategies for disrupting the biased processes that voters use to evaluate the qualifications of female candidates.

WHEN WOMEN WIN, AMERICA WINS!

The underrepresentation of women in political institutions has ramifications for the vibrancy of democratic institutions as well as the descriptive and substantive representation of women. Political institutions that systematically exclude half of the population will not be able to function efficiently. Shirley Chisholm, the first black woman to win election to Congress, aptly described the problem with political institutions that exclude women: "Our representative democracy is not working because the Congress that is supposed to represent the individuals does not respond to their needs. I believe the chief reason is that it is ruled by a small group of old men" (Chisholm 1970, p. 103). Rule by a "small group of old men" is hardly a fully representative democracy. A legislature that does not include women cannot effectively represent women, or really anyone.

Normative theorists argue that representative democracies gain more legitimacy when the legislature resembles the demographic characteristics of the population it represents (Mansbridge 1999; Pitkin 1967). Women in the electorate view the political system as more legitimate, participate more in politics, and have higher levels of political knowledge when women run for office or serve in legislatures (Fridkin and Kenney 2014; Wolak 2019). Female voters frequently prefer female candidates (Plutzer and Zipp 1996; Sanbonmatsu 2002a; Zipp and Plutzer 1985), though women of color largely drive this effect (Junn 2017). Clayton, O'Brien, and Piscopo (2019) found that both men and women viewed decisions made by all-male bodies as less legitimate compared with decisions made by gender-inclusive bodies.

Women in high-profile political positions serve as role models for women considering careers in politics or careers in other male-dominated institutions. When women run for political office, other women then consider running for political office (Bonneau and Kanthak 2018; Ladam, Harden, and Windett 2018; Sweet-Cushman 2019). These role-modeling effects often start when girls witness high-profile women pursuing political careers (Campbell and Wolbrecht 2006; Wolbrecht and Campbell 2017). While having a woman on the ballot, by itself, does not necessarily increase political engagement among women (Wolak 2015, 2019), evidence suggests that Clinton's loss coupled with Trump's misogyny had a positive role-modeling effect among adolescent girls and young women (Campbell and Wolbrecht 2019). Girls and young women who watched Hillary Clinton's 2016 presidential run may be more likely to consider running for political office decades from now.

There are also negative effects that come when women lose political office. Polls in the wake of Hillary Clinton's presidential loss found that 45 percent of women in professional, white-collar jobs felt significantly worse and 31 percent felt slightly worse about their career prospects. One woman's response to the survey question encapsulates the reverse role-modeling effect, succinctly stating that Clinton "made it far, but still lost to a man who is less qualified for the job. This is what we go through every day."[2] Witnessing a highly qualified woman lose to an, arguably, less qualified man is an experience many women share. It can be a profoundly demoralizing experience for many women: if Clinton cannot make it in politics, given her substantial qualifications, they also might not be able to succeed in their careers.

Putting more women in political office matters. Women are more productive lawmakers with the power to change how democratic institutions function. Women have the potential to bring more compromise and less gridlock to Congress. Female lawmakers are advocates for other women and marginalized communities (Pearson and Dancey 2011). The presence of women in legislative institutions can change the behavior of men in those institutions (Nugent 2019). One study found that when women deliver emotionally intense speeches in Congress, frequently about issues that affect the lives of women, male lawmakers were subsequently more likely to deliver more emotionally intense speeches in solidarity with their female colleagues (Dietrich, Hayes, and O'Brien 2019).

---

[2] Fortune magazine reported on this poll shortly after the 2016 elections. Kristen Bellstrom, "76% of Women Feel Worse about Their Career Prospects under a Trump Presidency," *Fortune.com*, November 16, 2016, http://fortune.com/2016/11/16/trump-women-career-prospects/.

Women prioritize a different set of issues on the legislative agenda (Dittmar, Sanbonmatsu, and Carroll 2018; Osborn 2012), and strategic alliances with male lawmakers help enshrine these issues into law (Volden, Wiseman, and Wittmer 2018). There are several important examples of these agenda-setting and strategic alliance effects. Congress did not consider Title IX until Representative Patsy Mink's election to the House. Mink was motivated to write the legislation based on her experiences with discrimination. She secured passage of the law by forging alliances with male senators, such as Senator Birch Bayh from Indiana, who was also a chief proponent of the Equal Rights Amendment and recognized the importance of the legislation. The Violence against Women Act, passed in 1994, was initiated by Congresswoman Louise Slaughter, and Senator Joe Biden was pivotal to securing passage of the law.

The presence of women can also transform conventionally masculine issues into more feminine issues. Kirsten Gillibrand often speaks of when she was a member of the House and served on the Armed Services Committee with several other female lawmakers. The committee dealt with a range of military issues, from the recruitment of troops to the procurement of weapons to deployments, and so on. The newly appointed women to the committee asked about the military's policies for families and dependents, especially regarding base housing policies. The issue fell within the purview of the committee, but it was not an issue the mostly male committee had considered before. Adding women to this pivotal House committee changed how the lawmakers of both political parties and across both genders thought about and legislated on issues seen as stereotypically masculine.

This book started with the empirical puzzle that the women who succeed in politics are among the most qualified candidates and that these women, on average, have better qualifications than their male counterparts. The women who make it to Congress tend to be highly effective at the task of legislating. But voters do not necessarily evaluate female candidates based on their ability to end gridlock, broker compromise, and craft legislation. Voters select political candidates based on how well these candidates meet a masculine standard of political leadership. This masculine standard of political leadership emphasizes the exercise of power for personal gain. These qualities not only disadvantage women but also do not necessarily make for good lawmakers or effective legislatures. Legislative institutions filled with hundreds of members aimed more at exercising power for personal gain rather than communal gain undermines the purpose of representative democracy – and limits the benefits that come from having not just more women in political office but a more fully representative democracy. When there are more women in political office, especially women from diverse racial, ethnic, religious, and social class backgrounds, democracy is more representative and responsive to constituents. Individuals feel more positively about government and democracy when their leaders look like them. The benefits are clear and simple: everyone wins when more women win political office.

BEYOND THE GENDERED QUALIFICATION GAP

This book builds a solid foundation for examining the barriers facing other types of nontraditional candidates who are also excluded from politics. Candidates may have many cross-cutting identities that do not perfectly fit into the masculine expectations voters have for political leaders. Stereotypes about race, ethnicity, religion, social class, sexual orientation, and gender identities, beyond just being male or female, can all create the perception that a candidate lacks the masculine qualifications needed for holding political office. A common identity for female candidates is that they are mothers, but the identities of women as mothers may affect perceptions of women's political qualifications (Bryant and Hellwege 2018; Deason, Greenlee, and Langer 2015; Greenlee 2014; Klar, Madonia, and Schneider 2014). Many nontraditional or, in other words, non-upper-middle-class white male candidates frequently have better qualifications than more conventional political candidates – suggesting that voters hold other types of candidates beyond just women to higher qualification standards. More work is needed to determine the barriers that nontraditional political candidates face in running for and winning political office.

A noteworthy outcome of the 2018 midterm elections is that it was not just that women won big but that women of color won tremendous victories. Stereotypes about race sharply intersect with stereotypes about gender. The gendered qualification gap likely exists for women of color who run for and win political office, but it is not clear how masculine and feminine stereotypes intersect with stereotypes about race to factor into voter decision-making. Voters assume that black female candidates, for instance, have more masculine qualities than a typical white woman, and this could benefit rather than hinder the electoral prospects for these candidates (Bejarano 2013; Brown 2014; Cargile 2016; Cassese 2019; Simien 2005). Lucy McBath won her race in Georgia's Sixth Congressional District as a mother whose son was a victim of gun violence.

Stereotypes about her race and femininity combined so that a message about being a black mother did not necessarily lead voters to doubt her masculine qualifications for office. Conducting more research that identifies the stereotypes held of people of color who run for political office can clarify how and when voter bias will affect whether voters see them as qualified for political office.

The 2018 midterm elections not only increased the number of women of color in political office but also increased the numbers of LGBTQ candidates who ran for and won political office. Christine Hallquist made history when she won the Democratic Party's nomination to run for the governor of Vermont as a transgender woman in 2018. Hallquist's candidacy, while ultimately not successful in securing a gubernatorial seat, brought to light the marginalization of the transgender community. There is relatively little scholarship tracing how voters apply stereotypes to candidates with nonconforming gender identities (for exceptions, see Haider-Markel et al. 2017; Jones and Brewer 2019; Jones et al. 2018). A candidate with a gender identity that does not match their biological sex may not be clearly categorized into feminine or masculine stereotype categories, and voters may not use gender-typicality and role-typicality standards to evaluate these political candidates. For example, stereotypes of gay women include a lot of masculine qualities that voters consider important for political leaders, such as being tough and strong, but stereotypes of gay women exclude a lot of feminine qualities that voters consider undesirable for political leaders, such as being emotional and weak. Sharice Davids, who won election in Kansas's Third Congressional District in 2018, ran as a gay Native American woman. In fact, her victory marked the first time a Native American woman won election to Congress.[3] The combination of multiple stereotypes may have worked to her benefit.

The research in this book did not test how gender-typicality and role-typicality standards affect races with two female candidates. The surge of women running for political office increases the likelihood of more races with women running against other women. I expect that gender-typicality and role-typicality standards will still shape how voters think about female candidates, but the use of these standards may not automatically disadvantage women. A few studies examine all-female electoral contexts

---

[3] Deb Haaland also won election in 2018 as the second Native American woman to win a seat in the House. Together, Haaland and Davids were first Native American women to go to Congress.

(Ditonto and Andersen 2018; Hennings and Urbatsch 2015; Palmer and Simon 2005), and this literature finds that voters see a female incumbent similarly to a male candidate. It is also possible that voters will shift to entirely different standards in an all-female race based on partisan stereotypes, especially if both women are challengers. All-female elections may also affect the partisan gender gap. Partisan-typicality standards do not adversely affect Democratic female candidates, but partisan-typicality standards may affect how voters choose between a Democratic and a Republican female candidate. Republican voters may feel less excitement and enthusiasm about supporting a Republican woman relative to Democratic voters.

This study examined only congressional races. Future work should explore whether voters have more feminine role-typicality expectations at other levels and across different types of political office. The level of office may adjust the gender-typicality and role-typicality framework. Role-typicality standards create a higher bar for female candidates when voters clearly associate masculinity with the level of office at stake. Empirical evidence suggests that voters hold masculine standards for candidates even at lower levels of office (Bauer 2020a; Oliver and Conroy 2017). It is thought that lower levels of political office are seen as more feminine, but voters stereotype even a low-profile city council office as masculine. Role-typicality expectations may become more strongly masculine as the level of office increases, especially because evidence shows that female candidates face more bias as the level of office increases, especially at the presidential level (Ono and Burden 2019). Conroy (2015) shows that the presidency, arguably the highest level of political office in the United States, is framed through the news media as a distinctly masculine political institution that values candidates with masculine traits. Thus, the electoral context of the office at stake can affect the stereotypic associations voters form about it (Badas and Stauffer 2018; Cargile and Pringle 2019).

Masculine pressures may not be as strong in a lower level of office that is not as prominent, powerful, or prestigious. Voters may hold strongly feminine expectations for an "ideal officeholder" for some specific types of offices, such as a school board member. School board positions are unique because this is an office that directly speaks to multiple stereotypic strengths of women. School boards deal with a stereotypic women's issue, education, which is an issue that directly affects the well-being of children (Lay 2015). It is not clear if voters stereotype these offices as more feminine compared with other types of offices. More work is needed that identifies how voters stereotype different types of political offices to see if the stereotypic expectations voters hold shift depending on the level of office at stake and the types of duties and responsibilities officeholders have at that level.

GENDERED QUALIFICATIONS OUTSIDE POLITICS

It is not just in the voting booth that voters apply gendered standards in a way that advantages men and disadvantages women. Women often feel pressured to "look like men" but be "better than men" anytime they enter an institution traditionally dominated by men, including business, STEM fields, the law, higher education, and a host of professions and institutions where men are the dominant gender or hold the gatekeeping power. Improving the status of women in politics has the potential to dramatically alter the ability of women to gain access to these institutions. Research at the nexus of social psychology and business frequently finds that women face qualifications biases (Milkman, Akinola, and Chugh 2015). Business managers and recruiters tend to favor resumes from male job applicants even if that applicant has less experience than a female job applicant. One study found that for new college graduates, the performance of men in college mattered little for their ability to get a job interview, and that even men with low GPAs received job interviews. But women college graduates with high GPAs were not as likely to receive a job interview compared with low-performing men (Quadlan 2018). These are situations where individuals may use role-typicality standards rooted in masculine expectations about who looks like a good or an ideal employee. These biases affect how graduate admissions committees select applicants for doctoral programs, especially in fields such as physics, biology, chemistry, computer science, engineering, philosophy, mathematics, and most other fields where one might pursue a graduate degree. In short, the image of who belongs in public life is one steeped in masculinity.

The marginal status of women in politics mirrors the marginal status of women in the workplace and the lower socioeconomic status of women. Working women can lose anywhere from $700,000 to $2,000,000 in lifetime salary earnings due to pay inequity, time off for maternity leave, and the slow pace of promotion up the managerial career ladder (AAUW 2012). Similar to female candidates, working women feel pressure to balance conflicting roles as competent and effective employees and managers with being caring and nurturing women (Eagly and Carli 2007; Phelan, Moss-Rascusin, and Rudman 2008). Communality can hinder the success of women in the business sphere. Successful female business leaders often must overcome the perception that they are not tough enough or competent enough to lead a company (Eagly and Karau 2002), and this is reflected in the scarcity of women serving as CEOs and on the boards of directors of corporations. High-profile female politicians can break down barriers for women in business through a role-modeling effect that normalizes the image of women as leaders. The theory advanced in this book applies to any setting stereotyped by agentic norms with an absence of women. These settings include positions of corporate leadership in the business sector, the mass media, academia, and even sports organizations. Women entering these traditionally agentic roles will likely have their qualifications scrutinized, downgraded, and even dismissed. To be successful, women entering agentic roles will likely need to be *more* qualified than their male counterparts.

Another ramification of women's political underrepresentation is the connection between gender and socioeconomic status. Women are more likely to be single parents and/or the recipients of government assistance (Fukuda-Parr 1999). Some 40 percent of all households have a woman as the primary breadwinner.[4] The rapid expansion of income inequality across the United States disproportionately affects the livelihoods of women. Women are aware of how economic issues affect their personal lives and increase their political participation in politics during an economic crisis (Box-Steffensmeier, Boef, and Lin 2004). Increasing the number of women in office means that pertinent economic issues affecting women may have a higher priority on the legislative agenda (Holman 2013; Swers 2002). Female legislators advocate for women (Mansbridge 1999), making it all the more important to understand how women can rise to positions of political influence.

The use of gendered standards to evaluate the qualifications of women has broad implications for how we value, as a community, culture, and society, the accomplishments of women. Downgrading or qualifying the accomplishments of women as good "for a girl" diminishes the achievements of women. These debates about valuing the roles women play are evident in the broad social discussions taking place about women. For

---

[4] Samantha Cooney, "More Women Are Their Family's Sole Breadwinner Than Ever Before," *Time.com*, December 20, 2016, http://time.com/4607876/female-breadwinners-rise-report/.

example, sports reporters debate whether Serena Williams, who has won twenty-three tennis titles as of the completion of this book, is the greatest tennis player of all time or just the greatest *female* tennis player of all time. Arguments against Serena Williams as the greatest tennis player of all time include that women's tennis just is not as tough, fierce, or competitive as men's tennis. Debates about great male tennis players, such as Roger Federer or Rafael Nadal, rarely include the qualification about whether they are the greatest tennis players of all time or just the greatest *men's* tennis players of all time. Accomplishments of men do not need to be qualified based on their sex.

Another example of disqualifying or downplaying women's accomplishments comes from the pay disparities between the US men's national soccer team and the US women's national soccer team. The men's soccer team received higher pay for its players in 2018 even though the team failed to qualify for the World Cup. The women's national soccer team won its fourth World Cup in 2019, but each player earns $23,000 less compared with the men's team. Many argue that women's soccer is not as aggressive, tough, or competitive as men's soccer. There are also arguments that the women's soccer team does not bring in as much revenue as the men's team. Both claims are verifiably inaccurate. Discounting the accomplishments of the women's team, and of women who excel in their chosen vocations, perpetuates the belief that women must be continually outperform their male counterparts just to be taken seriously as viable contenders, whether it is in sports, business, or politics.

CONCLUSION

The women who win elections have better qualifications than male candidates. This is due, in part, to subtle biases from voters. Voters hold female candidates to higher standards than male candidates due to the subtle influence of gender stereotypes. When electoral outcomes appear positive for female candidates, it does not necessarily mean that gender was absent from voter decision-making. Rather, gender affects many aspects of how voters think about politics. The masculinity that defines political leadership creates a fundamental tension in democratic decision-making. The very qualities that voters think are characteristic of good candidates are not necessarily qualities that make good legislators, governors, or presidents. Placing more valuing on feminine traits and experiences is fundamental to reducing the biases voters bring to the ballot and to encouraging more women to run for political office. The implications of women's political underrepresentation extend to nearly all aspects of the social, political, and economic status of women overall. Electing more qualified women to political office can bring positive benefits to women and can improve the overall quality of representation and democracy.

Appendixes

Qualifications and support for Clinton and Trump

	Clinton vote support	Trump vote support
Candidate knowledge	0.839***	0.657***
	(0.049)	(0.039)
Democratic respondent	1.269***	−1.523***
	(0.096)	(0.148)
Republican respondent	−1.433***	0.949***
	(0.158)	(0.097)
Respondent ideology	0.000	0.005***
	(0.001)	(0.001)
Female respondent	0.048	−0.091
	(0.090)	(0.090)
Age	0.003	0.020***
	(0.003)	(0.003)
White respondents	−0.224**	0.829***
	(0.098)	(0.124)
Income	0.018***	0.020***
	(0.006)	(0.006)
College degree	0.760***	0.117
	(0.100)	(0.100)
Constant	−4.912***	−4.752***
	(0.257)	(0.240)
Observations	3,916	3,910
Pseudo R^2	0.338	0.320

Partisan interactions and knowledge		
	Clinton vote support	Trump vote support
Candidate knowledge	0.956***	0.854***
	(0.068)	(0.053)
Democratic respondent	2.315***	−1.470***
	(0.412)	(0.152)
Republican respondent	−1.415***	2.272***
	(0.159)	(0.243)
Democratic respondent × candidate knowledge	−0.254*** (0.097)	−
Republican respondent × candidate knowledge	−	−0.453*** (0.076)
Respondent ideology	0.000	0.005***
	(0.001)	(0.001)
Female respondent	0.049	−0.067
	(0.089)	(0.090)
Age	0.003	0.021***
	(0.003)	(0.003)
White respondents	−0.219**	0.823***
	(0.098)	(0.124)
Income	0.019***	0.019***
	(0.006)	(0.006)
College degree	0.759***	0.132
	(0.100)	(0.100)
Constant	−5.410***	−5.305***
	(0.329)	(0.265)
Observations	3,916	3,910
Pseudo R^2	0.339	0.328

Note: Standard errors in parentheses.
* $p < 0.10$, ** $p < 0.05$, *** $p < 0.01$.

Perceptions of presidential candidate knowledge on voter decision-making, over time		
	Democratic candidate vote support	Republican candidate vote support
Candidate knowledge	0.218	0.619***
	(0.293)	(0.047)
Democratic respondent	1.273***	−1.160***
	(0.159)	(0.123)

Perceptions of presidential candidate knowledge on voter decision-making, over time

	Democratic candidate vote support	Republican candidate vote support
Republican respondent	−1.387***	1.373***
	(0.172)	(0.148)
Respondent ideology	−0.270***	0.234**
	(0.065)	(0.115)
Female respondent	0.087*	0.071
	(0.046)	(0.058)
Age	0.013***	0.010***
	(0.001)	(0.002)
White respondents	−0.586***	0.943***
	(0.162)	(0.089)
Income	0.062***	0.003
	(0.019)	(0.007)
College degree	0.402***	0.358***
	(0.124)	(0.131)
Constant	−1.726**	−5.308***
	(0.714)	(0.532)
Observations	19,117	15,085
Pseudo R^2	0.269	0.348

Note: Model estimated with the errors clustered by election year, in parentheses.
* $p < 0.10$, ** $p < 0.05$, *** $p < 0.01$.

APPENDIX TO CHAPTER 3

Study sample characteristics

	Visualizing leaders study (MTurk)	Gendered qualifications (MTurk)
% female	56	53
Age (mean)	38 years	38 years
% white	79	80
% college degree	66	63
% live in South	42	30
% liberal	41	47
Average political interest (ranges from 1 [low] to 7 [high])	2.28	5.68

Visualizing Leaders Protocol: "We are interested in how people think about political leaders. We'd like you to find an image using a Google image search that fits your perception of a political leader. In the box below, provide the link to the image that best exemplifies your perception of a political leader."

Gendered Qualifications Experiment Design

Gendered qualifications	
Biography	N
Feminine biography	91
Masculine biography	91

Feminine Qualifications: McCann is running for a seat to Congress. As a state legislator, McCann served as the party leader, chaired the education committee, and developed a reputation for bringing compromise to the legislature. Prior to serving in the legislature, McCann worked tirelessly as an advocate for women and children, and volunteered for many community organizations, including the Parent Teacher Organization. McCann's family are longtime residents of the state. McCann graduated from a small liberal arts college. McCann, throughout the campaign, has pledged to bring a caring approach to politics.

Masculine Qualifications: McCann is running for a seat to Congress. At the law firm, McCann was a partner, worked with major business clients in the state, and developed a reputation for an aggressive approach in the courtroom. Prior to serving in the law firm, McCann worked tirelessly as an advocate for the state's business interests and worked with military veterans. McCann is a longtime resident of the state. McCann graduated from a top law school at the top of the class. McCann, throughout the campaign, has pledged to bring a tough approach to politics.

How qualified is McCann to serve in the Senate? Very Qualified, Somewhat Qualified, Somewhat Unqualified, Very Unqualified

How favorable or unfavorable do you feel toward McCann? 1 (Extremely Unfavorable) to 7 (Extremely Favorable)

Vote Choice Question: If there were an election today, how likely is it you would vote for this candidate? Very Likely, Somewhat Likely, Somewhat Unlikely, Very Unlikely

APPENDIX TO CHAPTER 4

List of female candidates and opponents, 2016 Senate campaign

Female candidate	Opponent	State
Lisa Murkowski (R)	Joe Miller (Libertarian)	Alaska
Ann Kirkpatrick (D)	John McCain (R)	Arizona
Kamala Harris (D)	–	California
Loretta Sanchez (D)	–	California
Tammy Duckworth (D)	Mark Kirk (R)	Illinois
Patty Judge (IA)	Chuck Grassley (R)	Iowa
Kathy Szeliga (R)	Chris Van Hollen (D)	Maryland
Catherine Cortez Masto (D)	Joe Heck (R)	Nevada
Kelly Ayotte (R)	–	New Hampshire
Maggie Hassan (D)	–	New Hampshire
Wendy Long (R)	Chuck Schumer (D)	New York
Katie McGinty (D)	Pat Toomey (R)	Pennsylvania
Misty Snow (D)	Mike Lee (R)	Utah
Patty Murray (D)	Chris Vance (R)	Washington

Descriptive statistics for variables used in website and news analyses

Variable	Measurement	Descriptive statistics
Candidate and race characteristics		
Female candidate	1 = female 0 = male	33% female candidates
Democratic candidate	1 = Democrat 0 = Republican or other	50% Democrats
Incumbent candidate	1 = incumbent 0 = challenger	35% incumbents
Race competitiveness	1 = competitive 0 = not competitive	42% of races competitive
Campaign funds	Logged value of the total dollar amount of money raised by candidate	Mean = 15.06 (SD = 3.51)
Front-runner status	1 = clear trailer 2 = no clear trailer or front-runner 3 = clear front-runner	31% clear trailer 38% no clear trailer or front-runner 29% front-runner
News article characteristics		
Female author	1 = female author 0 = not female or unclear author gender	23% female authors

(continued)

(*continued*)

Descriptive statistics for variables used in website and news analyses		
Variable	Measurement	Descriptive statistics
National outlet	1 = national news outlet 0 = other outlet	24% national news coverage
International outlet	1 = international news outlet 0 = other outlet	16% international news coverage
Statewide outlet	1 = statewide news outlet 0 = other outlet	24% state news coverage
Local outlet	1 = local news outlet 0 = other outlet	34% local news coverage

Qualifications on campaign websites based on female candidate characteristics				
Qualification metric	Democratic female (%)	Republican female (%)	Female incumbent (%)	Female challenger (%)
Political experience	77	100	100	77
Professional experience	92	100	100	92
Academic qualifications	85	67	100	77
Feminine qualifications	85	100	100	85
Qualification metric	Democratic male (%)	Republican male (%)	Male incumbent (%)	Male challenger (%)
Political experience	65	60	63	61
Professional experience	59	77	69	71
Academic qualifications	53	69	56	67
Feminine qualifications	82	79	81	80

The table above displays the percentage of female candidates based on partisanship and incumbency status who used one of the qualification strategies on their campaign websites. It is important to note that these data are merely descriptive, as there are only three Republican women who ran for the Senate in 2016 and only three female incumbents. Thirteen of the women who ran for a Senate seat in 2016 were Democrats. Despite these limitations, there are some noteworthy patterns. First, on female incumbents' campaign websites, each of the four qualification metrics was highlighted. The similarity in the messaging strategies of female incumbents is particularly noteworthy because these three incumbents were running in very different types of elections. The three female incumbents include Republican Lisa Murkowski of Alaska, Republican Kelly Ayotte of New Hampshire, and Democrat Patty Murray of Washington. Murkowski's race was not at all competitive, and the incumbent easily won reelection. But Murkowski took no chances in the election, being sure to mention all the ways that she is qualified to represent Alaska in the Senate. The other Republican female incumbent, Kelly Ayotte, ran in a very competitive Senate race against a Democratic female challenger. Indeed, she lost the election by only some 700 votes. The close contest in New Hampshire may have pressured Ayotte to behave more like a challenger who needs to provide voters with information. Patty Murray, like Murkowski, ran in a noncompetitive election, and Murray's twenty-five years in the Senate made it unlikely that voters were unfamiliar with her qualifications. Nevertheless, Murray still discussed every aspect of her qualifications through her Senate website. Incumbency does not appear to provide female candidates with much security.

Female challengers and female Democrats, many of whom overlap in these two categories, were much less consistent in how they highlighted qualifications on campaign websites. Democratic and challenging women were those least likely to talk about their previous political experience. Many of the Democratic female challengers had ample levels of political experience in other levels of political office such as serving as a state attorney general, member of a state legislature, governor, or member of Congress. These women are not necessarily selling their experience. Democratic female challengers were most likely to talk about their professional experiences, such as their roles as accountants, lawyers, or nonprofit advocates. These experiences are certainly important but may not matter as much as political experience in voter decision-making.

The bottom half of the table shows the patterns of qualification messages among male candidates based on incumbency and partisanship. Male candidates are, overall, less likely to highlight qualifications on campaign websites. There is much less uniformity in the messages put forth by male candidates. Not all male candidates talk about their political, professional, academic, or family backgrounds. Male candidates, regardless of incumbency or partisan status, were most likely to talk about their family backgrounds, a feminine characteristic. This is a particularly interesting finding because there is no expectation that male candidates should talk about their families. Indeed, voters do not associate male candidates with feminine experiences. Talking about feminine experiences, however, is not necessarily risky for male candidates because voters will still assume that a male candidate is prepared to serve in political office regardless of his family background.

Differences between female and male candidate self-promotion on websites, logit models

	Political experience	Professional experience	Academic credentials	Feminine qualifications
Female	0.873	2.687**	1.123	0.705
candidate	(1.092)	(1.215)	(0.955)	(1.202)
Democratic	0.067	−1.715**	−0.668	−0.153
candidate	(0.690)	(0.809)	(0.652)	(0.836)
Competitive	1.086*	−1.786**	0.678	1.534*
race	(0.608)	(0.816)	(0.849)	(0.849)
Open seat	0.772	−0.027	−0.591	0.534
	(1.118)	(0.848)	(1.061)	(1.120)
Incumbent	−1.207	−0.478	−0.802	−0.182
candidate	(0.890)	(0.814)	(0.673)	(0.975)
Female	0.325	−0.487	−0.043	−0.472
opponent	(1.053)	(0.864)	(0.679)	(0.900)
Campaign	0.471	0.590**	0.212	0.135
funds, logged	(0.314)	(0.295)	(0.141)	(0.150)
Front-runner	−0.609	1.385***	0.297	0.007
status	(0.573)	(0.391)	(0.381)	(0.677)
Constant	−5.639	−8.924*	−2.813	−0.724
	(5.726)	(4.578)	(2.372)	(3.095)
Observations	61	61	61	61
Pseudo R^2	0.259	0.218	0.095	0.110

Note: Standard errors in parentheses.
* $p < 0.10$, ** $p < 0.05$, *** $p < 0.01$.

Differences between female and male candidate qualification news coverage, logit models

	Political experience	Professional experience	Academic experience	Feminine qualifications
Female	−0.865***	0.029	−1.039**	0.955***
candidate	(0.272)	(0.555)	(0.500)	(0.319)
Democratic	0.594**	−0.822**	0.207	−0.184
candidate	(0.264)	(0.396)	(0.587)	(0.371)
Incumbent	0.677**	−1.641***	−1.736***	−0.368
candidate	(0.345)	(0.392)	(0.402)	(0.483)

	Political experience	Professional experience	Academic experience	Feminine qualifications
Competitive race	−0.046 (0.209)	−0.150 (0.443)	−1.591*** (0.369)	0.066 (0.255)
Open seat	0.039 (0.311)	−1.127** (0.518)	−0.632 (0.553)	0.519 (0.386)
Female author	−0.015 (0.087)	0.304** (0.151)	−0.335 (0.515)	−0.096 (0.207)
National news outlet	−0.108 (0.091)	−0.470*** (0.168)	14.482*** (0.685)	0.060 (0.200)
State news outlet	−0.254* (0.142)	−0.636** (0.282)	14.682*** (0.565)	0.200 (0.311)
Local news outlet	−0.060 (0.115)	−0.424* (0.246)	14.864*** (0.566)	0.032 (0.316)
Constant	−0.440 (0.426)	−0.617 (0.691)	−17.490*** (0.466)	−3.220*** (0.492)
Observations	6,409	6,409	6,409	6,409
Pseudo R^2	0.040	0.042	0.112	0.046

Note: Standard errors in parentheses.
* p < 0.10, ** p < 0.05, *** p < 0.01.

Are the Men Just More Qualified?

Female and male Senate candidate qualifications			
	Female candidates	Male candidates	p-value
Political experience			
Statewide elected office	31.25%	7.69%	0.1281
Nonincumbent member of Congress	18.75%	61.54%	0.0173
State legislature	43.75%	38.46%	0.7832
Local office	12.5%	15.38%	0.8303
Number of elected offices held	1.25 (0.25)	1.77 (0.28)	0.1781
Professional experience			
Political pipeline job	81.25%	76.92%	0.7843
Feminine job	25%	15.38%	0.5419
Masculine job	75%	84.62%	0.5419
Academic experience			
Bachelor's degree	93.75%	92.31%	0.8841
Graduate degree	75%	61.53%	0.4539
Ivy League degree	18.75%	15.38%	0.8195

APPENDIX TO CHAPTER 5

	Experimental sample characteristics	
	Gender-typicality experiment	Role-typicality experiment
Sample	MTurk	SSI
% female	62	58
Age (mean)	37 years	40 years
% white	78	72
% college degree	59	56
% live in South	35	25
% liberal	43	31
Average political interest (ranges from 1 [low] to 7 [high])	2.54	2.29

Experimental Stimuli: Gender-Typicality Experiment

Challenger: Carol/Chris Hartley is running for a seat to Congress after having served in the state legislature for a single term. As a state legislator, Hartley did not serve in any leadership positions but was a member of several committees, though she/he sponsored no bills that became law. Before serving in the state house, Hartley had a small law practice with several clients throughout the state. Carol/Chris Hartley attended the State University where she/he received both her/his bachelor's degree and her/his law degree.

Incumbent: Congresswoman/man Carol/Chris Hartley is running for reelection. Hartley just finished her/his first term in the House of Representatives. Hartley serves on several committees. During the last legislative term, Carol/Chris Hartley sponsored bills to bring federal dollars to the district to repair roads and build a new community center – but was ultimately not successful. Hartley sponsored no bills that successfully became law. Carol/Chris Hartley has a reputation of refusing to work across the partisan aisle to get things done.

Role-Typicality Experimental Design

Female and male candidate photos

Carol Hartley   Tom Larson

Male candidate photos

Chris Hartley   Tom Larson

Democratic/Republican candidates Carol/Chris Hartley and Tom Larson continued campaigning throughout the state as they seek the party's nomination for the open seat to the House of Representatives.

Carol/Chris Hartley just completed her/his first term in the state senate. Before serving in the senate, Carol/Chris worked in finance, and received her/his bachelor's degree from the State University.

Hartley's opponent is Tom Larson, who also has experience in the state senate. Larson is certainly a formidable opponent, and also held several major events and rallies throughout the state.

The two candidates are tied in the polls, and the race is expected to remain close right up until the day of the primary.

Role-typicality experimental design $N = 226$			
Candidate party	Female or male candidate	Opposing candidate	n
Democratic	Carol Hartley	Tom Larson	75
Democratic	Chris Hartley	Tom Larson	73
Republican	Carol Hartley	Tom Larson	40
Republican	Chris Hartley	Tom Larson	38

Note: Study conducted via SSI, November 2016. This experiment matched participants into conditions based on shared partisanship.

Experimental Pretests

Candidate Names and Photos Pretest: I pretested the male and female photos used in the studies with a separate sample of participants on Amazon's Mechanical Turk in September 2012, $N = 129$. Comparing the photos of Carol and Chris Hartley in the productivity and competitive context study showed no significant differences in the average ratings of the female or male candidate in terms of age ($p = 0.1460$), education ($p = 0.9886$), or attractiveness ($p = 0.3630$).

I also compared the photos of Carol Hartley and Tom Laron used in the competitive context study. There were no significant differences in the age ($p = 0.5976$), education ($p = 0.7024$), and attractiveness ratings ($p = 0.8709$). There were also no significant differences in comparisons of Chris Hartley and Tom Larson, used in the competitive context study, across age ($p = 0.6941$), education ($p = 0.8767$), or attractiveness ($p = 0.2618$).

Gender-Typicality Pretest: The gender-typicality stimulus was pretested with a sample recruited through Amazon's Mechanical Turk in March 2016 ($N = 185$). The stimulus did not mention whether a candidate was female or male or partisanship, and this choice is intentional.

The pretest asked participants to indicate whether the candidate was female or male, partisanship, and ideology of the candidate. Participants rated the candidate as equally likely to be Democrat (37 percent) or Republican (37 percent). Participants also rated the hypothetical candidate as being ideologically moderate. On the question of whether the candidate was female or male, 76 percent of participants thought the candidate was male. This is not unexpected, given that 80 percent of members of Congress are male, and merely confirms the masculine expectations voters hold for political candidates.

Role-Typicality Pretest: The role-typicality stimuli were pretested in June 2016 with an MTurk sample ($N = 223$). The pretest included all four conditions of the experiment: Democratic candidates with a woman running, Republican candidates with a woman running, Democratic candidates with two men, and Republican candidates with two men. The pretest asked participants to rate the perceived ideology of the candidates. Here, I compare the female versus male conditions within candidate party. On ideology, there were no significant differences between the female and male conditions in the Republican conditions ($p = 0.3314$). There are significant differences between the female and male Democratic conditions, with the female candidate rated as more liberal than the male candidate ($p < 0.001$). This difference is not surprising and is in line with extant scholarship showing that voters rate Democratic female candidates as more liberal than their male counterparts (Koch 2000, 2002; McDermott 1997, 1998).

Minimum Skills Pretest: The legislative skills measure used in both experiments asked participants to rate whether the candidate possessed a set of specific skills. These items come from a pretest. The pretest asked respondents recruited on MTurk (in November 2016, $N = 80$) to list the skills a "typical member of Congress" needs to be an effective legislator.

Full Question Wordings and Response Options

Gender-Typicality Questions

Which skills from the list below does Hartley have, based on the brief biography you read?

Organized, Hardworking, Able to Manage Multiple Priorities, Able to Build Consensus among Colleagues, Comprising, Organized, Determined, Public Speaking, Working Well with Others, Bipartisan, Has Firm Principles, Willing to Stand Ground, Shares Credit with Others

Has This Skill/Does Not Have This Skill

Role-Typicality Questions
Which candidate do you think has the best chance of winning the primary/general election? Carol/Chris Hartley, Tom Larson

APPENDIX TO CHAPTER 6

Experimental Sample Demographics

Sample demographics	
% female	62
% Democrats	43
% Republicans	22
% Independents	35
% white	74
Age	
18–24	15%
25–44	59%
45–64	18%
65+	5%

Partisan-typicality experimental design, $N = 223$			
Candidate party	Female or male candidate	Opposing candidate	n
Democratic	Carol Hartley	Tom Larson	63
Democratic	Chris Hartley	Tom Larson	58
Republican	Carol Hartley	Tom Larson	55
Republican	Chris Hartley	Tom Larson	47

Note: Study conducted via MTurk, summer 2015. This experiment matched participants into conditions based on shared partisanship.

In your opinion, which of the two candidates is more experienced? Is more knowledgeable?

Hartley is extremely more experienced/likely to provide leadership/more knowledgeable

Hartley is somewhat more experienced/likely to provide leadership/more knowledgeable

Larson is somewhat more experienced/likely to provide leadership/more knowledgeable

Larson is extremely more experienced/likely to provide leadership/more knowledgeable

Which candidate do you think has the best chance of winning the primary/general election? Carol/Chris Hartley, Tom Larson

APPENDIX TO CHAPTER 7

Experimental sample characteristics

	Information	Context	Self-promotion
% female	58.76	57.30	50.81
Age (mean)	38.55 years	39.73 years	36.61 years
% white	83.62	73.78	70.36
% college degree	61.36	54.3	66.4
% liberal	37.29	50.94	41.93
N	254	267	413

Information experiment, $N = 256$

Candidate party	Female or male candidate	Information	n
Democratic	Diane Bailey	Information	43
Democratic	Diane Bailey	No information	43
Republican	Diane Bailey	Information	23
Republican	Diane Bailey	No information	22
Democratic	David Bailey	Information	40
Democratic	David Bailey	No information	40
Republican	David Bailey	Information	23
Republican	David Bailey	No information	22

Note: Study conducted via MTurk, summer 2014. This experiment matched participants into conditions based on shared partisanship. The analyses in the book collapsed participants across the partisan conditions.

Information-in-context experiment, $N = 275$

Candidate party	Female or male candidate	Information	n
Democratic	Diane Bailey	Information	50
Democratic	Diane Bailey	Context	40
Republican	Diane Bailey	Information	25
Republican	Diane Bailey	Context	20
Democratic	David Bailey	Information	50
Democratic	David Bailey	Context	43
Republican	David Bailey	Information	25
Republican	David Bailey	Context	22

Note: Study conducted via MTurk, October 2018. This experiment matched participants into conditions based on shared partisanship. The analyses in the book collapsed participants across the partisan conditions.

Self-promotion experiment, $N = 413$			
Candidate party	Female or male candidate	Information	*n*
Democratic	Carol Hartley	Self-promotion	66
Democratic	Carol Hartley	No self-promotion	62
Republican	Carol Hartley	Self-promotion	39
Republican	Carol Hartley	No self-promotion	38
Democratic	Chris Hartley	Self-promotion	41
Democratic	Chris Hartley	No self-promotion	40
Republican	Chris Hartley	Self-promotion	66
Republican	Chris Hartley	No self-promotion	61

Note: Study conducted via MTurk, August 2018. This experiment matched participants into conditions based on shared partisanship. The analyses in the book collapsed participants across the partisan conditions.

Experiment Pretests

The information and information-in-context experiments used the names Diane and David Bailey for the hypothetical candidates running for reelection. These experiments did not use photos to prime whether the candidate was male or female, but just relied on the gendered names. I pretested the names to be sure that participants perceived no differences in the images evoked by the hypothetical names Diane and David Bailey in terms of age, education levels, region of the country where the candidate resides, and candidate race. Participants thought Diane and David were between forty-five and fifty-four years old ($p = 0.7564$) and completed a graduate degree ($p = 0.2040$). Participants were equally likely to think Diane and David came from New England, the South, Midwest, or the West Coast ($p = 0.2373$), and a majority of participants thought Diane and David were equally likely to be white ($p = 0.6236$).

Information Stimulus

Treatment: Congresswoman Diane (David) Bailey, a two-term Democrat (Republican) in the House, is running for re-election. This legislative session, Bailey sponsored 21 bills and co-sponsored 26 bills with colleagues – three of these bills were passed into law. Bailey also chaired a major committee and secured $50 million in federal funding for projects in her (his) district.

Control: Congresswoman (man) Diane (David) Bailey, a Democrat in the House is running for re-election.

Context Stimulus

Female Treatment: Congresswoman Diane Bailey, a two-term Democrat in the House, is running for re-election. This legislative session, Bailey sponsored 21 bills and co-sponsored 26 bills with colleagues – three of these bills were passed into law. Bailey also chaired a major committee and secured $50 million in federal funding for projects in her district.

Bailey ranks far ahead of her male colleagues in terms of productivity. Research shows that, on average, female lawmakers in the U.S. Congress have higher levels of productivity than male lawmakers. Female members of Congress, in both the House and the Senate, sponsor and co-sponsor more legislation than male members of Congress. Women in Congress pass, on average, three more pieces of legislation into law and bring home 9 percent more in federal dollars to their districts compared to their male counterparts.

Male Treatment: Congressman David Bailey, a two-term Republican in the House, is running for re-election. This legislative session, Bailey sponsored 21 bills and co-sponsored 26 bills with colleagues – three of these bills were passed into law. Bailey also chaired a major committee and secured $50 million in federal funding for projects in his district.

Bailey lags far behind his female colleagues in terms of productivity. Research shows that, on average, female lawmakers in the U.S. Congress have higher levels of productivity than male lawmakers. Female members of Congress, in both the House and the Senate, sponsor and co-sponsor more legislation than male members of Congress. Women in Congress pass, on average, three more pieces of legislation into law and bring home 9 percent more in federal dollars to their districts compared to their male counterparts.

Control: Congresswoman Diane (David) Bailey, a two-term Democrat (Republican) in the House, is running for re-election. This legislative session, Bailey sponsored 21 bills and co-sponsored 26 bills with colleagues – three of these bills were passed into law. Bailey also chaired a major committee and secured $50 million in federal funding for projects in her (his) district.

Self-Promotion Stimulus

Race for the Senate Continues
Self-Promotion: Democrat (Republican) Carol (Chris) Hartley gave a speech to supporters attending a Get Out the Vote rally in advance of

Election Day. Hartley used the rally to highlight past legislative accomplishments. Speaking to supporters, Hartley said:

I, alone, passed legislation to build a new community center, repair the roads in the state, and provide support for our veterans. I am single-handedly responsible for attracting new businesses and thousands of jobs in our state. Many of the bills I introduced became law because I secured the support of my colleagues. Through my determination, I single-handedly improved the lives of people in our state.

Hartley is currently a member of the U.S. House of Representatives. Hartley is running for re-election in what is expected to be a close race.

No Self-Promotion: Democrat (Republican) Carol (Chris) Hartley gave a speech to supporters attending a Get Out the Vote rally in advance of Election Day. Hartley is currently a member of the U.S. House of Representatives. Hartley is running for re-election in what is expected to be a close race.

Outcome Questions/Response Options

Using the scale below, how would you rate Bailey's level of effectiveness as a legislator where 1 means Bailey was not very effective at all and 7 means Bailey was highly effective?

How well do you think the adjectives below fit Bailey? Use the scale below where 1 means not well at all and 7 means extremely well.

Experience, Knowledgeable, Strong Leadership

References

Aaldering, Loes, and Daphne Joanna van der Pas. 2017. "Political Leadership in the Media: Gender Bias in Leader Stereotypes during Campaign and Routine Times." *British Journal of Political Science* forthcoming. doi: https://doi.org/10.1017/S0007123417000795.

AAUW. 2016. *Barriers and Bias: The Status of Women in Leadership*. Washington, DC: American Association of University Women.

Alexander, Deborah, and Kristi Anderson. 1993. "Gender as a Factor in the Attribution of Leadership Traits." *Political Research Quarterly* 46 (3):527–545.

Andersen, David J., and Tessa M. Ditonto. 2018. "Information and Its Presentation: Gender Cues in Low-Information vs. High-Information Experiments." *Political Analysis* 26 (4):379–398.

Anzia, Sarah F., and Christopher R. Berry. 2011. "The Jackie (and Jill) Robinson Effect: Why Do Congresswomen Outperform Congressmen?" *American Journal of Political Science* 55 (3):478–493.

Armstrong, Cory. L. 2004. "The Influence of Reporter Gender on Source Selection in Newspaper Stories." *Journalism and Mass Communication Quarterly* 81:139–154.

Badas, Alex, and Katelyn E. Stauffer. 2018. "Someone like Me: Descriptive Representation and Support for Supreme Court Nominees." *Political Research Quarterly* 71 (1):127–142.

2019. "Voting for Women in Nonpartisan and Partisan Elections." *Electoral Studies* 57:245–255.

Baird, Chardie L. 2008. "The Importance of Community Context for Young Women's Occupational Aspirations." *Sex Roles* 58 (3–4):208–221.

Banaszak, Lee Ann. 1996. *Why Movements Succeed or Fail: Opportunity, Culture, and the Struggle for Women's Suffrage*. Princeton, NJ: Princeton University Press.

Bargh, John A. 1989. "Conditional Automaticity: Varieties of Automatic Influence in Social Perception and Cognition." In *Unintended Thought*, edited by J. S. Uleman and J. A. Bargh, 3–51. New York: Guilford.

1994. "The Four Horsemen of Automacity: Awareness, Intention, Efficiency, and Control in Social Cogniton." In *Handbook of Social Cognition*, edited by R. S. Wyer Jr. and T. K. Skrull, 1–40. Hillsdale, NJ: Erlbaum.

Barnes, Tiffany D. 2016. *Gendering Legislative Behavior: Institutional Constraints and Collaboration*. New York: Cambridge University Press.

Barnes, Tiffany D., and Emily Beaulieu. 2014. "Gender Stereotypes and Corruption: How Candidates Affect Perceptions of Election Fraud." *Politics & Gender* 10:365–391.

Barnes, Tiffany D., Emily Beaulieu, and Gregory W. Saxton. 2017. "Restoring Trust in the Police: Why Female Officers Reduce Suspicions of Corruption." *Governance* 31:1–19.

Barnes, Tiffany D., Emily Beaulieu, and Gregory W. Saxton. forthcoming. "Sex and Corruption: How Sexism Shapes Voters' Responses to Scandal." *Politics, Groups, and Identities* 8:103–121.

Barnes, Tiffany D., Regina P. Branton, and Erin C. Cassese. 2017. "A Re-examination of Women's Electoral Success in Open Seat Elections: The Conditioning Effect of Electoral Competition." *Journal of Women, Politics & Policy* 38 (3):298–317.

Bauer, Nichole M. 2015a. "Emotional, Sensitive, and Unfit for Office: Gender Stereotype Activation and Support for Female Candidates." *Political Psychology* 36 (6):691–708. doi: 10.1111/pops.12186.

2015b. "Who Stereotypes Female Candidates? Identifying Individual Differences in Feminine Stereotype Reliance." *Politics, Groups, and Identities* 3 (1): 94–110. doi: https://doi.org/10.1080/21565503.2014.992794.

2017. "The Effects of Counter-Stereotypic Gender Strategies on Candidate Evaluations." *Political Psychology* 38 (2):279–295. doi: 10.1111/pops.12351.

2018. "Untangling the Relationship between Partisanship, Gender Stereotypes, and Support for Female Candidates." *Journal of Women, Politics & Policy* 39 (1): 1–25.

2019. "The Effects of Partisan Trespassing Strategies across Candidate Sex." *Political Behavior* 41(4): 897–915. doi: https://doi.org/10.1007/s11109-018-9475-3.

2020a. "Running Local: Gender Stereotyping and Female Candidates in Local Elections." *Urban Affairs Review* 56(1): 96–123.

2020b. "Shifting Standards: How Voters Evaluate the Qualifications of Female and Male Candidates." *Journal of Politics* 82(1): 1–12.

Bauer, Nichole M., Laurel Yong Harbridge, and Yanna Krupnikov. 2017. "Who Is Punished? Conditions Affecting Voter Evaluations of Legislators Who Do Not Compromise." *Political Behavior* 39 (2):379–400. doi: 10.1007/s11109-016-9356-6.

Baxter, Sandra, and Marjorie Lansing. 1983. *Women and Politics: The Visible Majority*. Ann Arbor: University of Michigan Press.

Bederman, G. 1995. *Manliness and Civilization: A Cultural History of Gender and Race in the United States, 1880–1917*. Chicago: University of Chicago Press.

Bejarano, Christina. 2013. *The Latina Advantage: Gender, Race, and Political Success*. Austin: University of Texas Press.

Bernhard, Rachel, and Sean Freeder. 2020. "The More You Know: Voter Heuristics and the Information Search." *Political Behavior* 42:603–623.

Berry, Marie, and Erica Chenoweth. 2018. "Who Made the Women's March?" In *The Resistance: The Dawn of the Anti-Trump Opposition Movement*, edited by David S. Meyer and Sidney Tarrow. Oxford: Oxford University Press.

Biernat, Monica, and Diane Kobrynowicz. 1997. "Gender- and Race-Based Standards of Competence: Lower Minimum Standards but Higher Ability Standards for Devalued Groups." *Journal of Personality & Social Psychology* 72 (3):554–557.

Biernat, Monica, and Melvin Manis. 1994. "Shifting Standards and Stereotype Based Judgments." *Journal of Personality and Social Psychology* 66 (1):5–20.

Bigler, Rebecca S., and Lynn S. Lieben. 2006. "A Developmental Intergroup Theory of Social Stereotypes and Prejudice." In *Advances in Child Development and Behavior*, edited by R. V. Vail, 39–89. San Diego, CA: Elsevier.

Biroli, Flavia. 2018. "Violence against Women and Reactions to Gender Equality in Politics." *Politics & Gender* 14 (4):681–685.

Bittner, Amanda, and Elizabeth Goodyear-Grant. 2017. "Sex Isn't Gender: Reforming Concepts and Measurements in the Study of Public Opinion." *Political Behavior* 39 (4):1019–1041. doi: 10.1007/s11109-017-9391-y.

Blackstone, William. 1765. *Commentaries on the Laws of England*, vol. 1. Oxford: Clarendon Press.

Blair, Irene V. 2002. "The Malleability of Automatic Stereotypes and Prejudice." *Journal of Personality and Social Psychology Review* 6 (3):242–261.

Blair, Irene V., and Mahzarin R. Banaji. 1996. "Automatic and Controlled Processes in Stereotype Priming." *Journal of Personality and Social Psychology* 70 (6):1142–1163.

Bligh, Michelle C., Michele M. Shlehofer, Bettina J. Casad, and Amber M. Gaffney. 2012. "Competent Enough, but Would You Vote for Her? Gender Stereotypes and Media Influences on Perceptions of Women Politicians." *Journal of Applied Social Psychology* 42 (3):560–597. doi: https://doi.org/10.1111/j.1559-1816.2011.00781.x.

Bond, Jon R., Richard Fleisher, and Jeffrey C. Talbert. 1997. "Partisan Differences in Candidate Quality in Open Seat House Races, 1976–1994." *Political Research Quarterly* 50 (2):281–299.

Bonneau, Chris W., and Kristin Kanthak. 2018. "Stronger Together: Political Ambition and the Presentation of Women Running for Office." *Politics, Groups, and Identities* forthcoming.

Bos, Angela L. 2011. "Out of Control: Delegates' Information Sources and Perceptions of Female Candidates." *Political Communication* 28 (1):87–109.

2015. "The Unintended Effects of Political Party Affirmative Action Politics on Female Candidate's Nomination Chances." *Politics, Groups, and Identities* 3 (1):73–93.

Bourque, Susan C., and Jean Grossholtz. 1974. "Politics as Unnatural Practice: Political Science Looks at Female Participation." *Politics & Society* 4.

Box-Steffensmeier, Janet M., Suzanna De Boef, and Tse-min Lin. 2004. "The Dynamics of the Partisan Gender Gap." *The American Political Science Review* 98 (3):515–528.

Boydstun, Amber E., and Peter Van Aelst. 2018. "New Rules for an Old Game? How the 2016 US Election Caught the Press off Guard." *Mass Communication and Society* 21 (6):671–696. doi: 10.1080/15205436.2018.1492727.

Bracic, Ana, Mackenzie Israel-Trummel, and Allyson Shortle. 2019. "Is Sexism for White People? Gender Stereotypes, Race, and the 2016 Presidential Election." *Political Behavior* 41 (2):281–307. doi: doi.org/10.1007/s1110.

Branton, Regina, Ashley English, Samantha Pettey, and Tiffany D. Barnes. 2018. "The Impact of Gender and Quality Opposition on the Relative Assessment of Candidate Competency." *Electoral Studies* 54:35–43. doi: 10.1016/j.electstud.2018.04.002.

Brescoll, Victoria L., and M. LaFrance. 2004. "The Correlates and Consequences of Newspaper Reports of Research on Sex Differences." *Psychological Science* 15:515–220.

Brooks, Deborah Jordan. 2013. *He Runs, She Runs*. Princeton, NJ: Princeton University Press.

Brown, Elizabeth R., Amanda B. Diekman, and Monica C. Schneider. 2011. "A Change Will Do Us Good: Threats Diminish Typical Preferences for Male Leaders." *Personality and Social Psychology Bulletin* 37 (7):930–941.

Brown, Nadia. 2014. *Sisters in the Statehouse: Black Women and Legislative Decision Making*. New York: Oxford University Press.

Bryant, Lisa A., and Julia Marin Hellwege. 2018. "Working Mothers Represent: How Children Affect the Legislative Agenda of Women in Congress." *American Politics Research* 47 (3):447–470.

Burden, Barry C., Yoshikuni Ono, and Masahiro Yamada. 2017. "Reassessing Public Support for a Female President." *Journal of Politics* 79 (3):1–7.

Burns, Nancy, Kay Lehman Schlozman, and Sidney Verba. 2004. *The Private Roots of Public Action: Gender, Equality, and Political Participation*. Cambridge, MA: Harvard University Press.

Burns, Sarah, Lindsay Eberhardt, and Jennifer L. Merolla. 2013. "What Is the Difference between a Hockey Mom and a Pit Bull? Presentations of Palin and Gender Stereotypes in the 2008 Presidential Election." *Political Research Quarterly* 66 (3):687–701.

Campbell, Angus, Philip E. Converse, Warren E. Miller, and Donald E. Stokes. 1960. *The American Voter*. New York: Wiley.

Campbell, D. T., N. A. Lewis, and W. A. Hunt. 1958. "Context Effects with Judgmental Language That Is Absolute, Extensive, and Extra-Experimentally Anchored." *Journal of Experimental Psychology* 55:220–228.

Campbell, David E., and Christina Wolbrecht. 2006. "See Jane Run: Women Politicians as Role Models for Adolescents." *Journal of Politics* 68 (2): 233–247.

    2019. "The Resistance as Role Model: Disillusionment and Protest among American Adolescents after 2016." *Political Behavior* forthcoming.

Cargile, Ivy A. M. 2016. "Latina Issues: An Analysis of the Policy Issue Competencies of Latina Candidates." In *Distinct Identities: Minority Women in U.S. Politics*, edited by Nadia E. Brown and Sarah A. Gershon, 134–150. New York: Routledge.

Cargile, Ivy A. M., and Lisa Pringle. 2019. "Context Not Candidate Sex: A Case Study of Female Vote Choice for Mayor." *Urban Affairs Review* forthcoming.

Carlin, Diana B., and Kelly L. Winfrey. 2009. "Have You Come a Long Way, Baby? Hillary Clinton, Sarah Palin, and Sexism in 2008 Campaign Coverage." *Communication Studies* 60 (4):326–343. doi: 10.1080/10510970903109904.

Carnes, Nicholas, and Meredith L. Sadin. 2014. "The 'Mill Worker's Son' Heuristic: How Voters Perceive Politicians from Working-Class Families – And How They Really Behave in Office." *Journal of Politics* 77 (1):285–298.

Carnes, Nicholas, and Noam Lupu. 2015. "What Good Is a College Degree? Education and Leader Quality Reconsidered." *Journal of Politics* 78 (1): 35–50.

Carroll, Susan J., and Kira Sanbonmatsu. 2013. *More Women Can Run: Gender and Pathways to the State Legislatures*. New York: Oxford University Press.

Carson, Jamie L., Erik J. Engstrom, and Jason M. Roberts. 2007. "Candidate Quality, the Personal Vote, and the Incumbency Advantage in Congress." *American Political Science Review* 101 (2):289–301.

Cassese, Erin C. 2019. "Intersectional Stereotyping in Political Decision Making." In *Oxford Research Encyclopedia of Political Decision Making*, edited by David Redlawsk, Oxford University Press https://oxfordre.com/politics/view/10.1093/acrefore/9780190228637.001.0001/acrefore-9780190228637-e-773.

Cassese, Erin C., and Mirya R. Holman. 2018. "Party and Gender Stereotypes in Campaign Attacks." *Political Behavior* 40 (3):785–807. doi: 10.1007/s11109-017-9423-7.

2019. "Playing the Woman Card: Ambivalent Sexism in the 2016 U.S. Presidential Race." *Political Psychology* 40 (1):55–74.

Cassese, Erin C., and Tiffany D. Barnes. 2019. "Reconciling Sexism and Women's Support for Republican Candidates: A Look at Gender, Class, and Whiteness in the 2012 and 2016 Presidential Races." *Political Behavior* 41 (4): 677–700.

Chamberlain, Hope. 1973. *A Minority of Members, Women in the U.S. Congress*. New York: New York American Library.

Chambers, David Wade. 1983. "Stereotypic Images of the Scientist: The Draw-a-Scientist Test." *Science Education* 67 (2):255–265.

Chang, Edward H., Katherine L. Milkman, Dena M. Gromet, Robert W. Rebele, Cade Massey, Angela L. Duckworth, and Adam M. Grant. 2019. "The Mixed Effects of Online Diversity Training." *PNAS* forthcoming.

Chisholm, Shirley. 1970. *Unbought and Unbossed*. New York: Houghton Mifflin.

Claassen, Ryan L., and John Barry Ryan. 2016. "Social Desirability, Hidden Biases, and Support for Hillary Clinton." *PS: Political Science and Politics* 49 (4):730–735.

Clayton, Amanda, Diana Z. O'Brien, and Jennifer Piscopo, M. 2019. "All Male Panels? Representation and Democratic Legitimacy." *American Journal of Political Science* 63 (1):113–129.

Coleman, J. M., and Y. Y. Hong. 2008. "Beyond Nature and Nurture: The Influence of Lay Gender Theories on Self-Stereotyping." *Self and Identity* 7:34–53.

Conroy, Meredith, 2015. *Masculinity, Media, and the American Presidency*. New York: Palgrave Macmillan.

Cook, Elizabeth Adell, and Clyde Wilcox. 1994. *The Year of the Woman: Myths and Realities*. Boulder: Westview Press.

Corder, J. Kevin, and Christina Wolbrecht. 2016. *Counting Women's Ballots Female Voters from Suffrage through the New Deal*. New York: Cambridge University Press.

Crowder-Meyer, Melody. 2013. "Gendered Recruitment without Trying: How Local Party Recruiters Affect Women's Representation." *Politics & Gender* 9:390–413.

Crowder-Meyer, Melody, and Rosalyn Cooperman. 2018. "Can't Buy Them Love: How Party Culture among Donors Contributes to the Party Gap in Women's Representation." *Journal of Politics* 80 (4):1211–1224. doi: 10.1086/698848.

Darr, Joshua P. 2016. "Presence to Press: How Campaigns Earn Local Media." *Political Communication* 33 (3):503–522. doi: 10.1080/10584609.2015.1107158.

Deason, Grace, Jill S. Greenlee, and Carrie A. Langer. 2015. "Mothers on the Campaign Trail: Implications of Politicized Motherhood on Women in Politics." *Politics, Groups, and Identities* 3 (1):133–148.

Deckman, Melissa. 2016. *Tea Party Women: Mama Grizzlies, Grassroots Leaders, and the Changing Face of the American Right*. New York: New York University Press.

Devine, Patricia G. 1989. "Stereotypes and Prejudice: Their Automatic and Controlled Components." *Journal of Personality and Social Psychology* 56 (1):5–18.

Dietrich, Bryce J., Matthew Hayes, and Diana Z. O'Brien. 2019. "Pitch Perfect: Vocal Pitch and the Emotional Intensity of Congressional Speech on Women." *American Political Science Review* 13 (4): 941–962.

Ditonto, Tessa M. 2017. "A High Bar or a Double Standard? Gender, Competence, and Information in Political Campaigns." *Political Behavior* 39 (2): 301–325. doi: 10.1007/s11109-016-9357-5.

Ditonto, Tessa M., and David J. Andersen. 2018. "Two's a Crowd: Women Candidates in Concurrent Elections." *Journal of Women, Politics & Policy* 39 (3):257–284.

Ditonto, Tessa M., Allison J. Hamilton, and David P. Redlawsk. 2014. "Gender Stereotypes, Information Search, and Voting Behavior in Political Campaigns." *Political Behavior* 36 (2):335–358.

Dittmar, Kelly. 2015. *Navigating Gendered Terrain: Stereotypes and Strategy in Political Campaigns*. Philadelphia: Temple University Press.

Dittmar, Kelly, Kira Sanbonmatsu, and Susan J. Carroll. 2018. *A Seat at the Table*. New York: Oxford University Press.

Doan, Alesha E., and Donald P. Haider-Markel. 2010. "The Role of Intersectional Stereotypes on Evaluations of Gay and Lesbian Political Candidates." *Politics & Gender* 6 (1): 63–91.

Dolan, Kathleen. 2014. *When Does Gender Matter? Women Candidates and Gender Stereotypes in American Elections*. New York: Oxford University Press.

Druckman, James N., Martin J. Kifer, and Michael Parkin. 2009. "Campaign Communications in U.S. Congressional Elections." *American Political Science Review* 103 (3):343–366. doi: 10.1017/S0003055409990037.

Ducat, S. 2004. *The Wimp Factor: Gender Gaps, Holy Wars, and the Politics of Anxious Masculinity*. Boston: Beacon Press.

Duerst-Lahti, Georgia. 2007. "Masculinity on the Campaign Trail." In *Rethinking Madam President: Are We Ready for a Woman in the White House?*, edited by Lori Cox Han and Caroline Heldman. Boulder, CO: Lynne Rienner Publishers, p. 87–112.

Dunaway, Johanna, Regina G. Lawrence, Melody Rose, and Christopher R. Weber. 2013. "Traits versus Issues: How Female Candidates Shape Coverage of Senate and Gubernatorial Races." *Political Research Quarterly* 66 (3): 715–726. doi: https://doi.org/10.1177/1065912913491464.

Eagly, Alice H. 1987. *Sex Differences in Social Behavior: A Social Role Interpretation*. Hillsdale, NJ: L. Erlbaum Associates.

Eagly, Alice H., and Linda L. Carli. 2003. "The Female Leadership Advantage: An Evaluation of the Evidence." *The Leadership Quarterly* 14:807–834.

  2007. *Through the Labyrinth: The Truth about How Women Become Leaders*. Cambridge, MA: Harvard Business School Press.

Eagly, Alice H., and Steve J. Karau. 2002. "Role Congruity Theory of Prejudice toward Female Leaders." *Psychological Review* 109 (3):573–594. doi: 10.1037//0033-295X.109.3.573.

Ekstrand, Laurie E., and William A. Eckert. 1981. "The Impact of Candidate's Sex on Voter Choice." *The Western Political Quarterly* 34 (1):78–87.

Evans, Sara. 1979. *Personal Politics: The Roots of Women's Liberation in the Civil Rights Movement and the New Left*. New York: Random House.

Fenno, Richard F., Jr. 1978. *Home Style: House Members in Their Districts*. Boston: Little, Brown.

Fiske, Susan T., and Steven L. Neuberg. 1990. "A Continuum of Impression Formation, from Category-Based to Individuating Processes: Influences of Information and Motivation on Attention and Interpretation." In *Advances in Experimental Social Psychology*, edited by M. P. Zanna, 1–69. New York: Academic Press.

Fitzpatrick, Ellen. 2016. "The Unfavored Daughter: When Margaret Chase Smith Ran in the New Hampshire Primary." *The New Yorker*, February 6.

Folke, Olle, and Johanna Rickne. 2016. "The Glass Ceiling in Politics: Formalization and Empirical Tests." *Comparative Political Studies* 49 (5): 567–599.

Foschi, Martha. 1992. "Gender and Double Standards for Competence." In *Gender, Interaction, and Inequality*, edited by Cecilia L. Ridgeway. New York: Springer-Verlag, p. 181–207.

Fox, Richard L., and Jennifer L. Lawless. 2014a. "Reconciling Family Roles with Political Ambition: The New Normal for Women in Twenty-First Century U.S. Politics." *Journal of Politics* 76 (2):398–414.

  2014b. "Uncovering the Origins of the Gender Gap in Political Ambition." *American Political Science Review* 108 (3):499–519.

Freeman, J. 1975. *The Politics of Women's Liberation: A Case Study of an Emerging Social Movement and Its Relation to the Policy Process.* New York: D. McKay.

Fridkin, Kim L., and Patrick J. Kenney. 2009. "The Role of Gender Stereotypes in U.S. Senate Campaigns." *Politics & Gender* 5:301–329. doi: https://doi.org/10.1017/S1743923X09990158.

2014. "How the Gender of U.S. Senators Influences People's Understanding of Politics." *The Journal of Politics* 76 (4):1017–1031.

2015. *The Changing Face of Representation: The Gender of U.S. Senators and Constituent Communications.* Ann Arbor: University of Michigan Press.

Fukuda-Parr, Sakiko. 1999. "What Does Feminization of Poverty Mean? It Isn't Just Lack of Income." *Feminist Economics* 5 (2):99–103.

Fulton, Sarah A. 2012. "Running Backwards and in High Heels: The Gendered Quality Gap and Incumbent Electoral Success." *Political Research Quarterly* 65 (2):303–314.

2014. "When Gender Matters: Macro-dynamics and Micro-mechanisms." *Political Behavior* 36:605–630.

Fulton, Sarah A., Cherie D. Maestas, L. Sandy Maisel, and Walter J. Stone. 2006. "The Sense of a Woman: Gender, Ambition, and the Decision to Run for Congress." *Political Research Quarterly* 59 (2):235–248.

Funk, Carolyn L. 1999. "Bringing the Candidate into Models of Candidate Evaluation." *Journal of Politics* 61 (3):700–720.

Gehlen, Frieda L. 1977a. "Women Members of Congress: A Distinctive Role." In *A Portrait of Marginality: The Political Behavior of the American Woman,* edited by Marianne Githens and Jewel L. Prestage. New York: McKay, p. 304–319.

1977b. "Legislative Role Performance of Female Legislators." *Sex Roles* 3 (1):1–19.

Gershon, Sarah Allen. 2008. "Communicating Female and Minority Interests Online: A Study of Web Site Issue Discussion among Female, Latino, and African American Members of Congress." *The International Journal of Press/Politics* 13 (2):120–140.

2012a. "Press Secretaries, Journalists, and Editors: Shaping Local Congressional News Coverage." *Political Communication* 29 (2):160–183.

2012b. "When Race, Gender, and the Media Intersect: Campaign News Coverage of Minority Congresswomen." *Journal of Women, Politics & Policy* 33 (2):105–125.

2013. "Media Coverage of Minority Congresswomen and Voter Evaluations: Evidence from an Online Experiment." *Political Research Quarterly* 66 (3): 702–714.

Gertzog, Irwin. 1984. *Congressional Women: Their Recruitment, Treatment, and Behavior.* New York: Praeger.

Gilens, Martin. 1988. "Gender and Support for Reagan: A Comprehensive Model of Presidential Approval." *American Journal of Political Science* 32 (1): 19–49.

Glick, Peter, Maria Lameiras, Susan T. Fiske, Thomas Eckes, Barbara Masser, Chiara Volpato, Robin Wells, et al. 2004. "Bad but Bold: Ambivalent

Attitudes toward Men Predict Gender Inequity in 16 Nations." *Journal of Personality and Social Psychology* 86:713–728.

Golebiowska, Ewa A. 2003. "When to Tell?: Disclosure of Concealable Group Membership, Stereotypes, and Political Evaluation." *Political Behavior* 25 (4):313–337.

Greenlee, Jill S. 2014. *The Political Consequences of Motherhood*. Ann Arbor: University of Michigan Press.

Greenlee, Jill S., Tatishe M. Nteta, Jesse H. Rhodes, and Elizabeth A. Sharrow. 2018. "Helping to Break the Glass Ceiling? Fathers, First Daughters, and Presidential Vote Choice in 2016." *Political Behavior* forthcoming.

Groeling, Tim. 2010. *When Politicians Attack: Party Cohesion in the Media*. New York: Cambridge University Press.

Guttmann, A., and D. Thompson. 2012. *The Spirit of Compromise: Why Governing Demands It and Campaigning Undermines It*. Princeton, NJ: Princeton University Press.

Haider-Markel, Donald P., Patrick Miller, Andrew Flores, Daniel C. Lewis, Barry Tadlock, and Jami Taylor. 2017. "Bringing 'T' to the Table: Understanding Individual Support of Transgender Candidates for Public Office." *Politics, Groups, and Identities* 5 (3):399–417.

Hawkesworth, Mary. 2003. "Congressional Enactments of Race–Gender: Toward a Theory of Raced–Gendered Institutions." *American Political Science Review* 97 (4):529–550.

Hayes, Danny. 2005. "Candidate Qualities through a Partisan Lens: A Theory of Trait Ownership." *American Journal of Political Science* 49 (4):908–923. doi: https://doi.org/10.1111/j.1540-5907.2005.00163.x

2010. "Agenda Convergence and the Paradox of Competitiveness in Political Campaigns." *Political Research Quarterly* 63 (3):594–611.

2011. "When Gender and Party Collide: Stereotyping in Candidate Trait Attribution." *Politics & Gender* 7 (2):133–165. doi: 10.1017/S1743923X11000055.

Hayes, Danny, and Jennifer L. Lawless. 2016. *Women on the Run: Gender, Media, and Political Campaigns in a Polarized Era*. New York: Cambridge University Press.

Heilman, Madeline E., and Tyler G. Okimoto. 2007. "Why Are Women Penalized for Success at Male Tasks?: The Implied Communality Deficit." *Journal of Applied Psychology* 91 (1):81–92.

Heilman, Madeline E., Caryn J. Block, and Richard F. Martell. 1995. "Sex Stereotypes: Do They Influence Perceptions of Managers?" *Journal of Social Behavior and Personality* 10 (4):237–252.

Heldman, Caroline J., Susan J. Carroll, and Stephanie Olson. 2005. "'She Brought Only a Skirt': Print Media Coverage of Elizabeth Dole's Bid for the Republican Presidential Nomination." *Political Communication* 22:315–335. doi: https://doi.org/10.1080/10584600591006564.

Hennings, Valerie M., and R. Urbatsch. 2015. "There Can Be Only One (Woman on the Ticket): Gender in Candidate Nominations." *Political Behavior* 37 (3):749–766.

Herrick, Rebekah. 2016. "Gender Themes in State Legislative Candidates' Websites." *The Social Science Journal* 53:282–290.

Heyman, Gail D., and Jessica W. Giles. 2006. "Gender and Psychological Essentialism." *Enfrance* 58 (3):293–310.

Hibbing, John R., and Elizabeth Theiss-Morse. 2002. *Stealth Democracy*. New York: Cambridge University Press.

Holman, Mirya R. 2013. "Sex and the City: Female Leaders and Spending on Social Welfare Programs in U.S. Municipalities." *Journal of Urban Affairs* 36 (4):701–715.

Holman, Mirya R., and Monica C. Schneider. 2018. "Gender, Race, and Political Ambition: How Intersectionality and Frames Influence Interest in Political Office." *Politics, Groups, and Identities* 6 (2):264–280.

Holman, Mirya R., Jennifer Merolla, and Elizabeth J. Zechmeister. 2011. "Sex, Stereotypes, and Security: An Experimental Study of the Effect of Crises on Assessments of Gender and Leadership." *Journal of Women, Politics & Policy* 32 (3):173–192.

2016. "Terrorist Threat, Male Stereotypes, and Candidate Evaluations." *Political Research Quarterly* 69 (1):134–147. doi: https://doi.org/10.1177/1065912915624018.

2017. "Can Experience Overcome Stereotypes in Times of Terror Threat?" *Research and Politics* January–March 4:1–7.

Homola, Jonathan. 2019. "Are Parties Equally Responsive to Women and Men?" *British Journal of Political Science* 49 (3):957–975.

Huddy, Leonie, and Nayda Terkildsen. 1993. "Gender Stereotypes and the Perception of Male and Female Candidates." *American Journal of Political Science* 37 (1):119–147.

Jane, E. A. 2014a. "'Back to the kitchen, cunt': Speaking the Unspeakable about Online Misogyny." *Continuum* 28:558–570.

2014b. "Your a ugly, whorish slut." *Feminist Media Studies* 14:531–546.

Jennings, M. Kent, and Barbara G. Farah. 1981. "Social Roles and Political Resources: An Over-Time Study of Men and Women in Party Elites." *American Journal of Political Science* 25 (3):462–482.

Jerit, Jennifer, and Jason Barabas. 2017. "Revisiting the Gender Gap in Political Knowledge." *Political Behavior* 39 (4):817–838. doi: 10.1007/s11109-016-9380-6.

Jones, Phillip Edward, and Paul R. Brewer. 2019. "Gender Identity as a Political Cue: Voter Responses to Transgender Candidates." *Journal of Politics* 81 (2):697–701.

Jones, Phillip Edward, Paul R. Brewer, Dannagal Young, Jennifer L. Lambe, and Lindsay H. Hoffman. 2018. "Explaining Public Opinion toward Transgender People, Rights, and Candidates." *Public Opinion Quarterly* 82 (2):252–278.

Junn, Jane. 2017. "The Trump Majority: White Womanhood and the Making of Female Voters in the U.S." *Politics, Groups, and Identities* 5 (2):343–352.

Kahn, Kim Fridkin. 1992. "Does Being Male Help? An Investigation of the Effects of Candidate Gender and Campaign Coverage on Evaluations of US Senate Candidates." *The Journal of Politics* 54 (2):497–517.

1994. "Does Gender Make a Difference? An Experimental Examination of Sex Stereotypes and Press Patterns in Statewide Campaigns." *American Journal of Political Science* 38 (1):162–195. doi: DOI: 10.2307/2111340.

Kahn, Kim Fridkin, and Edie N. Goldenberg. 1991. "Women Candidates in the News: An Examination of Gender Differences in U.S. Senate Campaign Coverage." *The Public Opinion Quarterly* 55 (2):180–199.

Kanthak, Kristin, and Jonathon Woon. 2015. "Women Don't Run: Election Aversion and Candidate Entry." *American Journal of Political Science* 59 (3):595–612.

Karpowitz, Christopher, Quin Monson, and Jessica Preece. 2017. "How to Elect More Women: Gender and Candidate Success in a Field Experiment." *American Journal of Political Science* 61 (4):927–943.

Kaufmann, Karen M. 2002. "Culture Wars, Secular Realignment, and the Gender Gap in Party Identification." *Political Behavior* 24 (3):283–307.

Kerber, Linda K. 1980. *Women of the Republic*. Chapel Hill: University of North Carolina Press.

Kim, Jeong. 2019. "Direct Democracy and Women's Political Engagement." *American Journal of Political Science* 63 (3): 594–610.

Klar, Samara, and Yanna Krupnikov. 2016. *Independent Politics: How American Disdain for Parties Leads to Political Inaction*. New York: Cambridge University Press.

Klar, Samara, Heather Madonia, and Monica C. Schneider. 2014. "The Influence of Threatening Parental Primes on Mothers' versus Fathers' Policy Preferences." *Politics, Groups, and Identities* 2 (4):607–623.

Koch, Jeffrey W. 2000. "Do Citizens Apply Gender Stereotypes to Infer Candidates' Ideological Orientations?" *The Journal of Politics* 62 (2):414–429.

2002. "Gender Stereotypes and Citizens' Impressions of House Candidates' Ideological Orientations." *American Journal of Political Science* 46 (2): 453–462.

Koenig, Anne M., Alice H. Eagly, Abigail A. Mitchell, and Tiina Ristikari. 2011. "Are Leader Stereotypes Masculine? A Meta-Analysis of Three Research Paradigms." *Psychological Bulletin* 137 (4):616–642.

Krupnikov, Yanna, and John Barry Ryan. 2017. "Choice vs. Action: Candidate Ambiguity and Voter Decision Making 501." *Quarterly Journal of Political Science* 12 (4):479–505.

Krupnikov, Yanna, and Nichole M. Bauer. 2014. "The Relationship between Campaign Negativity, Gender and Campaign Context." *Political Behavior* 36 (1):167–188.

Krupnikov, Yanna, Kerri Milita, John Barry Ryan, and Elizabeth C. Connors. 2019. "How Gender Affects the Efficacy of Discussion as an Information Shortcut." *Political Science Research Methods* forthcoming.

Krupnikov, Yanna, Spencer Piston, and Nichole M. Bauer. 2016. "Saving Face: Identifying Voter Responses to Black and Female Candidates." *Political Psychology* 37 (2):253–273. doi: 10.1111/pops.12261.

Kunda, Ziva, Lisa Sinclair, and Dale Griffin. 1997. "Equal Ratings but Separate Meanings: Stereotypes and the Construal of Traits." *Journal of Personality and Social Psychology* 72 (4):720–734.

Kuperberg, Rebecca. 2018. "Intersectional Violence against Women in Politics." *Politics & Gender* 14 (4):685–690.

Ladam, Christina, Jeffrey J. Harden, and Jason H. Windett. 2018. "Prominent Role Models: High-Profile Female Politicians and the Emergence of Women as Candidates for Public Office." *American Journal of Political Science* 62 (2):369–381.

Lane, Robert. 1965. *Political Life*. New York: Free Press.

Lawless, Jennifer L. 2012. *Becoming a Candidate: Political Ambition and the Decision to Run for Office*. New York: Cambridge University Press.

Lawless, Jennifer L., and Kathryn Pearson. 2008. "The Primary Reason for Women's Underrepresentation? Reevaluating Conventional Wisdom." *Journal of Politics* 70 (1):67–82.

Lawless, Jennifer L., and Richard L. Fox. 2010. *It Still Takes a Candidate: Why Women Don't Run for Office*. New York: Cambridge University Press.

Lawrence, Regina G., and Melody Rose. 2010. *Hillary Clinton's Race for the White House: Gender Politics and the Media on the Campaign Trail*. Boulder, CO: Lynne Rienner Publishers.

2011. "Bringing out the Hook: Exit Talk in Media Coverage of Hillary Clinton and Past Presidential Campaigns." *Political Research Quarterly* 64 (4):870–883.

Lay, J. Celeste. 2015. "The Salience of Schools and Safety: Explaining Mayoral Voting among Women in Cities." In *Minority Voting in the United States*, edited by Kyle L. Krieder and Thomas J. Baldino, 168–189. Santa Barbara, CA: Praeger/ABC-Clio.

Lazarus, Jeffrey, and Amy Steigerwalt. 2018. *Gendered Vulnerability: How Women Work Harder to Stay in Office*. Ann Arbor: University of Michigan Press.

Levanon, Asaf, Paula England, and Paul Allison. 2009. "Occupational Feminization and Pay: Assessing Causal Dynamics using 1950–2000 U.S. Census Data." *Social Forces* 88 (2):865–891.

Lizotte, Mary-Kate, and Andrew H. Sideman. 2009. "Explaining the Gender Gap in Political Knowledge." *Politics & Gender*:127–151.

Lizotte, Mary-Kate, and Heather J. Meggers-Wright. 2019. "Negative Effects of Calling Attention to Female Political Candidates' Attractiveness." *Journal of Political Marketing* 18 (3): 240–266.

Lowande, Kenneth, Melinda Ritchie, and Erinn Lauterbach. 2019. "Descriptive and Substantive Representation in Congress: Evidence from 80,000 Congressional Inquiries." *American Journal of Political Science* 63 (3): 644–659.

MacKinnon, Catherine. 1979. *Sexual Harassment of Working Women: A Case of Sex Discrimination*. New Haven, CT: Yale University Press.

Maestas, Cherie D., and Cynthia R. Rugeley. 2008. "Assessing the 'Experience Bonus' through Examining Strategic Entry, Candidate Quality, and Campaign Receipts in U.S. House Elections." *American Journal of Political Science* 52 (3):520–535.

Maestas, Cherie D., Sarah A. Fulton, L. Sandy Maisel, and Walter J. Stone. 2006. "When to Risk It? Institutions, Ambition, and the Decision to Run for the U.S. House." *American Political Science Review* 199 (2):195–208.

Mahoney, Anna Mitchell. 2018. *Women Take Their Place in State Legislatures: The Creation of Women's Caucuses*. Philadelphia: Temple University Press.

Manne, Kate A. 2018. *Down Girl: The Logic of Misogyny* New York: Oxford University Press.

Mansbridge, Jane. 1985. "Myth and Reality: The ERA and the Gender Gap in the 1980 Election." *Public Opinion Quarterly* 49 (2):164–178.

1986. *Why We Lost the ERA*. Chicago: University of Chicago Press.

1999. "Should Blacks Represent Blacks and Women Represent Women? A Contingent 'Yes.'" *The Journal of Politics* 61 (3):628–657.

Mayhew, David R. 1974. *Congress: The Electoral Connection*. New Haven, CT: Yale University Press.

McCammon, Holly J., and Karen E. Campbell. 2001. "Winning the Vote in the West: The Political Successes of the Women's Suffrage Movements." *American Sociological Review* 66 (1):49–70.

McConnaughy, Corrine 2013. *The Woman Suffrage Movement in America: A Reassessment*. New York: Cambridge University Press.

McDermott, Monika L. 1997. "Voting Cues in Low-Information Elections: Candidate Gender as a Social Information Variable in Contemporary United States Elections." *American Journal of Political Science* 41 (1):270–283.

1998. "Race and Gender Cues in Low-Information Elections." *Political Research Quarterly* 51 (4):895–918.

2016. *Masculinity, Femininity, and American Political Behavior*. New York: Oxford University Press.

Milita, Kerri, Elizabeth N. Simas, John Barry Ryan, and Yanna Krupnikov. 2017. "The Effects of Ambiguous Rhetoric in Congressional Elections." *Electoral Studies* 46: 48–63. doi: 10.1016/j.electstud.2017.01.004.

Milkman, K. L., M. Akinola, and D. Chugh. 2015. "What Happens Before? A Field Experiment Exploring How Pay and Representation Differentially Shape Bias on the Pathway into Organizations." *Journal of Applied Psychology* 100 (6):1678–1712.

Miller, Arthur H., Martin P. Wattenberg, and Oksana Malanchuk. 1986. "Schematic Assessments of Presidential Candidates." *American Political Science Review* 80 (2):521–540.

Miller, Melissa K., and Jeffrey S. Peake. 2013. "Press Effects, Public Opinion, and Gender: Coverage of Sarah Palin's Vice Presidential Campaign." *International Journal of Press/Politics* 18:482–507.

Milyo, Jeffrey, and Samantha Schlosberg. 2000. "Gender Bias and Selection Bias in House Elections." *Public Choice* 105 (1–2):41–59.

Mo, Hyunjung Cecilia. 2015. "The Consequences of Explicit and Implicit Gender Attitudes and Candidate Quality in the Calculations of Voters." *Political Behavior* 37 (2):357–395.

Moss-Rascusin, Corinne A., Julie E. Phelan, and Laurie A. Rudman. 2010. "When Men Break the Gender Rules: Status Incongruity and Backlash against Modest Men." *Psychology of Men and Masculinity* 11 (2):140–151.

Nugent, Mary K. 2019. "When Does He Speak for She? Men Representing Women in Parliaments." PhD dissertation, Rutgers University.

Oliver, Sarah, and Meredith Conroy. 2017. "Tough Enough for the Job? How Masculinity Predicts Recruitment of City Council Members." *American Politics Research* 46 (6):1094–1122.

Ondercin, Heather L. 2016. "To Run or Not to Run: How the Likelihood of Winning Influences the Decisions of Female Candidates." Paper presented at the Midwest Political Science Association Annual Meeting, Chicago, IL.

    2017. "Who Is Responsible for the Gender Gap? The Dynamics of Men's and Women's Democratic Macropartisanship, 1950–2012." *Political Research Quarterly* 70 (4):749–761.

Ondercin, Heather L., and Daniel Jones-White. 2011. "Gender Jeopardy: What Is the Impact of Gender Differences in Political Knowledge on Political Participation?" *Social Science Quarterly* 92 (3):675–694.

Ono, Yoshikuni, and Barry C. Burden. 2019. "The Contingent Effects of Candidate Sex on Voter Choice." *Political Behavior* 41 (3):583–607.

Osborn, Tracy. 2012. *How Women Represent Women: Political Parties, Gender, and Representation in the State Legislatures.* New York: Oxford University Press.

Palmer, Barbara, and Dennis M. Simon. 2001. "The Political Glass Ceiling: Gender, Strategy, and Incumbency in U.S. House Elections, 1978–1998." *Women & Politics* 23 (1–2):59–78.

    2005. "When Women Run against Women: The Hidden Influence of Female Incumbents in Elections to the US House of Representatives." *Politics & Gender* 1:35.

Pearson, Kathryn, and Eric McGhee. 2013. "What It Takes to Win: Questioning 'Gender Neutral' Outcomes in U.S. House Elections." *Politics & Gender* 9:439–462.

Pearson, Kathryn, and Logan Dancey. 2011. "Speaking for the Underrepresented in the House of Representatives: Voicing Women's Interests in a Partisan Era." *Politics & Gender* 7:493–519.

Petrocik, John R. 1996. "Issue Ownership in Presidential Elections, with a 1980 Case Study." *American Journal of Political Science* 40 (3):825–850. doi: 10.2307/2111797.

Phelan, Julie E., Corinne A. Moss-Rascusin, and Laurie A. Rudman. 2008. "Competent yet out in the Cold: Shifting Criteria for Hiring Reflect Backlash toward Agentic Women." *Psychology of Women Quarterly* 32:406–413. doi: https://doi.org/10.1111/j.1471-6402.2008.00454.x.

Piston, Spencer, Yanna Krupnikov, John Barry Ryan, and Kerri Milita. 2018. "Clear as Black and White: The Effects of Ambiguous Rhetoric Depend on Candidate Race." *Journal of Politics* 82 (2):662–674.

Pitkin, Hannah. 1967. *The Concept of Representation.* Berkeley: University of California Press.

Plutzer, Eric, and John F. Zipp. 1996. "Identity Politics and Voting for Women Candidates." *The Public Opinion Quarterly* 60 (1):30–57.

Postman, L., and G. A. Miller. 1945. "Anchoring of Temporal Judgments." *American Journal of Psychology* 58:43–53.

Prentice, Deborah A., and Erica Carranza. 2002. "What Women and Men Should Be, Shouldn't Be, Are Allowed to Be, and Don't Have to Be: The Contents of

Prescriptive Gender Stereotypes." *Psychology of Women Quarterly* 26 (4): 269–291. doi: 10.1111/1471-6402.t01-1-00066.

Quadlan, Natasha. 2018. "The Mark of a Woman's Record: Gender and Academic Performance in Hiring." *American Sociological Review* 83 (2): 331–360.

Rahn, Wendy M. 1993. "The Role of Partisan Stereotypes in Information Processing about Political Candidates." *American Journal of Political Science* 37 (2):472–496.

Rheault, Ludovic, Erica Rayment, and Andreea Musulan. 2019. "Politicians in the Line of Fire: Incivility and the Treatment of Women on Social Media." *Research & Politics*:1–7.

Ridout, Travis N., Erika Franklin Fowler, and Kathleen Searles. 2012. "Exploring the Validity of Electronic Newspaper Databases." *International Journal of Social Research Methodology* 15 (6):451–466. doi: 10.1080/13645579.2011.638221.

Roberts, S. O., A. K. Ho, M. Rhodes, and S. A. Gelman. 2017. "Making Boundaries Great Again: Essentialism and Support for Boundary Enhancing Initiatives." *Personality and Psychological Bulletin* 43:1643–1658.

Rudman, Laurie A. 1998. "Self-Promotion as a Risk Factor for Women: The Costs and Benefits of Counter-Stereotypic Impression Management." *Journal of Personality and Social Psychology* 74:629–645.

Sadker, David, and Karen R. Zittleman. 2009. *Still Failing at Fairness: How Gender Bias Cheats Girls and Boys in School.* New York: Scribner.

Sadker, Myra, and David Sadker. 1986. "Sexism in the Classroom: From Grade School to Graduate School." *The Phi Delta Kappan* 67 (7):512–515.

Sanbonmatsu, Kira. 2002a. "Gender Stereotypes and Vote Choice." *American Journal of Political Science* 46 (1):20–34.

2002b. "Political Parties and the Recruitment of Women to State Legislatures." *The Journal of Politics* 64 (3):791–809.

2006. *Where Women Run: Gender and Party in the American States.* Ann Arbor: University of Michigan Press.

Sanbonmatsu, Kira, and Kathleen Dolan. 2009. "Do Gender Stereotypes Transcend Party?" *Political Research Quarterly* 62 (3):485–494.

Schlozman, Kay L., Nancy Burns, Sidney Verba, and Jesse Donahue. 1995. "Gender and Citizen Activity: Is There a Different Voice?" *American Journal of Political Science* 39:267–293.

Schneider, Monica C. 2014a. "The Effects of Gender-Bending on Candidate Evaluations." *Journal of Women, Politics, and Policy* 35:55–77. doi: https://doi.org/10.1080/1554477X.2014.863697.

2014b. "Gender-Based Strategies on Candidate Websites." *Journal of Political Marketing* 13 (4):264–290. doi: https://doi.org/10.1080/15377857.2014.958373.

Schneider, Monica C., and Angela L. Bos. 2014. "Measuring Stereotypes of Female Politicians." *Political Psychology* 35 (2):245–266. doi: https://doi.org/10.1111/pops.12040.

2016. "The Intersection of Party and Gender Stereotypes in Evaluating Political Candidates." *Journal of Women, Politics & Policy* 37 (3):274–294.

Schneider, Monica C., Mirya R. Holman, Amanda B. Diekman, and Thomas
    McAndrew. 2016. "Power, Conflict, and Community: How Gendered Views
    of Political Power Influence Women's Political Ambition." *Political Psych-
    ology* 37 (4):515–531. doi: 10.1111/pops.12268.
Searles, Kathleen, and Kevin K. Banda. 2019. "But Her Emails! How Journalistic
    Preferences Shaped Election Coverage in 2016." *Journalism* 20 (8):
    1052–1069.
Sellers, Patrick J. 1998. "Strategy and Background in Congressional Campaigns."
    American Political Science Review 92 (1):159–171.
Seltzer, Richard, Jody Newman, and Melissa Leighton. 1997. *Sex as a Political
    Variable: Women as Candidates and Voters in U.S. Elections.* Boulder, CO:
    Lynne Rienner Publishers.
Silva, Andrea, and Carrie Skulley. 2019. "Always Running: Candidate Emergence
    among Women of Color over Time." *Political Research Quarterly* 72 (2):
    342–359.
Simien, Evelyn M. 2005. "Race, Gender, and Linked Fate." *Journal of Black
    Studies* 35 (5):529–550.
Skocpol, Theda. 1992. *Protecting Soldiers and Mothers.* Cambridge, MA: Bel-
    knap Press of Harvard University.
Smith, Jessi, and Meghan Huntoon. 2014. "Women's Bragging Rights: Overcom-
    ing Modesty Norms to Facilitate Women's Self-Promotion." *Psychology of
    Women Quarterly* 38 (4):447–459.
Solowiej, Lisa, and Thomas L. Brunell. 2003. "The Entrance of Women to the
    U.S. Congress: The Widow Effect." *Political Research Quarterly* 56 (3):
    283–292.
Stoddard, Olga, and Jessica Preece. 2015. "Why Women Don't Run: Experi-
    mental Evidence on Gender Differences in Competition Aversion." *Journal
    of Economic Behavior & Organization* 117: 296–308.
Stone, Walter J., Sarah A. Fulton, Cherie D. Maestas, and L. Sandy Maisel. 2006.
    "Incumbency Reconsidered: Prospects, Strategic Retirement, and Incumbent
    Quality in U.S. House Elections." *Journal of Politics* 72 (1):178–190.
Stone, Walter J., L. Sandy Maisel, and Cherie D. Maestas. 2004. "Quality Counts:
    Extending the Strategic Politician Model of Incumbent Deterrence." *Ameri-
    can Journal of Political Science* 48 (3):479–495.
Streb, Matthew J., Barbara Burrell, Brian Frederick, and Michael A. Genovese.
    2008. "Social Desirability Effects and Support for a Female American Presi-
    dent." *The Public Opinion Quarterly* 72 (1):76–89.
Stromer-Galley, Jennifer, Philip N. Howard, and Steven M. Schneider. 2003.
    "The New Political Campaign Position: A Survey of Web Site Producers
    and Managers." International Communication Association, San Diego, CA.
Sweet-Cushman, Jennie. 2016. "Gender, Risk Assessment, and Political Ambi-
    tion." *Politics and the Life Sciences* 36 (2):1–17. doi: 10.1017/pls.2016.13.
    2018. "Where Does the Pipeline Get Leaky? The Progressive Ambition of
    School Board Members and Personal and Political Network Recruitment."
    Politics, Groups, and Identities forthcoming.
    2019. "See It; Be It? The Use of Role Models in Campaign Trainings for
    Women." *Politics, Groups, and Identities* 7 (4): 853–863.

Swers, Michele. 2002. *The Difference Women Make: The Policy Impact of Women in Congress*. Chicago: University of Chicago Press.

Taylor, Rothbart M. 1992. "Category Labels and Social Reality: Do We View Social Categories as Natural Kinds?" In *Language, Interaction, and Social Cognition*, edited by G. R. Semin and K. Friedler, 11–36. Thousand Oaks, CA: Sage.

Teele, Dawn Langan. 2018. "How the West Was Won: Competition, Mobilization, and Women's Enfranchisement in the United States." *Journal of Politics* 80 (2):442–461.

2019. *Forging the Franchise: The Political Origins of the Women's Vote*. Princeton, NJ: Princeton University Press.

Thomsen, Danielle M. 2015. "Why So Few (Republican) Women? Explaining the Partisan Imbalance in the US Congress." *Legislative Studies Quarterly* 50 (2):295–323.

2020. "Ideology and Gender in U.S. House Elections." *Political Behavior* 42: 415–442.

Tolley, Erin. 2016. *Framed: Media and the Coverage of Race in Canadian Politics*. Vancouver: University of British Columbia Press.

Turcotte, Jason, and Newly Paul. 2015. "A Case of More Is Less: The Role of Gender in U.S. Presidential Debates." *Political Research Quarterly* 68 (4): 773–784. doi: 10.1177/1065912915605581:1-15.

Valentino, Nicholas A., Carly Wayne, and Marzia Oceno. 2018. "Mobilizing Sexism: The Interaction of Emotion and Gender Attitudes in the 2016 US Presidential Election." *Public Opinion Quarterly* 82 (Special Issue):213–235.

Verba, Sidney, Kay Lehman Schlozman, and Henry E. Brady. 1995. *Voice and Equality*. Cambridge, MA: Cambridge University Press.

Vinkenburg, Claartje, Marloes L. van Engen, Alice H. Eagly, and Mary C. Johannesen-Schmidt. 2011. "An Exploration of Stereotypical Beliefs about Leadership Styles: Is Transformational Leadership a Route to Women's Promotion?" *The Leadership Quarterly* 22 (1):10–21.

Volden, Craig, Alan E. Wiseman, and Dana E. Wittmer. 2013. "When Are Women More Effective Lawmakers than Men?" *American Journal of Political Science* 57:326–341.

2018. "Women's Issues and Their Fates in the U.S. Congress." *Political Science Research Methods* 6 (4):679–696. doi: 10.1017/psrm.2016.32.

Vraga, Emily K. 2017. "Which Candidates Can Be Mavericks? The Effects of Issue Disagreement and Gender on Candidate Evaluations." *Politics & Policy* 45 (1):4–30. doi: https://doi.org/10.1111/polp.12192.

Ward, Orlanda. 2016. "Seeing Double: Race, Gender, and Coverage of Minority Women's Campaigns for the U.S. House of Representatives." *Politics & Gender* 12:317–343. doi: https://doi.org/10.1017/S1743923X16000222.

2017. "Intersectionality and Press Coverage of Political Campaigns: Representations of Black, Asian, and Minority Ethnic Female Candidates at the U.K. 2010 General Election." *The International Journal of Press/Politics* 22 (1):43–66.

Williams, Leonard. 1998. "Political Advertising in the Year of the Woman: Did X Mark the Spot?" In *The Year of the Woman: Myths and Realities*, edited by Elizabeth Adell Cook, Sue Thomas, and Clyde Wilcox, 197–215. Boulder, CO: Westview.

Wilton, Leigh S., Ariana N. Bell, Colleen M. Carpinella, Danielle M. Young, Cahel Meyers, and Rebekah Clapham. 2018. "Lay Theories of Gender Influence Support for Women and Transgender People's Legal Rights." *Social Psychological and Personality Science* 10 (7): 883–894.

Winter, Nicholas J. G. 2010. "Masculine Republicans and Feminine Democrats: Gender and Americans' Explicit and Implicit Images of the Political Parties." *Political Behavior* 32 (4):587–618. doi: 10.1007/s11109-010-9131-z.

Witt, Linda, Karen M. Paget, and Glenna Matthews. 1994. *Running as a Woman: Gender and Power in American Politics*. New York: Free Press.

Wolak, Jennifer. 2015. "Candidate Gender and the Political Engagement of Women and Men." *American Politics Research* 45 (3):872–896.

2019. "Descriptive Representation and the Political Engagement of Women." *Politics & Gender* forthcoming.

Wolbrecht, Christina. 2000. *The Politics of Women's Rights: Parties, Positions, and Change*. Princeton, NJ: Princeton University Press.

2002. "Explaining Women's Rights Realignment: Convention Delegates, 1972–1992." *Political Behavior* 24 (3):237–282.

Wolbrecht, Christina, and David E. Campbell. 2017. "Role Models Revisited: Youth, Novelty, and the Impact of Female Candidates." *Politics, Groups, and Identities* 5 (3):418–434. doi: http://dx.doi.org/10.1080/21565503.2016.1268179.

Wood, Wendy, and Alice H. Eagly. 2012. "Biosocial Construction of Sex Differences and Similarities in Behavior." In *Advances in Experimental Social Psychology*, edited by James M. Olson and Mark P. Zanna, 55–123. Burlington: Academic Press.

Zeldes, Geri Alumit, Frederick Zico, and Arvind Diddi. 2007. "Race and Gender: An Analysis of the Sources and Reporters in Local Television Coverage of the 2002 Michigan Gubernatorial Campaign." *Mass Communication and Society* 10 (3):345–363.

Zipp, John F., and Eric Plutzer. 1985. "Gender Differences in Voting for Female Candidates: Evidence from the 1982 Election." *The Public Opinion Quarterly* 49 (2):179–197.

Index

#MeToo movement, 142–143

abolition movement, 21–22
abortion, 123
academic credentials. *See also* higher
    education
  on campaign websites, 72–76
  levels of, 89
  masculinity and, 50–54, 61
Adams, Abigail, 19, 29, 39, 165
Adams, John, 19, 38
Affordable Care Act, 140
agency, 8, 53
Agenda Convergence Prediction, 82
agenda-setting effect, 80, 91
aggressiveness, 5, 116
  female candidates and, 43
  gender-typicality standards and, 98
  as masculine trait, 14, 161
  role-typicality standards and, 100
ambition-shaming, 63–65, 69
American National Election Study (ANES),
    20, 34, 37, 49
Anthony, Susan B., 22–23
appearance-based news coverage,
    80–81
Asian American women, 119; *see also*
    women of color
assertiveness, 5, 11, 116
authenticity, 44
Ayotte, Kelly, 86–88

Bachman, Michele, 120
backgrounds
  gendered, 57–60
  lack of diversity in, 52
Bayh, Birch, 169
Bayh, Evan, 87
bias, 4, 6, 10–12; *see also* implicit bias
    reduction; social desirability bias
  images of leaders, 45, 54–56
  perceptions of qualifications and, 15, 175
  qualification information and, 70
  racial, 144, 170–171
  shifting gendered standards and, 96
Biden, Joe, 169
Biernat, Monica, 98
black women, 119, 124, 131; *see also*
    women of color
Blackburn, Marsha, 163
Blackstone, William, 21
Boggs, Lindy, 26
Bos, Angela L., 9, 103–104
Boxer, Barbara, 27
Braun, Carol Mosley, 27, 119–120
Bright, Bobby, 132
broad inference assessments
  electoral viability and, 106, 111–115
  female politican standard and, 103
  masculine role-typicality standards and, 145
  partisan-typicality standards and, 132
  role-typicality standards and, 99–101
  vote choice and, 111–112, 115

Brown, Willie, 64
Burden, Barry C., 32
Burr, Richard, 79
Bush, George W., 42, 120

campaign contributions, 54
campaign websites, qualification
    information on, 16, 65–67, 70–79
Campbell, David, 39
Candidate Background Prediction, 57–60
candidates, female. *See also* Democratic
    female candidates; political office,
    women in; qualification information;
    Republican female candidates
  comparative context, 151–156
  deciding to run for office, 9, 68
  election rates, 6, 95
  feminine qualifications and, 74, 77, 85,
    87–88, 91–92
  higher qualification standard for, 4, 13,
    94–97, 114–116, 175–176
  level of qualification, 88–89
  masculinity and masculine traits, 43–44,
    66, 81–82
  number of qualification items on websites,
    77–79
  political experience, 5
  political experience coverage, 16
  professional backgrounds, 5
  qualification information on, 16–17,
    148–151
  self-promotion on campaign websites,
    65–79, 90–92
  underselling of qualifications, 67–79
candidates, male
  comparative context, 151–156
  election rates, 6
  qualification information on, 149–151
  role-typicality standards and, 115–116
candidates, nontraditional, 170
Cantrell, LaToya, 56–57
Capuana, Mike, 131
caregiving roles, 21
  femininity and, 16, 39
  gender essentialism and, 46–47
  qualifications and, 74
Carroll, Susan J., 68
Carter, Jimmy, 123
Carter, John, 148
child-rearing roles, 46–47, 64
Chisholm, Shirley, 30, 119–120, 162, 167

Christian Science Monitor, 90
civic skills, development of, 8, 53. *See also*
    minimum skill assessments
Clark, Wesley, 42
Clinton, Hillary
  gender bias and, 11, 52
  images of, 55
  knowledge ratings, 34–38, 40
  news coverage of, 81
  presidential campaigns, 1, 29, 32, 38,
    120, 164
  qualifications of, 1–3, 20, 33–34
  as role model, 39, 168
  self-promotion strategies, 160
Collins, Susan, 93, 114
communal social roles
  female candidates and, 11, 69, 74
  legislative institutions and, 59
  women's careers and, 8, 47, 174
comparative context, 151–156, 167
comparative context prediction, 152
competitiveness, 5
compromise, 5, 58, 69, 141, 168–169
Conroy, Meredith, 42, 50
consensus-building, 5, 53, 105
Conway, Kellyanne, 3
corruption, 22
counter-stereotypic information, 145,
    148–152, 157, 160
coverture, 21
credibility, 44
Crowley, Joe, 131

Davids, Sharice, 171
Deckman, Melissa, 128
Declaration of Sentiments, 22–23
Democratic female candidates. *See also*
    candidates, female; presidential
    candidates, female
  partisan gender gap and, 122, 124–127
  partisan stereotypes and, 12, 137
  recruitment of, 10, 127–128
Democratic partisan-typicality prediction,
    131. *See also* partisan-typicality
    standards
Democratic partisan-typicality standards,
    138–141
Democratic Party. *See also* partisanship
  feminine stereotypes and, 12, 17, 121,
    131, 138, 166
  gender equity and, 123

higher standards for, 52, 61, 169
marginalization and political
underrepresentation of, 4, 20, 38–39,
116, 140–141, 144, 167–170, 175
moral superiority arguments and,
22–24
qualification biases outside politics,
173–175
rights of citizenship, 15, 19–25, 38
and "women's work", 48–49
as working harder than men, 93–103
women of color. *See also* Asian American
women; black women

political candidates, 71, 81, 86, 119,
170–171
voting patterns, 124
Women's March, 38–39
women's movement, 122–123
Woodhull, Victoria, 29–30
World Anti-Slavery Convention, 21

Yamada, Masahiro, 32
Yeakel, Lynn, 27
Young, Todd, 87

Zechmeister, Elizabeth J., 12